Understanding
Local Area Networks
Fifth Edition

SAMS
PUBLISHING

201 West 103rd Street
Indianapolis, IN 46290

Understanding
Local
Area
Networks

Neil Jenkins
Stan Schatt

This book is dedicated to my wife, Christine, and my daughters, Kathryn, Holly, and Jessica for being my world.

—Neil Jenkins

This book is dedicated to my wife, Janie.

—Stan Schatt

Copyright © 1995 by Sams Publishing

FIFTH EDITION

International Standard Book Number: 0-672-30840-1

Library of Congress Catalog Card Number: 95-70103

98 97 96 95   4 3 2 1

Interpretation of the printing code: the rightmost double-digit number is the year of the book's printing; the rightmost single-digit, the number of the book's printing. For example, a printing code of 95-1 shows that the first printing of the book occurred in 1995.

Composed in AGaramond and MCPdigital by Macmillan Computer Publishing

Printed in the United States of America

Trademarks

Publisher and President *Richard K. Swadley*

Acquisitions Manager *Gregg Weigand*

Development Manager *Dean Miller*

Managing Editor *Cindy Morrow*

Marketing Manager *Gregg Bushyeager*

Acquisitions Editor
Brad Jones

Development Editor
Angelique Brittingham

Production Editor
Johnna L. VanHoose

Technical Reviewer
Scott Kunau

Editorial Coordinator
Bill Whitmer

Technical Edit Coordinator
Lynnette Quinn

Formatter
Frank Sinclair

Editorial Assistant
Sharon Cox

Cover Designer
Tim Amrhein

Book Designer
Alyssa Yesh

Production Team Supervisor
Brad Chinn

Production
Mary Ann Abramson, Michael Brumitt, Jeanne Clark, Terrie Deemer, Judy Everly, Kevin Laseau, Nancy Price, Tina Trettin, Mark Walchle, Angelina Ward

Indexer
Greg Eldred

Overview

Contents

Acknowledgments

For me, putting this book together was a real challenge. Many people provided factual information, technical notes, and plain old moral support. I would like to thank the following people who helped me complete this book.

I would specifically like to thank Andy Stewart, who helped me create some of the best LANs across Europe, and whose work on Novell and support seriously increased my own knowledge. Thanks also to Tony Iacobucci who provided much background knowledge on Novell that I stored up over the years.

I would like to thank Mark Mitchell for his help on e-mail, Kevin Holle for his many source books, Andrew Comerford at LANtastic, Mike Collins at IBM, Simon Lawless at ComputerLand, Julie Brennan at Brodeur & Partners, and the many people who helped me on CompuServe. A special mention goes to Corbin Glowacki at NetPro Computing who helped a lot in the final stages of the Banyan chapter. Andy Grieg made the Mac section possible.

I would also like to thank Alan Herbage at A.L.Solutions Ltd., and Kevin Keys who set me on the client/server path what seems an eternity ago, and have proved to be valuable friends.

Greg Guntle put me forward for this book, and Brad Jones believed in me to get it done. Thanks to them both and to Angelique Brittingham for supporting me in the writing. Scott Kunau as Technical Editor put my routers right, and Johnna VanHoose gave me great support from Sams.

Thank you, the reader, for purchasing this book. It is my hope that you find it an enjoyable read and that it helps you along the very interesting path of Local Area Networking.

The final thanks go to my wife, Christine. She put up with my tempers and manic typing and supported me wholly throughout. Her support makes everything for me possible.

—Neil Jenkins

I wish to acknowledge the technical expertise and generous help of Marc Covitt of Hewlitt-Packard; Steven Fox, David Guerro, and Randy Sprinkle of AT&T; Orval Luckey of IBM; and Bob Schulte of 3Com. I want to thank Sams for permission to reprint portions of *Understanding NetWare*.

—Stan Schatt

Trademark Acknowledgments

All terms mentioned in this book that are known to be trademarks or service marks are listed below. In addition, terms suspected of being trademarks or service marks have been appropriately capitalized. Sams cannot attest to the accuracy of this information. Use of a term in this book should not be regarded as affecting the validity of any trademark or service mark.

AppleShare, AppleTalk, LaserWriter, LocalTalk, ImageWriter, and Macintosh are registered trademarks of Apple Computer, Inc.

ARCnet is a registered trademark of Datapoint Corporation.

cc:Mail and Lotus 1-2-3 are trademarks of the Lotus Development Corporation.

COMPAQ is a registered trademark of Compaq Computer Corporation.

CompuServe Incorporated is a registered trademark of H&R Block, Inc.

The Coordinator is a trademark of Action Technologies.

DataFlex is a registered trademark of Data Access Corporation.

dBASE III Plus and dBASE IV are registered trademarks and MultiMate is a trademark of Ashton-Tate Corporation (now part of Borland International, Inc.).

DCA and 10Net are registered trademarks and IRMA and IRMAlink are trademarks of Digital Communications Associates, Inc.

DEC is a registered trademark and All-in-1 is a trademark of Digital Equipment Corporation.

eMAIL is a trademark of DaVinci Systems.

EPSON is a registered trademark of EPSON America, Inc.

Ethernet, 3+ Share, 3+ Mail, 3+ Backup, and 3+ Open are registered trademarks of 3Com Corporation.

Focus and PC Focus are trademarks of Information Builders, Inc.

Hewlett-Packard, HP LaserJet Plus, and HP Vectra are registered trademarks of Hewlett-Packard Co.

IBM, NetView, OS/2, and PROFS are registered trademarks and PS/2, NETBIOS, Systems Network Architecture, PC LAN Program, PC LAN, Token Ring Network, and LAN Server are trademarks of International Business Machines Corporation.

About the Author

Neil Jenkins

Neil Jenkins is a full-time PC Consultant specializing in client/server systems and local area networking. He has project managed and implemented client/server systems and networks in Europe, Latin America, and North America. He has developed business applications in Visual Basic, Powerbuilder, C, and Progress. Currently, he is the Senior Technical Consultant at A.L.Solutions Ltd., providing technical consultancy to clients regarding personal computers, local area networking, wide area networking, client/server development, and PC support. *Understanding LANs, 5E* is Neil's first book.

CompuServe UserId   100265,1327

Internet UserId   100265.1327@COMPUSERVE.COM

Introduction

Over the last 18 years, the DOS-based microcomputer has become a fixture in the business world, dramatically changing nearly every industry it has touched. Until recently, however, we lacked the technology to connect these units so that companies could share expensive resources and ensure data integrity. With the release of MS-DOS 3.1 several years ago (with its network features) and the development of faster microprocessors (such as the Intel 80486 and Pentium) to serve as the workhorses of network file servers, we now have the necessary software and hardware to implement cost-effective, efficient local area networks (LANs). These networks are becoming more and more critical to the operation of businesses and institutions throughout the 90's.

Understanding Local Area Networks explains how LANs and their various hardware and software components work. It will provide you with an understanding of

- the theory behind the various kinds of network architecture—the different forms networks take.
- data transmission methods—how information is sent through a network.
- the major LANs currently on the market and the degree of compatibility among them.

Finally, if you are a network administrator, this book will help you develop an understanding of whether or not a LAN is really a viable solution for your particular office setup.

What You Need To Know

You need no prior knowledge of local area networks to read this book. Early chapters provide a sound grounding in the basic building blocks of LAN hardware, software, and data transmission. In addition to focusing on the two major types of LANs found today (client/server and peer-to-peer), the book also examines future trends including such critical technology as

- wireless LANs
- remote LANs
- Asynchronous Transfer Mode (ATM) LANs
- fast Ethernet LANs

About This Book

This book is arranged somewhat like a textbook. Each chapter builds on the previous chapter's information. Try to master a chapter before moving on. If you want to explore the data communications topics in even more depth, a companion book in this series, *Understanding Data Communications*, should prove useful. If you want more information on Novell's NetWare (the LAN operating system with the major market share), the book *Understanding NetWare* provides a much more detailed description.

Local area networks have become an important part of our lives. If you are considering buying a LAN, this book will give you the necessary tools to make an informed purchase.

Overview

It can be helpful to study a roadmap and get your bearings before beginning a long journey. This book has been written to help you understand local area networks (LANs).

About This Chapter

Before starting this journey, I'll take a moment to explain how material in this book is organized and what type of material is covered. I'll use a fictitious company (The Widget Company) to illustrate some practical examples of the types of local area network functions that are described.

Distributed Processing and Networks

In three-and-a-half decades, the computer industry has evolved rapidly. Although only the arrival of the microcomputer had enabled companies to implement LANs, the concept is not new. It represents a logical development and evolution of computer technology. The first computers in the 1950s were *mainframes*. Large, expensive, and reserved for a few select users, these monsters occupied entire buildings.

These first computers were not designed for online response to a user's commands. They used a *batch* approach. Users submitted coded cards containing data and program commands. Computer professionals fed these cards into the computer and usually sent the printed results to the users the next day. A miscoded card usually meant that the user would have to resubmit the entire program the following day.

Initially, all processing was performed on mainframes using a batch approach. Time-sharing was an improvement, but the concept of distributed processing with minicomputers was a quantum leap in computer affordability and convenience. Many companies are replacing their mainframes and minicomputers with minicomputers and LANs.

At this time, there was little need to share computer resources such as printers and modems. Computers were so few (and so costly) that the average office could not afford one. One solution to this expense problem was *time-sharing*. During the 1960s, it became possible for an office to use a "dumb" terminal, modem, and card reader to connect with a mainframe computer through a telephone line. By leasing (or "sharing") time on this computer, the user was able to enjoy the benefits of computerization without massive capital expenditure.

The major problem with time-sharing was how long it took to send information over telephone lines. During the early 1970s, the production of the *minicomputer* (so called because it was smaller than a mainframe, though it worked in much the same way) avoided this problem. Because of the dramatic drop in prices, departments were able to have their own computers.

All a new user needed to become operational was a terminal and the cabling between it and the minicomputer. As Figure 1.1 illustrates, several users were able to use the same computer, and much higher speeds were possible than under time-sharing. The concept of distributing computer resources throughout a company by providing different departments with their own computers, rather than using one central computer for everybody became known as *distributed computing*. But even though several departments in a company might have their own minicomputers, providing communications among these computers still posed a problem. Therefore, companies began cabling these computers together and writing the software necessary for the units to communicate with each other.

FIGURE 1.1.

Distributed computing with a minicomputer.

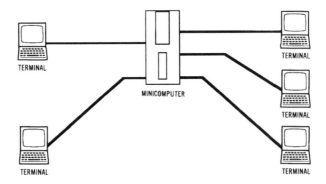

As microcomputers became much more powerful (and much less expensive) during the 1980s, companies began to take a second look at their minicomputers. Costing hundreds of thousands of dollars, these larger computers were not able to run the newer, more sophisticated business programs that were being produced for IBM PCs and compatibles.

By the mid-1980s, thousands of office workers began bringing their own personal computers to work in order to use the new business software written for PCs. As employees began exchanging floppy disks and keeping their own databases, companies began to have serious problems with maintaining the integrity of their data. Companies also found that they needed to develop faster, more flexible business systems in order to remain competitive in the market-place. The cost and size of mainframes and minicomputers became a problem in this environment. LANs offer a solution to such problems.

What Is a LAN? (Chapter 2)

Distributed computing, taken to its logical conclusion, came to mean linking microcomputers so that they could share information and peripherals. This was the idea behind the first local area networks. The broadest possible definition of a LAN is, "a communication network used by a single organization over a limited distance; this network enables users to share information and resources."

The first LANs were relatively primitive. Faced with a serious shortage of software designed for more than one user, these first LANs used *file locking*, which allowed only one user at a time to use a program. Gradually, however, the software industry has become more sophisticated; today's LANs can use powerful, complex productivity and business programs, usable by several hundred users at the same time (*record locking*).

Chapter 2 surveys the different types of physical configurations possible for a LAN. Whether PCs are arranged in the form of a star, a ring, or even a straight line, the speed of the network depends to a great extent on the media used to connect the units. This chapter also examines the various types of cabling available for LANs and the way each type affects network performance.

Widget's LAN

Now, take a look at a hypothetical company that has linked its PCs to form a LAN with which to share information and printers. (Virtually all the applications used in this example are explained in much greater detail in subsequent chapters, when you take a closer look at specific brands of LANs.)

Widget's LAN enables company employees to share data and peripherals (hard disk drives, printers, plotters, and so on). The Widget network enables dozens of workstations to share a variety of printers, including laser, inkjet, and dot-matrix, rather than each personal computer workstation having its own laser printer. Instead of buying dozens of copies of a word processing program, Widget buys a special network version of the program. This enables dozens of network users to share the program, and, more importantly, each other's documents.

A single computer's hard disk serves as the storage area for a *network file server*, which acts much like a waiter in a busy restaurant, serving the items requested by the customers. Widget can keep dozens of varying standard contracts on its network file server. Individual workstations can load these documents, make whatever changes are necessary to individualize the contracts, and then save them under appropriate names. The cost savings from these and other communal uses are impressive. To prevent degradation in a network's performance, a file server should be dedicated to this function and not used for any other purpose.

●
A LAN (local area network) covers a limited distance and facilitates information and resource sharing.

●
The savings a company such as Widget can realize by sharing hardware and software resources is staggering. Equally important is the increase in productivity that comes as the company runs more efficiently.

The Evolution of LAN Hardware (Chapter 3)

The growth of LANs has created the need for all kinds of devices specifically designed to work on these networks. In addition, several devices, such as disk drives, already designed for stand-alone microcomputers are now being re-designed and optimized for service on LANs. Chapter 3 provides some basic questions worth asking when selecting LAN hardware. As an example, not all *network interface cards (NICs)*, the circuit cards that link a microcomputer to a network, are the same. The chapter explains how key features help differentiate these NICs.

The sheer volume of LAN cabling within a company has created a demand for efficient cabling systems. Chapter 3 explains how cabling hubs, also known as wiring concentrators, work and how they enable administrators to manage network cabling.

Because so many companies have moved critical information from mainframe computers to LANs, the need to ensure that data isn't lost if a disk drive is damaged has become a major concern for network administrators. Chapter 3 explains some of the developments in network storage technology such as *redundant array of inexpensive disks (RAID)*. It also describes the different types of *uninterruptible power supplies (UPS)* available for LANs.

Network printers have emerged offering many sophisticated features enabling the printer to handle the complex printing requirements of diverse network users. Chapter 3 helps you understand some of the new features that can make network printers so valuable.

More and more users need to dial into a network at the office because they may be working at home, traveling, or at a client's office. Devices called *asynchronous communications servers* enable them to connect. These devices are becoming very important items on LANs. Chapter 3 explains the benefits of these peripherals.

LAN Software (Chapter 4)

Workgroup computing and dynamic data exchange are two key trends in LAN software.

LAN software requirements have grown over the past few years. Network users who previously were content to create simple documents and print them on a laser printer, now often demand sophisticated desktop publishing features as well as the ability to perform complicated printing tasks.

Users now find it much more efficient to use *workgroup* software, programs designed so that several people can perform a task while interacting with each other. As an example, all the members of a task force might want to view a proposal and see the comments of all the other group members. Similarly, employees might be working on different aspects of a project and want any changes in files to be reflected in a document that combines the work efforts of the group.

This concept of dynamic data linking means that when Bill changes a spreadsheet file, the data is updated automatically in a word processing document written by Sue. Chapter 4 describes some of the major requirements for various types of LAN software including a look at database software and electronic mail software.

Widget's Use of LAN Software

Every year Widget is required to produce an annual report that is printed and sent to stockholders. Since the company connected all departments with its LAN, that job has become much easier. Widget's LAN contains a number of Compaq PCs, IBM PCs, and Macintosh computers that are able to communicate with one another and exchange data over the network.

Since the accounting department's general ledger, accounts payable, accounts receivable, inventory, purchase order-and-receiving, and payroll programs are already installed on the network, its audited balance sheet is already available through the network for the annual report. The financial controller dynamically imports the balance sheet from the accounting programs into a word processing program in order to comment on several aspects of the company's financial position before saving the entire document on the company's file server.

Because many stockholders prefer to view financial information in graphic format, the company president asks two graphic artists in the marketing department to develop appropriate pie charts and bar charts to show the company's growth over the past few years. The artists use a graphics program on a Macintosh workstation to develop their charts based on a computer file from the researchers. Then they send the information to a plotter via the LAN.

The president receives a hard copy from the artists. The researchers receive the president's comments by electronic mail over the network, revise the charts, and save the files on the file server.

E-Mail

Everyone at Widget having a workstation connected to the LAN can receive and send mail electronically. As users enter the network (*log on*), the network alerts them if they have mail, so Widget employees can't use the excuse that they never saw a memo because it was lost in the mail.

The electronic mail program lets the sender know when a message has been received. It permits users to send blind copies (bcc) to other network users, and to send letters and reports to distribution lists. Secretaries who spent hours photocopying reports for distribution to managers now simply use electronic mail to send a copy of each report to each manager's workstation.

●
E-mail enables users to send information to each other across the network. It allows them to send all types of information including text, pictures, sound, and video.

Because Widget manufactures four different products designed for four very different markets, the president asks each of the four product managers to write a description of his or her product's current status and future plans. Each product manager saves his or her comments in a word processing file on the file server.

Meanwhile, the president is busy writing a letter to the stockholders analyzing Widget's performance and indicating the direction the company will take in the upcoming year. The researcher prints the requested material from the marketing and accounting departments; the president reads the documents and sends electronic mail to other employees requesting material to fill in the remaining gaps in the corporate report. After another round of revisions, the annual report is finished, printed with a laser printer that provides letter-quality text and crisp graphics, and sent to the print shop for reproduction. The whole process is faster and far more efficient because the company's LAN permits an almost-instant sharing of information.

Marketing and Financial Analysis

While Widget's salespeople are transmitting orders from customer locations, the marketing department's researchers and analysts are busy sifting through sales reports to discover trends and develop market forecasts.

The department's personnel share all their data on the LAN. Three analysts, for example, have used a Microsoft Excel spreadsheet program to analyze the buying patterns of the company's major distributors. Traditionally, Widget has offered volume discounts to encourage large purchases, but now it is considering offering monthly sales specials to help balance its inventory. By identifying specific items and the month when major customers purchase them, the marketing analysts will develop a 12-month sales plan.

Because the analysts are using the same Microsoft Excel program and saving their spreadsheet data on the network file server, the information can be shared among them. This means that after the researchers develop an item-by-item sales analysis, one researcher can access all three spreadsheets to develop a composite report that summarizes the information by product group. Using the Microsoft Excel spreadsheet and the LAN, the researcher prints a series of detailed graphs using the color laser printer in the sales office.

The Widget Company's accounting information is on the LAN, but many of the programs have additional file system security beyond the usual network level of security. For example, only a few employees in the accounting and personnel departments have access to payroll records. The information on customer orders and inventory usage is available only to certain employees in marketing, sales, and manufacturing.

New marketing analysts were able to use a special interface program to take information about sales orders and customers from the accounting programs, and convert this data into a form that could be used in Microsoft Excel. Note that while a copy of this valuable accounting information can be moved to another program, the original accounting data is protected from tampering or change. This is necessary in order to ensure that the accounting department maintains a clear audit trail, which means that all changes and/or additions to accounting program data must be done by the accounting department using a journal entry. This method leaves a permanent record that can be traced for answering future questions.

The financial controller has been delighted with the advantages of having all accounting programs available on the company LAN. During peak periods, accounting clerks can be shifted from doing payables to doing receivables. Each workstation in the department can access any accounting program, assuming the user has the proper level of file system security. Most of the clerks have the network security level that only permits them to perform routine tasks. Payroll clerks, for example, cannot change employee salaries, though they can prepare the monthly printing of salary checks.

The Role of the LAN Administrator

Every LAN requires a network administrator who is responsible for the network's overall management. The financial controller must consult the network administrator before providing newly hired accounting clerks with network access.

The administrator's tasks include adding new users and providing them with new passwords. If a department wants to add a new program to the LAN, the network administrator analyzes the effect of the program on the network as a whole, making sure (prior to approval) that the new program will integrate completely with the other programs already present.

Dependent on the size of the LAN, the network administrator may have other duties. Typically one person can administer and control a LAN of up to 200 users.

Network Management and Control (Chapter 5)

The growth of LANs has created an entirely new position: network manager. Chapter 5 examines some of the major tasks this individual must perform on a regular basis in order to maintain a LAN's health.

This chapter describes a number of network management and control programs that give the network manager the power to diagnose, repair, and maintain all elements of a complex local area network.

Enterprise Networking (Chapter 6)

One of the major trends in the networking industry has been the growth of *enterprise networks*. Corporate executives have come to realize that their computing resources consisted of too many isolated islands of incompatible computers and networks, each unable to communicate with others.

As an example, a company might have an IBM mainframe through which several users access a manufacturing program. A Digital Equipment Corporation VAX minicomputer might be found in the company's accounting department, while high-performance workstations linked to form a network are used in the engineering department for computer-aided design. Finally, several microcomputers could be linked to form a local area network for white collar workers to share laser printers and word processing and electronic spreadsheet programs.

Enterprise networks link all these different computing environments so that users have access to all computing resources. Because these computing environments are so very different, linking them involves handling several incompatible data formats. The IBM mainframe, for example, codes data using a coding scheme known as EBCDIC while PC data is coded using a completely different ASCII format. Obviously, some very complex forms of translation are needed to achieve an enterprise network.

Chapter 6 focuses on how gateways can be created to link mainframes to LANs. It also describes how bridges can link LANs to other LANs. Finally, LANs might be running incompatible software (network operating system) that packages data differently so that two LANs might require a special device known as a *router* to facilitate communication. Chapter 6 covers gateways, bridges, and routers to help you understand the difficulties in building an enterprise network.

The rise in popularity of information networks such as the Internet and CompuServe has led to companies' need to connect to these networks to do business. Chapter 6 looks at how access to these networks can be added to a LAN.

Widget's Efforts To Create An Enterprise Network

Using an access server, Widget salespeople are able to enter orders from remote customer locations and update current inventory levels online. Salespeople can use the access server to connect to the LAN and use its word processing and database programs to generate personalized sales letters.

The ability to share information is particularly valuable in a competitive sales environment. Each of Widget's outside salespeople has a portable computer with a built-in modem able to access the LAN over a phone line. Widgets come in an assortment of colors and configurations, and the company previously lost several thousand dollars' worth of orders each year through cancellations. A salesperson would take a large order, drive to Widget headquarters, and submit the order to the sales manager. Only after the order was input into Widget's mainframe computer would the salesperson learn that several of the ordered items were back-ordered. When customers were informed of the substantial delay before delivery, they usually cancelled the entire order.

As Figure 1.2 shows, the situation has changed dramatically. Widget's LAN contains a *remote asynchronous connection server*, a communications link between the network and the outside world. The salespeople use their portable computers to connect to the network using their customers' regular telephone lines. They enter an order while talking with the customer. If an item is back-ordered, the computer indicates a possible alternative: "The yellow widgets are back-ordered two weeks, but green is very popular this time of year and is available immediately." Because the customer is in a buying mood, and the salesperson is present (and very persuasive), it isn't surprising that many customers choose an alternative or agree to wait for a back-ordered item.

FIGURE 1.2.

The Widget dial-in example.

When a customer's order is entered into the computer, a file is established for that customer. Salespeople find this information invaluable, because they are able to determine buying trends and preferences. Frequently, they will send out individualized form letters to announce new product releases, or to indicate that the old widget might need an overhaul.

Because the customer list is integrated with the company's accounting programs including accounts receivable, occasionally the accounting department will ask a salesperson to contact a delinquent customer about an overdue account. The receivables clerk simply sends the account information by electronic mail to the salesperson. Widget's accounting program on the LAN contains a useful safeguard to keep its receivables low. When a salesperson inputs an order from a customer site, the order entry program flashes a message on the screen if the customer has an overdue account. Frequently, the salesperson can collect a check and then override the message to enter the new order.

Peer-to-Peer Networks (Chapter 7)

Many network industry experts have been surprised by the growth of peer-to-peer networks. These networks consist of microcomputers linked together so that each of these computers can share the hardware and software resources of the other computers on the network.

In other words, Bob can share his C:\SPREADST directory containing his spreadsheet files with other users on the network, and Sue can share her C:\DOCS directory containing her word processing documents. Under this scheme, Mary can also share the laser printer directly connected to her personal computer (PC).

Chapter 7 covers the major peer-to-peer network operating systems on the market. You learn the major features offered by Microsoft's Windows for Workgroups, Windows 95, Artisoft's LANtastic, and Macintosh's System 7. These programs differ considerably in how they share printers and directories, the security available, and their ability to communicate with LANs that utilize different network operating system software.

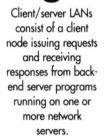

Client/server computing consists of a graphical user interface and front-end programs running on a client node and companion back-end server programs running on one or more network servers.

Client/Server Computing (Chapter 8)

Many companies in the mid-90s found that their LANs provided access to completely different computer systems. These systems may have been their own mainframes or mini-computers, or computers owned by other companies. Because their business demanded that they remain competitive, a new style of computing evolved. This style became known as *client/server computing*. Chapter 8 defines what client/server is, how it benefits businesses, and how it impacts networks.

Client/Server LANs (Chapters 9-12)

There are many situations where peer-to-peer networks are inadequate. Medium-sized and large companies have embraced the enhanced security, optimized print and file services, and specialized application servers available with a network operating system that utilize the client/server architecture.

Client/server LANs consist of a client node issuing requests and receiving responses from back-end server programs running on one or more network servers.

Networked PCs (nodes) run client software that provides an easy-to-use display (user interface) as well as links to software running on the centralized network server. When users request a specific customer record, the server software locates this record and sends only that specific record over the network.

Chapters 9 through 12 examine the major client/server network operating systems including NetWare, Windows NT Server, IBM LAN Server, and Banyan VINES. Designed to handle LANs consisting of hundreds or even thousands of users, these products offer a wealth of features. These chapters help you differentiate between these products and determine which one is appropriate for your company's needs.

The Future of Networking (Chapter 13)

LANs in the late 1990s and later will be far different than those found today. Chapter 13 explores several significant trends that, while still in their infancy, should have considerable impact on future networks. The use of multimedia and more sophisticated databases dictates the need for greater bandwidth over which to transmit data. Among the new technologies explored in Chapter 13 are fast Ethernet, asynchronous transfer mode (ATM), copper fiber distributed data interface (CDDI), and LAN switching.

A study of many large corporations would reveal that many corporate users dial into LANs from remote locations. This trend toward mobile computing is increasing and will continue to increase during the late 1990s. Chapter 13 explores how remote computing works today and how it will work in the future.

LANs will have a significant impact on our home environments. Chapter 13 explores the rise in LAN-based entertainment and the effect LAN technology will have on the home.

Wireless LANs are still in their infancy, but already the signs are present that indicate this technology will become very important in the near future. Chapter 13 also explains why wireless LANs will grow.

Selecting a Local Area Network (Chapter 14)

One of the major purposes of this book is to make readers more knowledgeable as LAN users and buyers. Chapter 14 provides a series of handy checklists to help readers determine their own local area network needs. By reading the book sequentially and studying the future network trends discussed in Chapter 13, the reader should be able to use the material in Chapter 14 not only to plan for today's LAN but also to ensure that this network will not become obsolete in the future.

Supporting a Local Area Network (Chapter 15)

Once a network has been implemented into an organization, it has to be supported. Chapter 15 discusses some ground rules for maintaining a healthy, reliable network environment.

What Have You Learned?

1. A local area network (LAN) is a communications network used by a single organization over a limited distance, which permits users to share information and resources.

2. Before microcomputers (personal computers), time-sharing with terminals and modems enabled companies to share mainframe resources.

3. Minicomputers were the first computers to permit distributed computing in a cost-effective way.

4. Peer-to-peer networks enable users to share each other's hardware and software resources.

5. Workgroup software enables several users to work on the same data and see and share each other's work.

6. Outside computers can use a remote bridge to communicate with computers on the LAN.

Quiz for Chapter 1

1. Handing in program cards and receiving the results the next day is characteristic of

   a. batch processing.

   b. online processing.

   c. distributed processing.

   d. remote processing.

2. Time-sharing was not a very effective way for a company to do its data processing because

   a. it required a computer at every station.

   b. communication over a phone line with a modem was too slow.

   c. computers were constantly breaking down.

   d. computers do not like to share.

3. Distributed computing means

   a. computers distributed to different users and departments.

   b. computer cards distributed to different departments.

   c. a mainframe computer doing all the work.

   d. a computer doing nothing but computing.

4. Centralized file servers are found under

   a. peer-to-peer networks.

   b. client/server computing.

   c. master/slave computing.

   d. matrix computing architecture.

5. Linking all computing resources within a company creates a(n)

   a. enterprise network.

   b. network segment.

   c. wide area network.

   d. metropolitan area network.

UNDERSTANDING

LAN Primer

The Basics of a Local Area Network

About This Chapter

This chapter describes the building blocks of a LAN. It explores how computer workstations are cabled together and how they share resources. It takes a close look at the rules that all LANs follow to ensure that information does not become garbled or lost. Finally, this chapter looks at a number of standards that are establishing some order in what is currently a chaotic field.

The Changing Focus of Local Area Networks

Recall from Chapter 1 that a LAN is a system that allows microcomputers to share information and resources within a limited (local) area. This area is generally less than one mile from the file server to a workstation. A LAN requires that the individual workstations (microcomputers) be physically tied together by cabling (usually coaxial or twisted pair), or by a wireless link, and that some network software is on the workstation's hard disk. (This permits the sharing of peripherals, data, and application programs.)

Because sharing peripheral equipment such as printers, hard disk drives, and plotters, is the major use of LANs, and hardware represents the major microcomputer cost in most offices, early primitive networks more than justified their cost. They made certain that valuable equipment did not remain idle. Today, some networks (such as Novell's) further increase office savings by allowing "diskless" workstations; these do not have a hard disk drive or floppy disk drives. A special *remote boot ROM* chip, inserted onto the *network interface card*, permits the computer to be part of the network, and to use the network's disk drive.

The LAN is now the main environment a company needs to use to supply flexibility and effectiveness to its business areas. The LAN enables a company to use varied equipment and systems to deliver solutions for its business. This potentially makes the company more profitable faster.

It is difficult to generalize about microcomputer networks. Compatibility problems have plagued the industry despite efforts by the Institute for Electrical and Electronics Engineers (IEEE) to standardize how information can be transmitted within a network. In this chapter, I will look at the components all networks require and the various forms they can take.

The Individual Network Workstation

An individual network workstation can work independently as a personal computer or share network information and resources through the LAN. Usually it is linked to the network's file server or disk server by a network interface card and by cabling.

Most companies decide to install a LAN because they already have a major investment in microcomputers, peripherals, and software. Rather than scrap everything and start again with a minicomputer, these companies opt to tie the existing equipment together to share hardware and software resources. This enables staff who previously may have been self-contained to work much more effectively as a team; the benefits come from sharing information or data and by using peripherals located on the network.

Each microcomputer attached to the network retains its ability to work as an independent personal computer running its software. It also becomes a network workstation capable of accessing information located on the network file server. As Figure 2.1 illustrates, this ability to function as a network station requires a special interface (usually a circuit board). The board plugs into one of the microcomputer's expansion slots and cables link it to a server.

While the Apple Macintosh is used as a network workstation in a number of Fortune 1000 companies, this chapter focuses on IBM and IBM-compatible personal computers. Chapter 7, "Peer-to-Peer Networks," contains information on the Macintosh and Macintosh networks.

The workstations in Figure 2.1 are IBM-compatible PCs containing network interface cards. The network program they are using works in conjunction with MS-DOS. A cable connects each workstation (through its network interface card) to the network file server. The user can choose to use the microcomputer as an independent unit or as part of the network. By running the network software program and *logging on* (identifying oneself as an authorized user with a user ID and password), the user becomes an active part of the network. Once this has been done they may begin to use that network's resources.

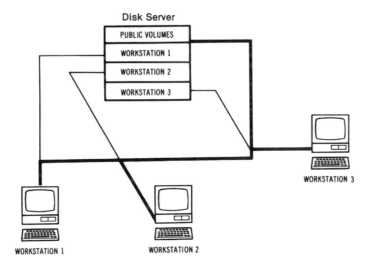

FIGURE 2.1.

Workstations connected with Network Interface Cards and cabling to a file server.

Network Disk Servers

Some early LANs used a *disk server*, a hard disk containing information that can be shared by the workstations on the network. To the individual workstations, this disk server looks like another hard disk drive. If it was designated as drive E, for example, Frank Jones would save his business expense spreadsheet as E:busexp. The E tells Jones's DOS software to send the data to the network hard disk for storage.

The workstation's accessing of network drive E, is identical to a PC's access of its own disk drives for file storage. The procedure becomes a bit more complex, however, when a workstation wants a particular file residing on the disk server.

IBM and IBM-compatible PCs running DOS use a *file allocation table (FAT)* to keep track of exactly where a particular file is stored. Without seeing a copy of this valuable table, an individual workstation has no idea where its files are stored. The network disk server keeps its own FAT and sends a copy to each workstation. Each workstation then stores the copy in RAM, which it uses as "work space" when running programs. As needed, the workstation's operating system uses the network FAT to access its files on the disk server.

Imagine what would happen if dozens of workstations received copies of the FAT and began saving documents back to the disk server. Each copy of the FAT saved back to the disk server would overwrite (and thus erase) the FAT file that existed before the new copy's arrival. Without a safeguard for this important table's integrity, determining which was the original FAT would prove almost impossible.

With a disk server, the integrity of its FAT is maintained by dividing (partitioning) this hard disk drive into several user volumes. Each volume is reserved for a particular workstation's exclusive use to preserve the integrity of the FAT for that particular volume. Although certain volumes might be established as public volumes, usually they are classified as *read-only* to safeguard their integrity; individual workstations can view this

Some early networks used a disk server to store files and provide workstations with information upon request.

A file allocation table (FAT) helps the disk server keep track of where a particular file is located.

Disk servers partition hard disk drives into separate volumes for each user. A public volume is available so that different workstations can share information.

information but cannot change it. An example of a typical public volume use is a large customer database file. Several different departments might need to view this information, but the network administrator has declared the file read-only so that no one inadvertently changes or destroys the data.

File Servers

A file server uses software to form a shell around the computer's normal operating system. To an individual workstation, the file server represents a very large disk drive. Workstations don't need to be concerned with a particular file's location.

File servers are far more efficient and sophisticated than disk servers. A file server contains software that forms a shell around the computer's normal disk operating system. This shell software filters out commands to the file server before the operating system can receive them. The file server maintains its own file system. When a workstation demands a specific file, the file server already knows where the file is because of its file system. It sends the file directly to the workstation. Note that the individual workstation does not designate the file server as another disk drive as is the case with a disk server. The workstation maintains a connection table of logically designated mapped drives that point to file system directories in the file server. A file request is made by the user, and the file server responds with the file.

The file server is more efficient than the disk server because there is no longer a need to send copies of the FAT to each workstation requesting a file. Also, there is no longer a need to partition the network hard disk drive into volumes, because the individual workstations no longer need to worry about where a particular file resides. As Figure 2.2 illustrates, a file server provides greater efficiency in a LAN.

FIGURE 2.2.

Workstations connected to a file server.

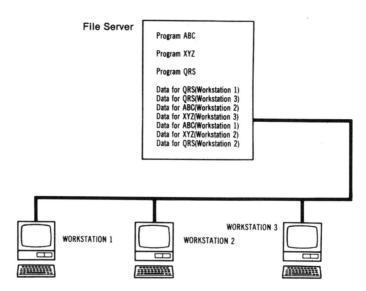

Distributed File Servers

For most small office networks, a single file server is more than adequate. This is known as a *centralized server*. It functions like a minicomputer; one unit handles all the file serving, and each workstation waits its turn. If the LAN is designed to handle several different departments, or a larger network, then adding more file servers to the network is usually more efficient.

These additional units are known as *distributed file servers* because they divide (or distribute) the file serving duties for the entire network. For example, all accounting department workstations use the same accounting programs and access the same data. Sending this information several hundred feet away to a file server is inefficient. A distributed file server located in the accounting department can speed access time and reduce the load on the rest of the network. This approach maintains optimum speed for other network users as well. Accounting personnel no longer need to request files from a central file server that also services other users' requests. Because the accounting department's distributed file server is only concerned with accounting files, it has fewer files to search. It can find and deliver requested information much more quickly. Finally, the information arrives sooner because the file server is located right in the department it services.

Distributed file servers have one other important advantage. If one file server becomes inoperative, the LAN is not necessarily shut down. Another distributed file server (provided it has sufficient disk space) can service the entire LAN temporarily.

While distributed file servers can provide a number of advantages, they can make security more difficult. The network administrator must now ensure that all file servers' hard disk drives are protected from unauthorized entry. Chapter 5, "Network Management and Control," addresses the major issue of network security.

> ●
> A network may contain one centralized file server or several distributed file servers.

Dedicated and Nondedicated File Servers

A *dedicated file server* is a microcomputer (with a hard disk drive) used exclusively as a file server. By dedicating all its memory and processing resources to file serving, the particular computer usually provides increased network speed and efficiency. In the business world, dedication was not always prized; it was very expensive. However, with the price of microcomputers continually falling, companies are using dedicated file servers.

When a file server is *nondedicated*, it is used as a workstation along with its file-serving functions. This means that RAM must be partitioned so that some of it is available for running programs. It also means that a network workstation might have to wait for a file to be sent while the file server user loads a program from memory using the machine's microprocessor. The faster the microprocessor, the faster the server can perform its tasks. Because file servers generally are the fastest and most expensive computers in the network, deciding whether to dedicate the unit is difficult. Money that might be saved by making the machine nondedicated is lost many times over by the degradation of the entire LAN.

> ●
> A dedicated file server is used only for that function, while a non-dedicated file server also serves as a workstation. More efficient dedicated file servers are more expensive because they require a PC to be set aside for their use.

The time lost by users of the other workstations in the network soon shows the folly of trying to economize on this very critical network element. Generally, a centralized file server for more than three or four workstations should be dedicated.

File Servers on a Peer-to-Peer Network

On a *peer-to-peer* LAN, users determine which computer resources to share with other network users. A user might wish to share his or her hard disk drive as a file server for other network users. Any network user can then use the files on that hard disk drive as if they were on their own local drive. A peer-to-peer network might consist of several nondedicated file-server workstations whose resources the owners have decided to share with other network users. Similarly, other users might select their printers as resources they wish to share with network users. Examples are: Windows for Workgroups, Windows 95, Lantastic, or Windows NT Workstation.

As previously discussed, if a user allows network users to access their resources such as the hard disk drive, the computer's RAM divides into RAM available for sharing and RAM for the machine's user. The machine may not work as fast or as efficient as before. Usually users do not share the running of applications, rather they just share directories containing data files.

Print Servers

Just as a network file server permits the sharing of a single network hard drive, a network *print server* can enable dozens of workstations to share various types of printers. A manager might use a laser printer for his daily correspondence, but once a month he might need a wide-carriage dot-matrix printer to print a critical spreadsheet. An accountant on the same network might use a wide-carriage dot-matrix printer daily to produce balance sheets, financial reports, and charts. Once or twice a month he might need to write a business letter using a laser printer. With a LAN and its print server software, both the manager and the accountant may choose any printer on the network.

A network print server may be a dedicated microcomputer running print server software only, or it may be a piece of software running on the network file server.

To speed up the network printing process, many network managers often install printers with their own NIC cards. Such printers can receive data from the network at the rate of several million bits per second. They are particularly useful for printing large graphics files containing so much data that they can congest other network traffic while printing. Because they are connected directly to the network rather than to a computer, they can usually be positioned anywhere within an office.

Using print server software doesn't mean that a workstation can't have its own dedicated printer. Let's say that a marketing analyst uses a thermal color printer almost exclusively to print transparencies of charts for presentations. This printer, connected by a parallel

---

⬤
Workstations on a peer-to-peer network can choose to share their hard disk drives as file servers for other network users.

⬤
Network print servers enable workstations to share several different printers. These printers do not have to be the same type.

⬤
Some high-speed network printers contain their own network interface cards enabling them to connect directly to the network rather than to a computer on the network.

interface and cable to the analyst's workstation, can remain a dedicated *local printer* and not a network printer, so it is always available to the specific user. If the analyst needs to produce a letter-quality report, he can send his word processing file via the network to a laser printer.

Another major reason for dedicating a printer to a particular workstation and not including it as part of the network: a user may need to print special pre-printed continuous-feed forms. A purchasing agent, for example, might need to print dozens of purchase order forms or an accounts payable clerk might need to print continuous-feed company checks. It would be a lot of trouble for these individuals to have to remove the continuous-feed forms in order to print an occasional letter.

The network administrator ensures that when a program is installed on the network, it is installed with a default printer driver. This means that usually the program's files are printed on a particular printer. Word processing programs, for example, might routinely send files to the office letter-quality printer or a laser printer. Spreadsheet programs might send files to a wide-carriage dot-matrix printer.

Printer-sharing software should contain a *print spooler*, software that creates a buffer for storing print jobs while waiting to be printed. Think of this as a list of print jobs. As each file is printed, the next file in line takes its place. Sophisticated print spoolers have additional capabilities, including moving a job to the front of the line if it requires immediate printing. On a large office network, time-consuming printing jobs such as daily reports often are placed in the print spooler to be printed in the evening so they don't tie up a printer during peak hours.

Communications Servers

LANs are being used more and more to connect microcomputers to the larger minicomputers and mainframes within a company. Because these larger computers do not run the same operating systems as microcomputers, some translation must be done between the microcomputer and the mini/mainframe. This enables the microcomputer to talk with the larger computers.

This translation can be handled by each microcomputer, or it can be handled by a *network communications server* also called a *gateway*. A network communications server can allow many microcomputers to communicate with a single mini/mainframe computer. Gateway servers allow easy access to mainframe data and simply require a file server computer running specialized software. An example of this software is Novell's Netware for SAA.

Other Servers

Other servers that may form part of a network include facsimile servers—a fax server. This is essentially a fax machine running on a microcomputer. Its function is to send and receive faxes.

Printers can be limited to certain users on a network. These printers usually perform very specific tasks.

Print spooler software enables network users to place files in a buffer for printing later.

A high-performance file server can also act as a fax server, communication server, and database server.

A database server is usually a server specifically running a database. This type of server does not usually handle both file and printer sharing. A database server is usually configured differently from a file server.

New types of servers are beginning to appear. In nearly all cases these are servers specifically configured to manage a particular function. Notable examples include *mail servers*—servers that act as mailboxes on the network, and *graphics servers*—servers that handle and transport high quality images around the network.

Most high-performance modern file servers can adequately handle all the server functions outlined above. From a management and ease-of-use viewpoint on larger networks typically over 100 users, it becomes practical to split these functions onto distributed servers.

A Guide to LAN Cabling

The LAN must have cabling to link the individual workstations with the file server and other peripherals. If there were only one type of cabling available, the decision would be simple. Unfortunately, there are many different types of cabling—each with its own vocal supporters. Because there is a considerable range in cost and in capability, this is not a trivial issue. This section examines the advantages and disadvantages of twisted-pair, baseband, and broadband coaxial cable, as well as fiber-optic cabling.

Twisted-Pair Cable

Twisted-pair cable is inexpensive and easy to install. It is an ideal selection when interference is not a major consideration.

Twisted-pair cable is by far the least expensive and most common type of network medium. As Figure 2.3 illustrates, this cabling consists of two insulated wires twisted together so that each wire receives the same amount of interference from the environment. This "noise" in the environment becomes part of the signal being transmitted. Twisting the wires together reduces (but does not eliminate) this noise. Twisted-pair wire comes in a wide range of pairs and gauges. Wires have an American Wire Gauge number (AWG) based on their diameter. For example, 26-gauge wire has a diameter of 0.01594 inch. For networks, 22- and 24-gauge are the two most common types of twisted-pair cabling.

Twisted-pair cable is bundled in groups of pairs. The number of twisted pairs per group can range from 2 to 3,000; many LANs use 25 pairs. Some LANs use the very same inexpensive, unshielded twisted-pair cable used for telephones, while others require higher data-grade quality. As one option for its token ring network, for example, IBM supports Type 3 unshielded twisted-pair cable (telephone wire) for its token ring network but requires 22 AWG or 24 AWG with a minimum of two twists per linear foot (the more twists, the less interference). It recommends four twisted pairs when new wire is installed, but existing telephone twisted-pair wire must have two spare pairs that can be dedicated to the token ring network.

SHEATH

PLASTIC INSULATION
(COLOR CODED)
TWISTED PAIRS

FIGURE 2.3.

*Twisted-pair wire
(two pair).*

On the other hand, AT&T's STARLAN requires higher data-grade quality cabling. AT&T specifies that its network requires 24-gauge *shielded* two-twisted-pair wire—one pair of wires to transmit data and one pair to receive data. Higher grade cabling makes a difference in data transmission quality over longer distances. For example, compare AT&T's higher grade twisted-pair standard and IBM's Type 3 twisted-pair telephone-wire standard. AT&T's workstations can be up to 990 feet from a wiring closet, while IBM's workstations must be within 330 feet.

The major limitations of twisted-pair wiring are its limited range and its sensitivity to electrical interference. When standards were first proposed for twisted-pair networks, the medium was able to handle transmission speeds of approximately one million bits per second (mbps) over several hundred feet. Today, the industry standard known as 10baseT reflects the technological advances that make it possible to transmit information at 10 mbps over twisted-pair wire and 100 mbps transmission over unshielded twisted-pair wiring is emerging as a new standard.

Coaxial Cable

Coaxial cable is almost as easy to install and maintain as twisted-pair and is the medium of choice in many major LANs. As Figure 2.4 illustrates, "coax" is based on a central copper core encased in a plastic sheath that is then surrounded by an outer jacket composed of copper or aluminum acting as a conductor. This also provides protection. The signal is transmitted along the central core with the outer jacket forming a screen from outside electrical interference. This type of cable is commonly found in the home as an integral part of cable television.

Originally, coax was the most common LAN cable due to its high capacity and resistance to interference. Its thickness means it is limited in its ability to be run through small cable ducts and around tight angles. While coax is still widely used, most of the networks that specified this cable type are now able to operate on various other types such as fiber-optic and twisted-pair. The result of which is that coax as a LAN cabling system is beginning to decline.

Coaxial cable is used in both baseband and broadband networks. While more expensive than twisted-pair, it can transmit data significantly faster over a much longer distance.

FIGURE 2.4.
Coaxial cable.

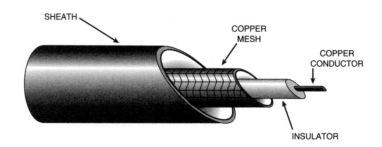

Baseband Cable

Baseband cable can send data very fast (10–80 mbps) but is limited to a single channel. It isn't possible to send integrated voice, data, and video signals over baseband cable.

Baseband coaxial cable has one channel that carries a single message at a time at a very high speed. Its carrier wire is surrounded by a copper mesh, and usually the entire cable's diameter is approximately 3/8 inch. Digital information is sent one bit at a time across a baseband cable's bandwidth in serial fashion. Depending on the LAN, it is possible for baseband coaxial cable to handle a data rate of 10–80 mbps. Ethernet, which was the first major LAN with nonproprietary communications interfaces and protocols, uses baseband coaxial cable.

Because the Ethernet standard was developed by Xerox Corporation and has been supported by both Xerox Corporation and Digital Equipment Corporation, baseband cabling is a popular choice for a LAN medium. Because of baseband's single channel limitation, it isn't possible to send integrated signals composed of voice, data, or video over baseband cable. One advantage of baseband cabling is how easy it is to tap into this cable and connect or disconnect workstations without disturbing network operations. Although the maximum recommended distance for a baseband LAN is approximately 1.8 miles (3 kilometers), 1,500 feet (500 meters) might prove to be a more realistic figure if the network is heavily used. While baseband's inability to send integrated signals as well as its distance limitations must be considered when configuring a network, these disadvantages may not be significant if data transmission speed and cost are primary criteria in media selection.

Broadband Cables

Broadband cables can carry integrated voice, data, and even video signals. Because amplifiers are used, broadband has a greater range than baseband.

Unlike baseband, *broadband coaxial cables* have the capacity to carry several different signals broadcast at different frequencies simultaneously. Cable television companies have taken this approach using 75-ohm broadband coaxial cable. Subscribers can select from several different stations, each broadcasting on its own designated frequency. All broadband systems can use a single cable with bi-directional amplifiers, as shown in Figure 2.5, or a dual cable system. In either case, carrier signals are sent to a central point known as the *headend* (a translating and broadcasting device), from which they are re-transmitted to all points on the network.

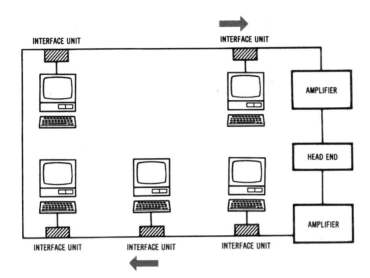

FIGURE 2.5.

Single broadband coaxial cable with bi-directional amplifiers.

The *single-cable* approach splits a cable by frequency to achieve bi-directional transmission of data. Commercial cable companies use 6 MHz channels for each communication path. Even with some frequencies designed as *guard bands* between the different channels, it is possible to allocate 346 MHz for forward communications (6 MHz/channel × 56 channels) and 25 MHz for the return data path (6 MHz/channel × 4 channels). The 25 MHz devoted to returning data can be used for several narrow-band channels.

Dual-broadband cable uses one cable for inbound data moving toward the headend, and a second cable looped at the headend for the outbound carriers. The full-frequency spectrum is available for both inbound and outbound signals. Because of the duplication of cabling, amplifiers, and hardware, dual-broadband cable is much more expensive than the single cable approach, but it makes twice as many usable channels available, and some networks might require them. Let's take a closer look at this particular broadband approach.

With a dual-cable configuration, coaxial cable forms a two-way highway composed of two bands. Each of these bands contains several channels. Standard television channels transmit at 6 MHz. Because we have a band with a range of approximately 300 MHz, it is possible to have as many as 50 channels broadcasting at a data rate of 5 mbps. The *inbound band* carries data from the LAN's *nodes* (individual workstations) to the headend; the *outbound band* carries data to the network nodes as illustrated in Figure 2.6.

Broadband cable installation requires more planning than baseband. Because the broadband signals are being broadcast, amplifiers need to be installed to maintain the signal strength. In a company with several departments, each department would have a *drop line* with tap lines coming from this line to each node. These taps contain resistors to ensure that all workstations receive signals at the same strength. If the Widget Company planned to add another building soon, it would want to add a *splitter* (as shown in Figure 2.7), which divides the signal into two paths. Because the splitter would be added to ensure future LAN growth, the unused port would be sealed until needed. Because splitters affect transmission quality across the entire network, splitters for later use should be included in the LAN's initial plan.

FIGURE 2.6.

Dual-broadband cable configuration.

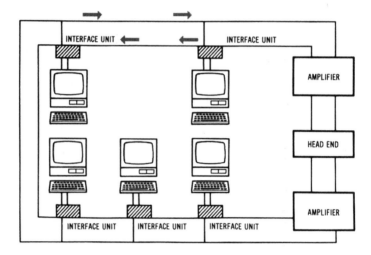

FIGURE 2.7.

Coaxial cable configuration with splitters.

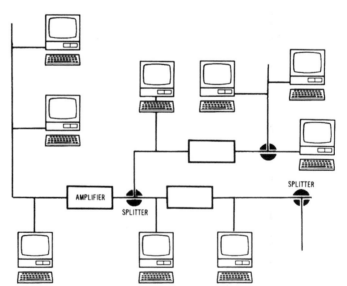

Fiber-Optic Cable

One of the most exciting advances in media is the use of fiber optics in LANs. This type of data transmission has a number of advantages over twisted-pair and coaxial cable. Besides data transmission rates far higher than either of these older media, *fiber-optic* cabling is immune to electromagnetic or radio-frequency interference and capable of sending signals several miles without loss. This mode of transmission is also virtually immune to unauthorized reception.

A fiber-optic cable is made of pure glass drawn into very thin fiber forming a core. As Figure 2.8 illustrates, these fibers are surrounded by *cladding*, a layer of glass with a lower refractive index than the glass in the core.

A fiber-optic network uses a laser or *LED (light-emitting diode)* to send a signal through the core portion of the cable. *Optical repeaters* are often used along the path to amplify the signal, so it arrives at its destination at full strength. At the receiving end of the cable, the message is translated back into a digital or analog signal by a photodiode. The cabling can consist of a single fiber (*monomode*), several fibers (*multimode*), or a variation of multimode (*graded index*) in which the index of refraction drops slowly from the center of the fiber toward the outside.

> Fiber-optic technology offers immunity from electromagnetic interference as well as error-free transmission for several miles with the highest network security level. Unfortunately, it currently is the most expensive medium for designing a LAN.

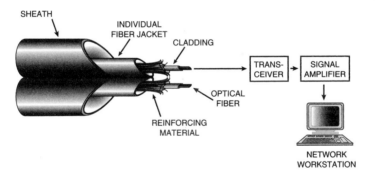

FIGURE 2.8.

Fiber-optic cabling.

Monomode fiber has a very wide bandwidth, but its tiny core makes it extremely difficult to splice without special kits and technical expertise. Also, monomode requires a laser, rather than an LED, as a signaling source, which is more expensive. Multimode fiber has a smaller bandwidth but is much easier to splice. Graded index multimode fiber is the most expensive medium, but it provides the highest transmission rate over the greatest distance.

Multimode fiber optics for network cabling come in groups of 2 to 24 fibers, with groups of 2 to 4 fibers being the norm. Each fiber is unidirectional, because a beam of light is transmitted in only one direction. Two-way communication requires another fiber within the cable so that light can also travel in the opposite direction. The American National Standards Institute (ANSI) has established a standard for the *physical media-dependent (PMD)* layer of the *fiber data distributed interface (FDDI)* to work in conjunction with data transmission of 100 mbps. It is possible to achieve rates up to 1 gigabit/second (Gbps).

At present, fiber-optic cabling is expensive for most installations, and its sophisticated technology makes it difficult to add new workstations after initial installation. If a company has a serious interference problem, however, or requires absolute network security or the capability of sending signals several miles, fiber optics might be the only solution. Fiber-optic cabling is currently mainly used to connect different LANs together rather than individual machines to a file server. This connection is a high-speed interconnection of computing devices, and fiber-optic may also be used as a *backbone* connecting low speed LANs together. While at its present costs fiber cannot compete with either coax or twisted-pair. As demand and higher speed optical fiber use increases, the price will undoubtedly drop.

Wireless Networks

●
In some environments where cabling is not desirable or even possible, wireless networks are becoming more popular.

Some environments are difficult to cable. For instance, offices that frequently relocate personnel might find it difficult to use conventional network cabling schemes. One solution is the "wireless" network. Microcomputers can be outfitted with small microwave transmitting circuit cards. These units transmit network signals through the air to other network workstations that also have microwave equipment. Token ring and Ethernet LANs are growing in popularity, but their cost is still prohibitive compared to systems using conventional cabling.

Network Architecture

Just as there are several different ways to cable a LAN, there are also several different network forms. These different shapes are known as *network architecture* or *topology*. Keep in mind that the form of the LAN does not limit the transmission media. Twisted-pair, co-axial, and fiber-optic cable all lend themselves to these different topologies.

The Star

●
The star topology makes it easy to add new workstations and provide detailed network analysis.

One of the oldest types of network topologies is the star, which uses the same approach to sending and receiving messages as a telephone system. Just as telephone calls from one customer (workstation) to another customer (workstation) are handled by a central switching station, all messages in a LAN star topology must go through a central connecting device known as a hub or concentrator that controls the flow of data. As Figure 2.9 illustrates, this architecture makes it easy to add new workstations to the LAN. A cable from the central connection point (concentrator) to each new microcomputer's network interface card is all that is needed.

Another advantage of star topology is that the network administrator can assign certain nodes higher status than others. The central computer will then look for signals from these higher-priority workstations before recognizing other nodes. For networks with a few key users requiring immediate response from on-line inquiries, this feature of star topology can be extremely useful.

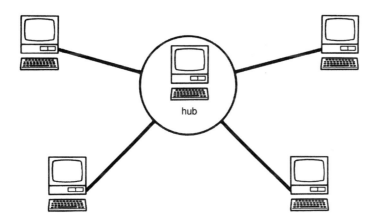

FIGURE 2.9.

A star network topology.

Finally, a star architecture makes it easier to have centralized diagnostics of all network functions. Because all messages come through the central concentrator, it's easy to analyze all workstation messages and produce reports revealing the files each node uses. This type of report can prove valuable as a means of ensuring network security.

The major weakness of a star architecture is that the entire LAN fails if anything happens to the central concentrator. This is precisely the same weakness of multi-user minicomputer systems relying on a central processor.

> The failure of the central concentrator results in the entire network's failure.

The Clustered Star

The *clustered star* topology consists of several stars linked together. The failure of any one star does not result in the failure of the entire network, though workstations linked to the failed star will not be able to operate on the network.

> An alternative to the star is the clustered star topology. Several stars can be linked together.

The Bus

Another major network topology is the *bus*, shown in Figure 2.10. Think of it as a data "highway" that connects several LAN workstations. In many such networks, the workstations check whether a message is coming down the highway before sending messages. Because all workstations share this bus, all messages pass other workstations on the way to their destinations. Each workstation checks the message's address to see if it matches its own address. A workstation copies messages addressed to it to the RAM on its network interface card and then processes the information.

> A bus topology is like a data highway. It's easy to add new workstations but difficult to maintain network security. It requires the least amount of cabling of any topology.

Unlike the star topology, where dozens of cables can cause logistical problems when they congregate near the central computer, bus cabling is simple. It requires the least amount of cabling of any major topology, and many low-cost LANs use a bus architecture and twisted-pair wire cabling. Another advantage of the bus topology is that the failure of a single workstation may not cripple the rest of the network, it depends on the type of failure. Cabling failure at the workstation will cripple the network. Ethernet is an example of a network that uses the bus approach.

FIGURE 2.10.

A bus network topology.

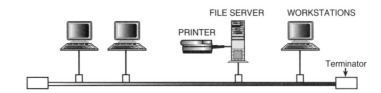

A bus topology disadvantage is that generally there must be a minimum distance between taps so workstations can avoid signal interference. Also, there is no easy way for a system administrator to run diagnostics on the entire network. Finally, a bus architecture does not have the network security features within a star topology, because all messages are sent along a common data highway. Security could be compromised by an unauthorized network user.

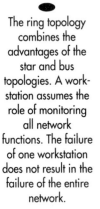

The ring topology combines the advantages of the star and bus topologies. A workstation assumes the role of monitoring all network functions. The failure of one workstation does not result in the failure of the entire network.

The Ring

Figure 2.11 illustrates yet another major type of network architecture: the *ring*. A ring topology consists of several nodes joined together to form a logical circle. Messages move from node to node, in one direction only. Some ring networks are capable of sending messages bi-directionally, but they still can only send messages in one direction at a time.

The ring topology permits verification that a message has been received. When a node receives a message addressed to itself, it copies the message and then sends the message back to the sender with a flag that indicates its receipt.

One of the major issues in a ring topology is the need to ensure that all workstations have equal network access. In a token ring LAN, a data packet known as a *token* is sent from the transmitting workstation throughout the network. The token contains the sender's address and the receiving node's address. When the receiving station has copied its message, it returns the token to the originating workstation, which then sends the token on to the next workstation in the ring. If it has nothing to send, the token goes to the next workstation.

FIGURE 2.11.

A ring network topology.

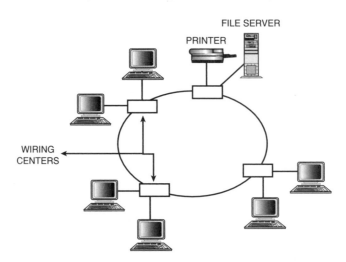

For system administration purposes, one workstation is designated as the monitoring node in the network. The monitoring node handles all diagnostic functions. This station is called the active monitor.

There are many advantages to a ring topology. Should the monitoring node fail, the network remains operative because it's possible to designate another workstation for this task. With bypass software, the network may withstand the failure of various workstations by bypassing them. Additional ring networks can be linked through bridges that switch data from one ring to another. (The mechanics of a bridge are discussed in Chapter 6, "Connectivity and the Enterprise Network.")

Previously, if several workstations were cabled together to form a ring, it was extremely difficult to add new workstations. The entire network had to be shut down while a new node was added and the cabling was reattached. Most token ring networks now come with connectors called wire centers (shown in Figure 2.11). These enable network administrators to add and remove workstations by connecting them to (or disconnecting them from) the appropriate wire centers. The network remains intact and in operation.

Network Standards and Protocols

So far in this chapter I have examined the major components of a LAN. If the computers, application software, network software, and cabling were all manufactured by the same vendor, there would be few problems in making everything work together smoothly. Today's reality, however, is usually that network software from one LAN manufacturer does not work on a competitor's network, while application programs and even cabling must be selected for a specific LAN.

To provide some level of uniformity among network vendors, the International Standards Organization (ISO) has developed *Open Systems Interconnection (OSI)* standards. Computers networked together need to know in what form they will receive information. When will a particular word begin, when will it end, and when will the next word begin? Is there a way for one computer to check if its message was garbled in transmission? The OSI model answers these questions (and more) with a set of standards enabling the public to buy network products from different vendors with some assurance that they will work together. The model achieves two objectives. It provides a useful and commonly agreed way of understanding and analyzing the various functions of communications systems like LANs, and it provides a framework for the aforementioned internationally agreed standards.

The OSI Model

As Figure 2.12 illustrates, the OSI model consists of seven layers of specifications describing how data is to be handled during different transmission stages. Each layer provides a service for the layer immediately above it.

●
Over the past few years, a number of standards have been developed. Some governing organizations in this field have developed protocols, or rules, that ensure compatibility for different vendors' network hardware and software.

FIGURE 2.12.
The OSI Model.

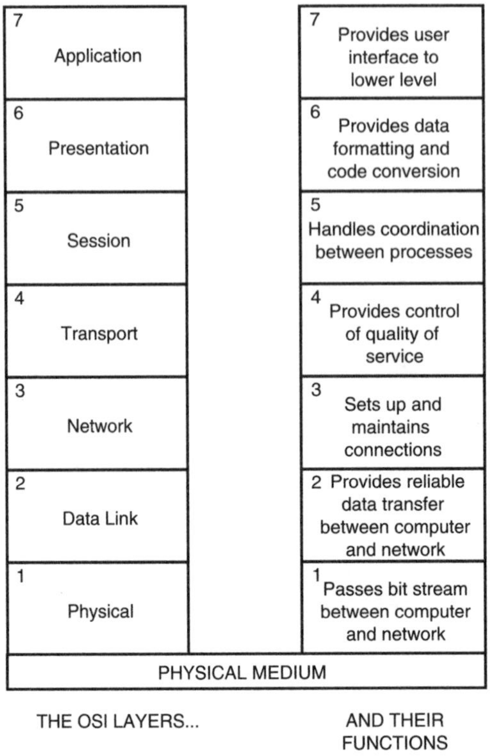

THE OSI LAYERS...	AND THEIR FUNCTIONS
7 Application	7 Provides user interface to lower level
6 Presentation	6 Provides data formatting and code conversion
5 Session	5 Handles coordination between processes
4 Transport	4 Provides control of quality of service
3 Network	3 Sets up and maintains connections
2 Data Link	2 Provides reliable data transfer between computer and network
1 Physical	1 Passes bit stream between computer and network
PHYSICAL MEDIUM	

● The Open Systems Interconnection (OSI) standards consist of a seven-layer model that ensures efficient communication within a LAN and among different networks.

An example better illustrates this principle. When someone uses a citizen's band radio (CB) to communicate with another person, he or she is using a set of agreed-upon standards very much like the OSI model. Let's look more closely at how Frank's call to Betty follows a series of uniform standards.

By pressing his send button and announcing "Breaker breaker," Frank indicates that he wants to send a message. He then uses his commonly agreed-upon nickname to identify himself before asking for his friend Betty by her particular nickname: "This is Happy Hacker, can you read me PC Woman?" After establishing communication with Betty, Frank tells her to "switch over to Channel 25 because it's clearer." Betty acknowledges her understanding of the message with a "That's a 10-4, Happy Hacker."

At the physical level, Frank had to press certain buttons to broadcast a message, using radio hardware equipment that includes transistors. His use of nicknames established a concrete address for the recipient of his message, and identified him as the sender. Frank then established that his communication was being received clearly (identified the quality of transmission). After establishing an error-free channel of communication, Frank began talking (with a slight Brooklyn accent) to Betty about his new communications program. Betty was kept very busy translating Frank's technical jargon and his Brooklyn slang into standard American English. She was able to do this because Frank followed certain rules; he used American English grammatical patterns.

Frank followed a series of generally accepted standards while conversing with Betty over their CB radios. The OSI layers of standards only work when all vendors adhere to them and do not use "shortcuts." Note that these standards are not hardware, and they are not software; they are simply a set of generally accepted conventions.

The OSI model assigns seven different layers to the complex procedures necessary for data communications along a network. The model is designed to make it easier to achieve initial agreement on the lower layers and ultimately on the entire seven layers. The layer hierarchy runs from the general at the highest layer, to the specific at the lowest level. Changes can be made in one layer without affecting the other layers.

The Physical Layer

The first layer of standards—the Physical layer—is a set of rules regarding the hardware used to transmit data. Among the items covered at this level are the voltages used, the data transmission timing, and the rules for establishing the initial "handshaking" communication connection. The Physical layer establishes whether bits are to be sent *half duplex* (very similar to the way data is sent across a CB) or *full duplex* (which requires simultaneous sending and receiving of data). You get a closer look at this process in Chapter 6, when we examine communications between LANs and mainframe computers.

Other hardware descriptions covered in the Physical layer standards include the acceptable connectors and interfaces to media. At this layer, the OSI model is concerned with electrical considerations and bits (1s and 0s). The bits don't really have any meaning at this level. Assigning meaning is the responsibility of the next OSI layer.

●
The Physical layer's standards cover the hardware standards for network compatibility. These include the voltage used, the data transmission timing, and handshaking requirements.

The Data Link Layer

Earlier you saw that the OSI model has been developed so that each layer provides the layer above it with a key element. The Physical layer provides the *Data Link layer* with bits. Now it is time to give these raw bits some meaning. At this point we no longer deal with bits but with data frames, packets containing data as well as control information.

The Data Link layer adds flags to indicate the beginning and end of messages. This layer's standards perform two important functions: they ensure that data is not mistaken for flags, and they check for errors within the data frame. This error-checking can take the form of sending information about a data frame to the receiving machine, and receiving an acknowledgment if everything has been received correctly.

●
The Data Link layer is concerned with packaging data into data frames for transmission and ensuring that they are transmitted and received correctly.

The Network Layer

This third layer of the OSI model, the *Network layer*, is concerned with packet switching. It establishes virtual circuits (paths between two computers or terminals) for data communications. At the sending end, the Network layer repackages messages from the

●
The Network layer is concerned with packet switching. It establishes virtual circuits between computers or terminals for data communication and ensures that the data frames arrive at the right place.

Transport layer (above it) into data packets, so that the lower two layers can transmit them. At the receiving end, the Network layer reassembles the message. To understand this use of data packets, it is necessary to look at an industry standard found at the lower three OSI model layers: the X.25 standard.

The Transport Layer

The *Transport layer* of the OSI model has many functions including several orders of error recognition and recovery. At the highest order, the Transport layer can detect (and even correct) errors, identify packets that have been sent in incorrect order, and rearrange them in correct order. This layer also multiplexes several messages onto one circuit, then writes a header to indicate which message belongs to which circuit. The Transport layer also regulates information flow by controlling the messages' movement. The layers above the Transport layer are not concerned with the mechanics of data transfer; this level and below takes care of it all. This level provides a quality service to the upper layers with an improved set of features above those of the lower three levels.

●
The Transport layer is primarily concerned with error recognition and recovery but also handles the multiplexing of messages and the regulating of information flow.

The Session Layer

So far, you have seen that the OSI model is concerned with bits and data messages, not with recognizing particular users on the network. Think of the Session layer as the layer concerned with network management. It has the ability to abort a session, and controls the orderly termination of a session. The user communicates directly with this layer.

●
The Session layer is concerned with network management. It handles password recognition, logon and logoff procedures, and network monitoring and reporting.

The *Session layer* can verify a password typed in by a user, and enable a user to switch from half-duplex transmission to full duplex. It can determine who speaks, how often, and for how long. It controls data transfers, and even handles recovery from a system crash. Finally, the Session layer can monitor system usage and bill users for their time.

The Presentation Layer

The *Presentation layer* of the OSI model is concerned with network security, file transfers, and formatting functions. At the bit level, the Presentation layer is capable of encoding data in a variety of different forms, including ASCII and EBCDIC.

●
Network security, file transfers, and format functions are dealt with by the Presentation layer.

The American Standard Code for Information Interchange (ASCII) is a seven-bit-plus-parity-bit character code for data transmission. It's the convention used most universally. Many of the larger IBM computers use Extended Binary Coded Decimal Interchange Code (EBCDIC). The Presentation layer must be able to handle both of these standards for data transmission.

For true communication, both communicating computers' Presentation layers must contain the same *protocols*, or rules for handling data. This layer handles protocol conversion between different computers using different formats. Most word processing functions we associate with formatting text (including pagination, number of lines per screen, and even cursor movement across the screen) are also handled in the Presentation layer.

Terminal Protocol

The proliferation of terminals with incompatible codes is treated at this level. A *terminal protocol* resolves these differences by enabling each data terminal to map the same virtual terminal. In effect, this procedure means that a set of translation tables exists between a local terminal and a remote terminal. The local terminal sends a data structure defining its current screen in terms of how many characters per line are displayed. This number can vary considerably; many terminals display 132 characters per line, but other formats are available. The data structure goes to the remote terminal's corresponding control object, which translates this number into a code that its terminal can understand and implement. Other codes indicate boldface, underline, graphics, and so on.

The Application Layer

The *Application layer* handles messages, remote logons, and the responsibility for network management statistics. At this level, you find database management programs, electronic mail, file server and printer server programs, and the operating system's command and response language. You will not find application software like word processing or spreadsheets at the application layer, only the protocols that allow them to work.

For the most part, the functions performed in this layer are user-specified. Because different user programs establish different needs, it is difficult to generalize about the protocols found here. Certain industries (such as banking) have developed sets of standards for this level.

● Network programs found at the Application layer include electronic mail, database managers, file server software, and printer server software.

CCITT X.25 Standard

The Consultative Committee for International Telephony and Telegraphy (CCITT) has developed a set of international telecommunications standards. As Figure 2.13 illustrates, the first three layers of the X.25 standard (Physical, Frame, and Packet) correspond to the OSI model's first three layers (Physical, Data Link, and Network).

● X.25's *Physical layer* corresponds to OSI's Physical layer. It uses the CCITT's X.21 recommendation to define the RS-232 standard for asynchronous data transmission, as well as full-duplex point-to-point synchronous transmission between the DTE and a public switched network. These are communications standards discussed at length in *Understanding Data Communications*, from Sams Publishing.

● The CCITT X.25 standard establishes rules for data packets that are to be sent to public switched networks. The X.25 set of three layers corresponds to the first three protocol layers of the OSI model.

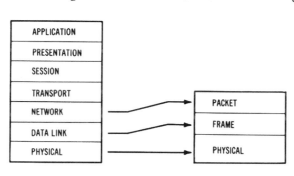

FIGURE 2.13.
The X.25 standard and the OSI model.

● X.25's *Frame layer* corresponds to the OSI model's Data Link layer. Here the data is actually exchanged between a DTE and the network.

● In X.25's *Packet layer* (corresponding to the OSI's Network layer), data is in packet form, which is a requirement for public switched networks. The X.25 standard ensures that information sent from *data termination equipment (DTE)* can be understood when received by a *public packet network*.

These data packets contain several discrete types of information that distinguish one message from another. A packet contains an *ADDRESS field* indicating its destination. A *CONTROL field* provides several kinds of information, including indications that a message is beginning or ending, that the message has been received successfully, or that an error has occurred and is acknowledged.

The X.25 standard is designed for packet switching. Using this particular convention, the Network layer of the OSI model functions very much like a gigantic mail room. Messages from a host computer are placed in packets, addressed, and sent to the bottom two layers for transmission. Because there may be several different ways (circuits) to route a message to a particular workstation, special *routing tables* monitor traffic to balance the workload. The major use of the X.25 standard is in conjunction with mainframe communications and public switched networks, a subject covered in Chapter 6.

The Network layer contains other conventions besides X.25. There are procedures for recognizing message priorities and sending messages in proper order. Finally, this layer controls network congestion by preventing the sending computer from sending information faster than it can be received or stored.

High-Level Data Link Control Procedure (HDLC)

● High-level Data Link Control procedure (HDLC) defines the standards for linking a DTE and a DCE.

The X.25 standard, found particularly at the Data Link and Network layers of the OSI model, defines the standards for linking a DTE device such as a computer, and a DCE device such as a modem, using *High-level Data Link Control procedure (HDLC)*.

Under HDLC, all information is sent in *frames*. A frame consists of six fields, with flags composing the beginning and ending fields. As Figure 2.14 illustrates, the flags are identical bit patterns, characterized by six straight one-bits.

FIGURE 2.14.
An HDLC frame's format.

01111110	ADDRESS	CONTROL	INFORMATION	FRAME-CHECK SEQUENCE	0111110

The ADDRESS field consists of the destination address if the frame is a command, and a source address if the frame is a response. The CONTROL field contains information indicating whether the frame contains a command or a response. The INFORMATION field usually contains integral multiples of 8-bit characters, but this is not always the case. There is a significant difference between HDLC and the subset of it used by IBM (called SDLC).

The FRAME-CHECK SEQUENCE field is used to ensure that the receiving station can distinguish information from garbage. It is necessary to have a way to handle situations with information containing more than five straight one-bits. How can the receiving station determine whether the data is really information or simply a flag indicating the end of a frame?

The solution to this problem is called *bit stuffing*. The HDLC protocol ensures that a zero-bit is inserted in any word containing more than five straight one-bits. The information contained in the FRAME-CHECK SEQUENCE field tells the receiving station where to eliminate the zero-bits that have been stuffed into the frame before reading the information.

●
"Bit stuffing" ensures that data in a packet will not be mistaken for control bits.

The HDLC protocol is designed to handle data exchange between a controlling central computer and its secondary stations. The central computer is responsible for error checking, as well as for polling the secondary stations at designated times. When it receives a signal that a station has a message to send, it sends a *poll bit* that permits a response from that station. This mode of operation is called *Normal Response Mode (NRM)*.

A second mode of operation permits all secondary stations to send messages at any time, without waiting for a poll bit from the central computer. This method is called *Asynchronous Response Mode (ARM)*.

Synchronous Data Link Control (SDLC)

IBM's computers that run under its Systems Network Architecture use Synchronous Data Link Control (SDLC), a subset of HDLC. While it contains the same basic HDLC frame—consisting of beginning and ending flags, with the same HDLC bit pattern—there are some differences. SDLC's information field contains data that can only be integral multiples of 8-bit characters. An equally significant difference is that SDLC contains several commands and responses not found under HDLC. (Chapter 6 returns to SDLC when it examines the link between LANs and the IBM world of Systems Network Architecture.)

●
Synchronous Data Link Control (SDLC) data packets contain some control codes unique to IBM.

IEEE Network Standards

Several IEEE committees have developed standards for LAN topologies and access methods using the OSI set of layered standards as a foundation. Three of these IEEE 802 standards are of particular interest to us: 802.3 (the CSMA/CD bus standard), 802.4 (the token bus standard), and 802.5 (the token ring standard). A fourth standard, 802.6, is concerned with standards for a metropolitan area network, a subject beyond the scope of this book. The complete set of 802 standards can be ordered directly from the IEEE, whose address is listed in the bibliography.

●
IEEE has developed standards for a bus LAN (802.3), a token bus LAN (802.4), and a token ring LAN (802.5).

Why did IEEE develop four different—and even contradictory—standards? Because by 1980, when the 802 committee's subcommittees first met, a wide range of incompatible LAN products already existed. Some vendors had opted for bus topologies, while others had chosen token rings or stars. The vendors had also chosen widely divergent methods of handling a very significant problem facing a LAN: avoiding data collisions among network nodes that have information to send.

So many different kinds of LANs had proliferated because no one topology or data access method is best for all LAN applications. IBM has illustrated this fact by offering a bus topology network a few years ago (PC network) as well as a token ring topology (token ring network). Each network was designed to meet a different set of customers' needs.

For the end user, the major advantage of the IEEE 802 standards is that they will eventually result in the standardization of the Physical and Data Link layers in the OSI model. This means different manufacturers who comply with these standards will produce hardware that can work in the same system. For network software to work, however, vendors will have to follow the standards established by the higher layers of the OSI model. This may take some time.

IEEE 802.3 and Ethernet

When the IEEE 802 committees began their deliberations, they were faced with a *de facto* standard, Xerox's Ethernet LAN. By 1980, Intel and Digital Equipment Corporation had joined Xerox in indicating that all their products would be Ethernet compatible. The original published specifications were known as DIX (Dec, Intel, Xerox) Ethernet Specifications Version 1 and 2. Rather than requiring that all LANs follow the Ethernet standard, a subcommittee provided 802.3 as an acceptable Ethernet-like standard.

As discussed earlier, the IEEE 802 subcommittees developed standards based on the first three layers of the OSI model. They developed the Data Link layer into two sublayers: a *Logical Link Control (LLC)* sublayer and a *Media Access Control (MAC)* sublayer. The LLC standard is very much like the HDLC standard we described earlier, while the MAC sublayer is concerned with detecting data collisions.

●
The IEEE 802.3 committee defined an Ethernet data packet's format, the cabling to be used, and the maximum distance for the network.

The Ethernet Data Packet

The IEEE 802.3 standard describes a LAN using a bus topology. This network uses 50-ohm coaxial baseband cable capable of sending data at 10 mbps. As Figure 2.15 illustrates, the committee specified exactly how a frame should be composed. Notice the similarity between this frame and the HDLC protocol discussed earlier in this chapter.

FIGURE 2.15.

The Ethernet frame format.

PREAMBLE	DESTINATION ADDRESS	SOURCE ADDRESS	TYPE	DATA	FRAME-CHECK SEQUENCE

The Ethernet packet begins with a PREAMBLE consisting of eight bytes used for synchronization. The DESTINATION ADDRESS can be a single workstation's address, a group of workstations, or even several groups of workstations. The SOURCE ADDRESS is critical so that the workstation receiving the message recognizes the originator. The TYPE field is important because there must be a way of designating which type of format the data is using. Without this information, it is impossible to decipher the packet when it arrives. The DATA field is strictly limited; it can only hold a minimum of 46 bytes and a maximum of 1,500 bytes of information. Finally, the FRAME-CHECK SEQUENCE field ensures that the data in the other fields arrives safely. In addition to specifying the type of data frames that can be packed in a packet and the type of cable that can be used to send this information, the committee also specified the maximum length of a single cable (1,500 feet) and the ways that repeaters could be used to boost the signal throughout the network.

The CSMA/CD Protocol

The IEEE 802.3 subcommittee specified how a LAN using the bus topology should construct its information frames (and send them over the network) in order to avoid collisions. The protocol is known as Carrier-Sense Multiple Access with Collision Detection (CSMA/CD).

To illustrate the CSMA portion of this protocol, imagine a network user who wants to send a message. In terms of the OSI model (incorporated into the IEEE 802.3 standard), the Physical layer of the user's workstation model generates a signal. It listens to detect another carrier signal from another user who is about to send a message. If no other signal is detected, the first user's message is sent.

There are problems with this seemingly tidy solution to traffic control on a network. What happens if two network users are located fairly far apart? It is possible for their network interface cards to issue a carrier-sense signal, listen and hear nothing, and then send their messages only to have the data collide? To avoid this type of accident, the committee added Collision Detection (CD) to the Carrier-Sense Multiple Access approach. This means that two users' network interface cards listen while they transmit a message. If a user detects a collision, the card listens for the other workstation to send a transmission and then transmits the message again.

There is still another problem with this approach. Imagine two drivers who arrive at the same intersection where there are four-way stop signs. Both drivers arrive simultaneously, come to a complete stop, wait a reasonable time, and then begin to move again, only to have to slam on their brakes to avoid a collision. Embarrassed by the near collision, the two drivers pause before starting again. Unfortunately, they start again at precisely the same time, and once again narrowly avoid a collision.

While the two drivers' adventure at an intersection sounds like a silent-movie comedy plot, the reality of collision after collision is certainly not funny to network administrators. To avoid this possibility, network planners have designed their CSMA/CD approach so that each workstation waits a random amount of time after a data collision before once again transmitting a message. After a collision, a special signal called a *jam* is sent through the network. This signal ensures that all network stations, no matter how far apart, are aware there has been a collision.

After repeated collisions, the network doubles its random delays before permitting stations to transmit once again. This approach does not eliminate collisions completely, because it is still theoretically possible for two well-separated workstations to wait different

●
Carrier-Sense Multiple Access with Collision Detection (CSMA/CD) is a protocol for defining the ways that networks avoid collisions.

amounts of time and still transmit messages that collide. These accidents, however, become much less frequent, thus more manageable.

Despite the ingenuity of this approach to collision avoidance, there is one additional consideration. A heavily used bus network using CSMA/CD can begin to look very much like a Los Angeles freeway during rush hour. Even though data is supposed to move at 10 mbps, the doubling and redoubling of the delay duration after a few collisions could reduce the network's throughput to as low as 1–3 mbps. Also, if the number of users is increased, then obviously the likelihood of collision also increases.

IEEE 802.3 10Base5

When the 802 committee developed its standard for a bus network, thick coaxial cabling was the norm for Ethernet. As a result, sometimes the original set of IEEE 802.3 specifications is referred to as *10Base5* because it describes a bus network with thick baseband coaxial cabling that can transmit data at 10 mbps over a maximum length of 500 meters.

IEEE 802.3 10Base2

Many network vendors have found it much easier and less expensive to use thin baseband coaxial cabling when installing an 802.3 bus network. The IEEE 802.3 *10Base2* specifications describe a bus network composed of thin coaxial cabling that can transmit data at 10 mbps for a maximum distance of 200 meters.

The IEEE 802.3 STARLAN Standard

The IEEE 802 committee has developed a standard for a CSMA network that uses a *clustered star topology* in which stars are linked to each other. Sometimes known as *1Base5*, this set of specifications describes a network that can transmit data at 1 mbps for a distance of 500 meters using two pairs of 24-gauge twisted-pair unshielded wire.

IEEE 802.3 10BaseT

The IEEE 802.3 *10BaseT* set of specifications combines the best features of a star and a bus network. While the network is logically a bus with data being transmitted over the entire network, it is configured as a physical *distributed star*, using inexpensive twisted-pair wire. 10BaseT networks can transmit data at 10 mbps for a maximum distance of 100 meters.

What makes 10BaseT so attractive to network managers is that workstations are linked to a hub that contains built-in diagnostics. When a hub recognizes that a workstation is faulty, it can bypass that workstation so that the entire network is not disrupted.

IEEE 802.4 Token Bus

The IEEE 802.4 subcommittee developed a standard for a different type of bus network that does not have the contention approach of the 802.3 model. This type of network is desirable if it is absolutely necessary that there be no data collisions.

To understand how this token approach is in sharp contrast to the CSMA/CD bus approach, imagine a public forum on a very controversial issue. Under the CSMA/CD method (by analogy), several people might try to speak simultaneously only to stop politely when they heard another speaker begin. With dozens of speakers trying to speak (but not wanting to interrupt each other), the process would become chaotic and inefficient. Under the token approach, there would be a token that serves as a symbol of authority enabling a particular person to speak. A speaker would hold the token and make his or her speech. When finished, the speaker would pass the symbol of authority through the room to the next person who had indicated a desire to speak. No one who did not have the token physically in hand would attempt to speak. The token bus approach works in much the same way.

Figure 2.16 illustrates the token bus frame format under IEEE 802.4. The PREAMBLE field is used primarily to synchronize the signal. The START FRAME DELIMITER and END FRAME DELIMITER fields define the limits of the frame. The FRAME CONTROL field carries information from either the Logical Link Control (LLC) or Media Access Control (MAC) sublayers, while the DESTINATION and SOURCE ADDRESS fields function identically with those found in the 802.3 Ethernet frame. The DESTINATION ADDRESS field can contain a specific workstation's address, a group address for several workstations, or addresses for several different groups (a broadcast address). The INFORMATION field and the FRAME-CHECK SEQUENCE fields both are identical to those discussed under the 802.3 model.

PREAMBLE	START FRAME DELIMITER	FRAME CONTROL	DESTINATION ADDRESS	SOURCE ADDRESS	INFORMATION	FRAME-CHECK SEQUENCE	END FRAME DELIMITER

The token is actually a data packet. A workstation sends the token to the receiving workstation's address. This station copies the message and then returns the token to the sending station. Figure 2.17 illustrates how a token is passed in a bus topology.

The network maintains a table of workstation addresses. These addresses may bear no resemblance to the station's physical location on the bus network. They indicate the order in which each station receives the token.

IEEE 802.4 defines a bus topology using a data packet "token" that is passed from workstation to workstation. Because only the workstation owning the token can transmit information, this effectively eliminates the possibility of data collisions.

FIGURE 2.16.

The token bus frame format.

FIGURE 2.17.

How a token is passed in a bus topology.

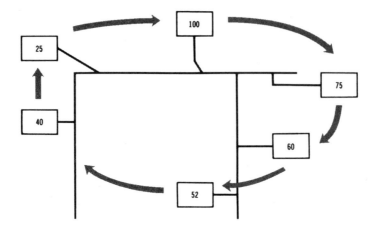

The token is passed to the station with the next lower address. When the station at address 100 sends the token to address 75, it listens to make sure that the token was received satisfactorily. If a workstation uses the network more than other workstations and requires the token more frequently, it can be listed several times in the network address table, so it receives the token more often.

Remember that the token is really a bit pattern. If a station does not receive a reply from the station to which it sent a token, it sends a second token. If there is still no reply, the sending station sends a special message down the network, requesting the address of the next station to receive the token by sending what is called a *who follows* frame. If this fails to invoke a response, it sends a general request through the network, asking any station that wants to send a message to respond to receive the token. This is known as a *solicit successor* frame. The sending workstation then changes the token's address to match this address and sends the token.

Notice that the topology of this 802.4 standard is a bus, yet the token passing is in the form of a logical ring. The last address workstation to receive the token sends it back to begin the process again. In a smoothly working token bus, each workstation receives the token, inserts the information it is sending, and then sends it to its destination where the workstation copies the information before once again sending the token through the network.

Problems can occur with this approach. The most serious are caused by malfunctioning hardware, which can result in missing tokens or even multiple tokens. To keep such a situation from crippling the network, the network controller assumes responsibility for monitoring and error checking.

Other weaknesses inherent in the token bus approach include some specific distance limitations as well as limitations on how many new workstations can be "tapped" into the bus. Under Ethernet, for example, there are minimum distance requirements between individual workstations. There are also limitations on how many new workstations can be added to the bus, because each new workstation creates a certain amount of signal distortion. The token bus approach is not widely used.

ARCnet

Attached Resource Computer Network (ARCnet) was developed in 1977 by Datapoint and is a proprietary LAN. Today it is available from a number of vendors, including Standard Microsystems, Acer Technologies, Earth Computers, and Thomas-Conrad. ARCnet provides inexpensive, very reliable network hardware that supports a wide range of network operating systems, including NetWare. The ARCnet Trade Association (ATA) has standardized on Performance Technology's NetBIOS, so that ARCnet users can run virtually any NetBIOS-compatible network operating system on ARCnet.

What makes ARCnet particularly interesting is that while it has existed outside the IEEE 802 body of standards, its vendors have made a major effort to make it a de facto industry standard. Because of its low cost, flexibility, and reliability, they have succeeded.

> ●
> ARCnet is a popular LAN topology that is a variant of the IEEE 802.4 standard. It is not an IEEE standard.

Topology

ARCnet offers bus, star, and distributed star topologies, using thin coaxial cable, twisted-pair wire, or fiber-optic cable. This flexible network permits the intermixing of all these topologies and media.

The star is the most common ARCnet topology. Up to eight workstations can be connected to a central hub with a 2,000-foot maximum cable length between workstations. A passive hub can be used if distances do not exceed 100 feet. Active hubs can be joined together by way of an interface on the back of the hub, or through one of the eight ports. In total, the network can stretch up to four miles.

Because of the number of ARCnet vendors, there are a wide range of product configurations available. Active hubs, for example, can be purchased with anywhere from 4 to 32 ports.

A bus configuration that uses coaxial cabling can contain up to eight workstations. If a company's computing needs grow, this bus can be linked to a star-configured ARCnet network. A repeater, called an *active link* can expand a coax bus network by linking two bus cables, or a star network by increasing point-to-point distances. Active links can be purchased with various combinations of connectors. Twisted-pair, coax, and optic-fiber segments can all be linked into one ARCnet network. Figure 2.18 illustrates a star configuration linked to a coax bus network under ARCnet.

> ●
> ARCnet's topologies can take the form of a bus, star, or distributed star.

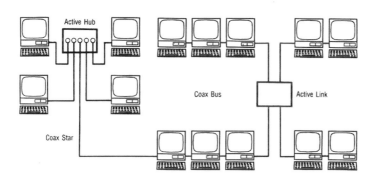

FIGURE 2.18.

Star configuration linked to coax bus under ARCnet.

At one time it was limited to RG-62 A/U thin coaxial cabling, but today's ARCnet is popular in part because it's also able to use existing unshielded twisted-pair wire, as well as IBM types 6, 8, and 9. Its star configuration makes it easy for a network supervisor to diagnose cabling problems, because a cabling problem is localized to a particular hub-to-node link and reflected on most ARCnet cards by an LED.

ARCnet's Access Method

ARCnet uses a token bus protocol that considers the network to be a logical ring. The permission to transmit a token is passed in a logical ring according to the workstation's network interface card address, which must be set between 1 and 255 using an eight-position DIP switch. Each network interface card knows its own address, as well as the address of the workstation to which it will pass the token. The highest-addressed node closes the ring by passing the token to the lowest-addressed node. Figure 2.19 illustrates how this process works.

FIGURE 2.19.

ARCnet's access method.

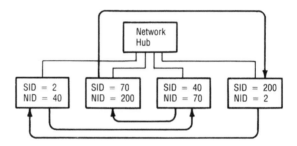

ARCnet is a character-oriented protocol with five different types of frame formats, including:

● An Invitation to Transmit, which passes the token from one node to another
● A Free Buffer Enquiry (FBE), which inquires whether the next workstation can accept a data packet
● The Data Packet itself (up to 507 bytes)
● An Acknowledgment (ACK), indicating a packet has been received correctly
● Negative Acknowledgment (NAK), used to decline an FBE

An *alert burst* of six 1s identifies the ARCnet data packet. The other parts follow sequentially. Figure 2.20 illustrates the ARCnet packet format.

Following the alert burst is the Start of Header (SOH), which comprises one byte. The Source Node ID (SID), which identifies the node sending the packet, is also one byte, though the packet's recipient is specified by a two-byte Destination Node ID (DID). A one- or two-byte count indicates the data field size, and it is followed by the Error Check Characters (CRC). These last two bytes play a role in where the token goes next.

ALERT BURST	SOH	SID	DID	DID	COUNT	DATA	CRC	CRC

FIGURE 2.20.
ARCnet's packet format.

When node 100 receives the token, for example, it might need to send a packet to node 222. It would first send an FBE to node 222, to confirm its ability to receive a message. When it received an ACK as a response, it would transmit its packet. Upon receipt of the packet, node 222 would respond by verifying the error-checking information (CRC) and replying with an ACK.

If node 222 is silent, node 100 knows there must have been an error in transmission. When node 100 does receive an ACK, it can issue an FBE to the next node to use the token, node 101.

IEEE 802.5 Token Ring Network

The IEEE 802.5 standard was developed to cover LANs with ring topologies that use a token to pass information from one workstation to another. At this point, we will examine the theory behind this set of standards.

As Figure 2.21 illustrates, the sending workstation in a token ring network places a message on the token, and directs it to its destination address. The receiving workstation copies the message and then sends the token back to the originating workstation which, in turn, removes its message and passes the token to the next station.

Because it is crucial that an originating station knows whether its message has been received, the frame format is slightly different. Figure 2.22 reveals that there is an ACCESS CONTROL field.

●
IEEE 802.5 defines a token ring network in which workstations pass a token around a physical and logical ring. The token ring uses amplifiers to boost signals so it has a greater range than a bus network.

FIGURE 2.21.
How a token is transmitted on a token ring network.

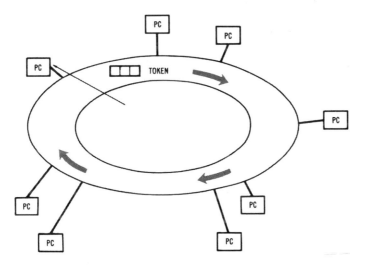

FIGURE 2.22.

Format for a token.

STARTING DELIMITER	ACCESS CONTROL	ENDING DELIMITER

This field controls the actual passing of the token. The ENDING FRAME DELIMITER field also contains a new wrinkle. Two bits in this frame are used to indicate whether the station receiving a message recognized the address, and whether it copied the message successfully.

In a smoothly running token ring network, each station receives the token and checks to see if the message address matches its own. If its address matches, it copies the message and sends the token on by repeating the signal. If the message is for another workstation, it repeats the signal and sends it on. There has to be provision in the network to handle an inactive or defective workstation; otherwise, the entire network would fail if one workstation were disabled. One way to handle this situation is to use hardware that enables the network to bypass a nontransmitting workstation. Earlier we discussed the use of wire centers as a method to keep the token moving past inactive stations.

A major advantage of a token-ring over a token bus is that it can cover a greater distance without loss of signal because each workstation repeats the signal.

Besides the potential problem of a malfunctioning station that is not able to receive or send a message, another major negative feature of a token ring network is that large installations require significantly more cable than a corresponding bus topology. In a very large network, however, there may not be another viable alternative.

The IBM Token Ring Network

The IBM Token Ring Network can transmit at 4Mbps or 16Mbps and supports up to 260 workstations.

The IBM token ring network uses a star-wired ring topology and follows the baseband signaling and token passing protocols of the IEEE 802.5 standard. The network can utilize a variety of cabling from unshielded twisted-pair telephone wire (designated by IBM as Type 3 cabling) to fiber-optic. The token ring network operates at both 4 and 16 mbps and supports up to 260 devices by using shielded twisted-pair, or 72 devices using telephone twisted-pair.

At 16 mbps, the token ring network supports frame sizes up to 18K (compared to the limit of 2K in the 4-mbps ring). These larger frame sizes are ideal for transmission of images in an engineering environment.

The 16-mbps network uses a technique known as early token release. A workstation may transmit a token immediately after sending a frame of data instead of waiting for the original token to return. Using more than one token on the same ring at the same time increases network efficiency and speed; tokens are timed to avoid collision.

The fundamental differences between token ring and Ethernet in the U.S. marketplace are highlighted in Table 2.1 below.

Table 2.1 Token Ring and Ethernet differences.

	Token Ring	*Ethernet*
Network Hardware	Token Ring	Ethernet
Protocol	Token Ring	CSMA/CD
Typical wiring	Shielded/Unshielded Twisted Pair	Coaxial/Unshielded Twisted Pair
Speed	4,16 mbps	10 mbps
Typical Topology	Ring	Bus
IEEE Specification	802.5	802.3

The PC Adapter

The token ring network requires an adapter card in an expansion slot of each node. Figure 2.23 illustrates the configuration of this circuit card. There is an exchange of data buffers and control blocks between the network workstation's memory (RAM) and the adapter card. The card's RAM is mapped into the workstation's memory in a section IBM calls shared RAM. This technique reduces the overhead required for I/O between adapter card and workstation.

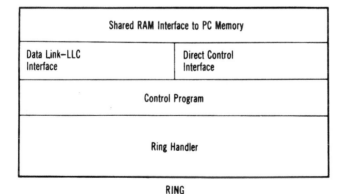

FIGURE 2.23.

Token ring adapter card structure (Courtesy of IBM Corporation).

Figure 2.23 also reveals the two interfaces found on the adapter card. The Data Link LLC Interface contains some microcode (ROM) that supports these logical link control functions (as defined by the IEEE 802.2 standards). The direct interface allows a user program to read logs on such matters as error status information maintained by the adapter card.

The adapter card in each network workstation handles token recognition and data transmission. Among the adapter's network responsibilities are frame recognition, token generation, address recognition, error checking and logging, time-out controls, and link fault detection.

One adapter on each network ring is designated as the active monitor in contrast to the other adapters, which function as passive monitors. Should normal token activity become disrupted, the station that is the active monitor becomes responsible for error recovery procedures. Note that any one of the remaining adapter cards can assume an active role should something happen to the active token monitor.

The adapter card comes with two different diagnostic programs. The Adapter Diagnostics Program is used before the adapter card is attached to the ring. It simply checks the adapter and the attaching cable, and ensures that the card can perform self-diagnostics successfully. A second program checks the adapter card after it has been connected to the ring, and ensures it can perform the "Open" functions required to connect it to the ring media.

The adapter itself can detect permanent errors such as loss of receive signal, and then generate a notification signal to initiate automatic network recovery. The adapter detects recoverable errors such as bit errors in the transmitted message and reports them to a ring diagnostic program.

Token ring network PC adapters are available from a variety of vendors including IBM. PCs are attached directly to the token ring through this adapter.

Multistation Access Unit (MSAU)

The *multistation access unit (MSAU)* is a wiring concentrator that permits up to eight network workstations to be either inserted or bypassed on the ring. This unit is mounted either on a rack located in a nearby wiring closet or in a housing on a wall or tabletop. The MSAU is actually a passive device; it contains bypass circuitry designed to detect the presence or absence of a signal from a network workstation. Should the MSAU detect a defective device or damaged cable, it bypasses this particular workstation to avoid losing data and the token that circulates throughout the ring.

Figure 2.24 illustrates how the workstations are attached to the MSAU. Although up to eight different workstations can be connected in what looks like a star architecture, notice that the topology within the MSAU is really a ring.

Each multistation access unit contains 10 connector jacks. Eight of these ports are used to connect network workstations, and the remaining two ports are used to connect other multistation access units.

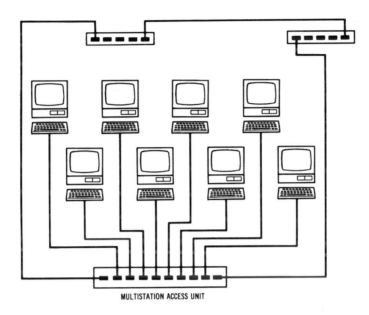

FIGURE 2.24.

Three Multistation Access Units.

MULTISTATION ACCESS UNIT

Data Transmission

Token ring network is a non-contention network. Because of the nature of a token ring architecture, only one network node can send information at any given time. I will take a close look at how information is transmitted and received on this network and also at how network problems are diagnosed.

Information to be sent across the network is formatted into frames. Figure 2.25 illustrates the fields found within these frames. Notice that the frame contains both the destination node address and the address of the source workstation. In very large networks, in which multiple rings are tied together with bridges, an optional routing information subfield (RI) follows the address fields, indicating the sequence of bridges that must be traversed to reach the correct ring.

STARTING DELIMITER	STARTING PHYSICAL CONTROL FIELD	DESTINATION ADDRESS	SOURCE ADDRESS	DATA	FCS	ENDING DELIMITER	ENDING PHYSICAL CONTROL FIELD

FIGURE 2.25.

A token ring information frame.

When a mailbox's flag is up, the postman knows that there is a letter to be picked up. In much the same fashion, the token that circulates around the ring has a bit sequence that tells the various nodes whether it is carrying a message or is free to be used. The first byte of the physical control field, the starting delimiter field, and the ending delimiter field comprise a special token identifier. One of these bits is known as the token bit. When it is set to zero, it means the token is identified as a token and is ready to be used. When a node has information to send, it captures this token and then adds the source and destination addresses, as well as the other fields seen in Figure 24.16. It then changes the zero to a one, meaning that this frame is now an information frame.

The information frame moves through the ring until it reaches the destination node, a workstation that recognizes its own address in the destination address field. This workstation copies the information that has been sent and then returns the information frame to the sender as a token.

Upon return receipt, the sender removes the header (first 15 bytes) and issues a new token. This new token is ready to circulate to the next node that needs to send a message. Each network node gets a chance to use the token, because no one node is allowed to transmit continuously.

Errors can occur on a token ring network, and IBM has developed safeguards to prevent network downtime. As indicated earlier in the discussion of the adapter cards, the circuit cards required in each network node perform such tasks as frame recognition and token generation. A node designated as the active token monitor runs the IBM Token-Ring Manager program. This program monitors the network for transient errors and permanent errors.

A transient error is a "soft" error, often intermittent, which usually can be corrected by retransmission. A node detects soft errors by monitoring all frames, verifying the validity of the frame-check sequence that accompanies the message. Each node keeps track of these errors and reports them if they exceed a threshold amount. An operator can use a function called Soft Error Conditions to display the conditions of all stations reporting transient errors. The node detecting these errors sets the *error detected* flag in the physical trailer portion (6 bytes) of the frame.

In contrast to these soft errors, there are also permanent errors that represent a serious threat to the network's continued operation. When a node sends a message and receives the token back, it examines it to see if the address-recognized flag has been set by the destination node. If the flag has not been set, the location of this defective node is identified. The wire concentrators are able to bypass such faults in the network, and keep the network operating.

A complete disruption of the network signal can be caused by the complete failure of an active node's receiver and/or transmitter, or by a break in the wiring. The next network node downstream from the defective node sends out a special network signal called a beacon. This frame contains the address of the node sending this special message as well as the address of the node immediately upstream from it (presumably the defective node). The normal response to this signal is for the wiring concentrator involved to bypass the defective node.

Breaks in the actual wiring of the network may not be as easy to resolve. The entire ring may have to be reconfigured to bypass a particular break. Because each node has the ability to perform self-diagnostic tests that can identify errors in its wiring, it is a good idea to run these tests if there is no obvious break apparent in the network wiring. Modern wiring concentrators or *hubs* are discussed in more detail in Chapter 4, "A Guide to Network Software." These hubs can reconfigure themselves when an error occurs, effectively disconnecting the faulty workstation from the network.

What Have You Learned?

1. File servers offer many advantages over disk servers in a LAN.

2. The major LAN media include twisted-pair wire, coaxial cable, and fiber optics.

3. Broadband coaxial cable can transmit several different messages simultaneously using different frequencies.

4. In a star topology, the entire LAN fails if the central computer fails.

5. CSMA/CD is a method for detecting and avoiding data collisions on a LAN.

6. X.25 is a standard for packet switching with layers of standards corresponding to the first three layers of the OSI model.

7. The OSI model consists of seven layers of standards designed to ensure LAN compatibility of hardware and software.

8. HDLC consists of protocols for placing a message in a packet for transmission.

Quiz for Chapter 2

1. The X.25 set of standards covers how many layers of the OSI model?

    a. One

    b. Two

    c. Three

    d. Four

2. Which OSI model layer concerns itself with hardware specifications?

    a. Data Link

    b. Network

    c. Physical

    d. Presentation

3. Bit stuffing is used to

    a. pad insufficient information.

    b. distinguish beginning and ending flags from information.

    c. convert 8-bit words into 16-bit words.

    d. fill a data turkey.

4. When a central computer polls a station to see if it has a message to send, this is an example of

    a. Asynchronous Response Mode (ARM).

    b. Normal Response Mode (NRM).

    c. Infrequent Polling Proce dure (IPP).

    d. Polling by Authorization (PBA).

5. A protocol is really

    a. a set of demands.

    b. a set of rules.

    c. a translation book for diplomats.

    d. a call with very high authorization.

6. A CB radio call is very much like

    a. full-duplex transmission.

    b. half-duplex transmission.

    c. quarter-duplex transmission.

    d. no duplex transmission.

7. In the OSI model, error recognition and recovery is really the responsibility of

    a. the Physical layer.

    b. the Application layer.

    c. the Session layer.

    d. the Transport layer.

8. In the OSI model, password verification is the responsibility of

    a. the Session layer.

    b. the Physical layer.

    c. the Data Link layer.

    d. the Network layer.

9. Distributed file servers are

    a. special file servers designed for LANs.

    b. multiple file servers designed to speed up the network.

    c. inexpensive file servers.

    d. file servers also used as workstations.

10. A dedicated file server is

    a. a hard-working file server.

    b. a file server used as a workstation and as a file server.

    c. a file server used only for serving files to workstations in a LAN.

    d. a file server that never breaks down.

11. A print spooler is really

    a. a buffer used to store files for printing.

    b. the central processing unit.

    c. a printer's spooling mechanism.

    d. a place for assembling and disassembling printer material.

12. To send simultaneous voice and data signals, a LAN should use

    a. twisted-pair wire.

    b. baseband coaxial cable.

    c. broadband coaxial cable.

    d. two coffee cans with lots of string.

13. A data highway is a good description of which network topology?

    a. A bus

    b. A star

    c. A ring

    d. A token ring

14. A dead workstation on a token ring network can cripple the network without

    a. special software.

    b. wire centers or special bypass hardware.

    c. extra tokens.

    d. a dead station token (DST).

15. A broadcast address enables a message to go to

    a. a single workstation.

    b. a single group of workstations.

    c. several groups of workstations.

    d. a selected peripheral.

16. A jam signal sent through a network means

    a. the network traffic is too congested.

    b. there has been a data collision.

    c. it's time to go.

    d. the printer's paper feeder is jammed.

17. The IEEE 802.3 standard is most similar to

    a. IBM's Token Ring network.

    b. Xerox's Ethernet LAN.

    c. a generic star network.

    d. a generic token ring network.

18. For a relatively large network covering a long distance, the best network topology would be

    a. a bus.

    b. a token ring.

    c. a token bus.

    d. a superbus.

19. If interference is a major problem, a network designer should consider

    a. baseband coaxial cable.

    b. broadband coaxial cable.

    c. twisted-pair wire.

    d. fiber optics.

20. Database management software and electronic mail software would be found in which layer of the OSI model?

    a. The Application layer

    b. The Presentation layer

    c. The Data Link layer

    d. The Network layer

A Guide to Network Hardware

About This Chapter

This chapter explains some of the hardware found on most networks, including network interface cards (NICs), wiring hubs, backup hardware, uninterruptible power supplies (UPS), and network printers. File servers and communications servers are also discussed. What options do network managers have when considering these products? What are some of the features that help differentiate one product from another product? This chapter has the answers to these critical questions.

Network Interface Cards (NICs)

Network interface cards (NICs) have become commodities, low-priced and readily available. Still, there are important features that help differentiate NIC products:

Is the NIC software configurable?

All but a few die-hard traditionalists prefer the ease-of-use of NICs that accompany software programs that can be used to configure them, rather than the alternative of switches on the cards that must be manually set.

Is a 32-bit card needed to improve performance?

Many network managers have discovered that the sluggish performance of a file server can be improved dramatically by replacing the server's 16-bit NIC with a full 32-bit card. The use of more advanced bus technologies such as PCI further improves both client workstations and servers.

Are any network management or security features included?

Some vendors have sought to differentiate their NICs by adding software that makes it possible to make messages on the network more secure. Also, these cards sometimes contain information that can be used as part of overall network management.

Are combo cards needed?

Network managers with LANs containing mixed media such as 10BaseT and thin coaxial cabling often find it advantageous to buy combo cards, cards that contain multiple interfaces for different media. The advantage of such cards is that they can be used on different segments of a LAN regardless of the different types of media on these segments. Buying cards with multiple interfaces is cost advantageous if an environment has different media types or is planning on migrating from one media to another.

What is the throughput available with the card?

Not all 16-bit or 32-bit cards have the same performance because they use different algorithms. Industry periodicals such as *PC Week* or *InfoWorld* often run stories containing benchmarks based on tests their labs have conducted. This information can be valuable to help differentiate NIC products that might look identical and be priced comparably.

Network Wiring Hub

● The wiring hub or wiring concentrator makes it easy to centralize the control of network cabling.

One major trend in the network industry has been the popular acceptance of wiring hubs as the predominant method of cabling a local area network. The *wiring hub*, also known as a wiring concentrator, is a product that centralizes a network's wiring to make it easier to manage this critical network function. While token ring was the first type of network topology to offer the convenience of this cabling approach, a popular version of Ethernet known as 10BaseT also uses this cabling approach. Figure 3.1 illustrates how PCs on a corporate LAN encompassing a number of floors can be managed using hubs.

A major advantage of a wiring hub is that it provides an easy way to handle employees' moves and changes. If an employee moves from the Accounting department to the Operations department, the LAN need not be re-wired. Instead, the employee's PC is moved to the new location and its network interface card connected to a wiring outlet. At the wiring hub, the wiring for this PC is plugged into a different portion of the hub.

Another major advantage of a wiring hub is that it usually can handle malfunctioning network interface cards so that they do not disrupt the entire network. A wiring hub can sense when a PC's network interface card is malfunctioning. It can then re-route network traffic so that other PCs on the network will not receive the signals generated from this dysfunctional unit.

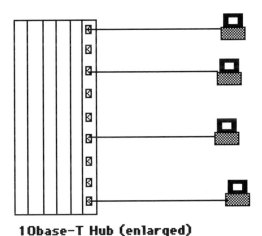

10base-T Hub (enlarged)

FIGURE 3.1.

PCs on a LAN using wiring hubs.

Intelligent Hubs

Intelligent hubs provide the same functionality as outlined above, but, in addition, contain built-in intelligence to communicate network management information to a software package. This enables a network administrator to manage and control all hub functions. The ability to view all hub activity on a single display is particularly valuable in the case of a large network that might contain hundreds of network nodes and multiple LANs that are bridged within the hub.

There are a number of features that could prove desirable in an intelligent hub depending on a company's network needs. The network manager must ask the right questions to ensure that the appropriate wiring hub is selected.

What network topologies are supported?

A large company might require support for both an Ethernet and token ring network immediately. With the need for greater bandwidth looming on the horizon, a network administrator might want to ensure that the intelligent hub purchased also supported FDDI and that the vendor promises to support the 155 mbps asynchronous transfer mode (ATM) architecture in the future.

Is internetworking permitted within the hub?

A company with different types of LANs probably requires the ability to bridge or route packets over its entire enterprise network. Is it possible, for example, to route AppleTalk LAN packets to another network within the hub?

Is mainframe-to-LAN connectivity within the hub required?

Some hub vendors offer products with the ability to route SNA mainframe information to LANs that are managed within their hubs. For companies where mainframe to LAN traffic is heavy, this feature can be valuable.

How many LANs must the hubs accommodate?

Some hubs might be able to accommodate multiple Ethernet and token ring LANs while others are more limited. What kind of growth does the company anticipate in the future?

Do PCs running certain applications on LANs in the hub require dedicated bandwidth?

PCs requiring extensive dedicated bandwidth for certain LAN applications require a feature known as a *switching hub*. Switching hubs provide a point-to-point connection between two PCs on a LAN, very much like a telephone connection, so that these PCs can enjoy as much as a full 10 mbps transmission speed under Ethernet.

Network Backup Systems

Because networks store companies' mission-critical data, backup systems are required. There are several different types of backup technologies available. Quarter-inch cartridge (QIC) tape backup systems are very popular because they are inexpensive and reliable. A limitation is that many vendors offer tape cartridges with only a 600M capacity if the data is also compressed when it is backed up. For a large network, this limitation is clearly a very serious one.

Companies with larger networks requiring media with greater backup capacity often consider 4mm and 8mm digital audio tape (DAT) cartridge drives. These drives can support up to 8G of compressed data storage. Combine this with a suitable six cartridge autochanger, and a storage capacity of 48G becomes available. Unlike quarter-inch tape drives which record information in a linear fashion, these drives utilize helical scan recording technology. A rotating head is used to write data diagonally across slowly moving tapes.

Some companies may invest in a Storage Management System (SMS). These systems automatically archive unused files to cheaper media, and then retrieve them if and when they are required. All this is transparent to the user.

● Redundant arrays of inexpensive disks (RAID) consist of multiple disks used in parallel.

Network Storage and RAID

Network managers are very concerned about their LANs' fault tolerance. If a file server disk drive fails, they want to know that data will not be lost. A solution today that is growing in popularity is known as *redundant arrays of inexpensive disks (RAID)*. RAID can be implemented at either the hardware level or software level. Hardware RAID is most efficient. A RAID system consists of multiple disk drives used in parallel. This arrangement provides the network with redundancy because parity bits spread across the entire range of disks make it possible to reconstruct the data found on a specific disk should it be damaged. While not all levels of RAID provide complete redundancy of data, they do provide enhanced I/O performance over a single, very large file server. There are six different levels of RAID available.

RAID 0

Data is striped (spread) across several disks to improve I/O performance. Unfortunately, this level of RAID does not provide any data redundancy. The failure of a single disk will result in lost data.

RAID 1

RAID 1 consists of disk mirroring. Data is written simultaneously to a pair of drives. If one drive fails, the data can be retrieved from the mirrored drive. The disadvantage of RAID 1 is that a network with an expensive, large file server would require an expensive second drive with the same capacity to act as the mirrored drive.

RAID 2

Error correction is implemented to provide fault tolerance. A failed disk can be rebuilt from the error correction data spread across several disks.

RAID 3

Error correction is included in drive-controller hardware as well as with a parity drive. Data is transferred to the array disk drives one byte at a time; parity is calculated and stored on the dedicated parity drive. A single drive controller is used for reads and writes so that only one write at a time to an array drive takes place. RAID 3 is best suited for handling very large blocks of data.

RAID 4

This level is similar to RAID 3 except it offers better performance with less fault tolerance. Reads and writes can take place independently on any of the array drives. One disadvantage of RAID 4 is that parity information must be updated for every write to every drive.

RAID 5

This level of RAID spreads data and parity information across all the drives in an array. There is no single dedicated parity disk that performs error checking. Performance is boosted because it is possible to have simultaneous reads and writes of data. RAID 5 is better suited for handling smaller files. Figure 3.2 illustrates the difference between RAID 3 and RAID 5.

FIGURE 3.2.

RAID 3 and RAID 5.

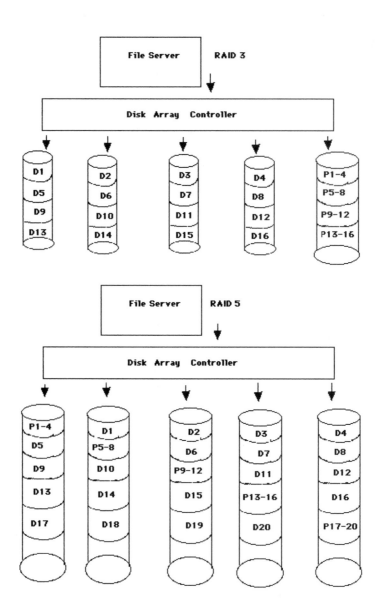

Network Uninterruptible Power Supply

Local area networks require much the same security found on mainframe systems. If the power fails, network administrators want to ensure that data is not lost. The *uninterruptible power supply (UPS)* is a device that contains a battery pack that can provide backup power for a network's file server should electricity fail. This power gives the network administrator time to save all open data files before shutting down the LAN's file server.

There are two different types of uninterruptible power supplies. The *standby UPS* functions very much like an insurance policy. It remains inactive until there is power failure, at which time it springs into action.

The *on-line UPS* is connected directly to the file server and operates all the time. Power entering this type of UPS, charges the UPS's batteries. The UPS filters (conditions) the power before it passes this power on to a LAN's file server. This type of UPS is more expensive than the standby UPS, but it does provide the additional function of conditioning the power. The file server is protected from power spikes that could damage the machine. Some modern UPS's can shutdown a file server if there is power loss; this occurs in a controlled manner protecting the data.

Network Printers

As local area networks have become larger and printing jobs have increased in size and complexity, a market has developed for printers designed specifically for the demands of a network printing environment. These printers generally offer built-in network connectivity, high-speed printing, and enhanced resolution.

The following section highlights some features desirable for network printers.

Duty Cycle

Because of the heavy volume of printing on a network, many network printers now offer a duty cycle of at least 50,000 pages per month. The QMS 860 and HP 4si both have duty cycles of 75,000 pages per month. Several printer manufacturers now offer printers designed for larger networks, with duty cycles upward from 250,000 pages per month.

Direct Network Connections

Many network printers offer slots for network interface cards so that these printers can become nodes connected directly to a network. The advantages of this approach include much faster throughput for these printers with rates from 500,000 bytes per second to

2Ms. Some network printers now come with built-in network interface cards for the major topologies including Ethernet, Token Ring, and LocalTalk.

While most network printers with multiple interfaces have the ability to automatically switch interfaces to receive incoming data, only one interface is active at a time. QMS's network printers offer a multitasking feature that enables them to receive data from multiple interfaces simultaneously and then spool the data on these interfaces to internal memory or to a disk.

Multiple Protocol Support

Large local area networks rarely have only one protocol running over them. If the LAN is using NetWare as its network operating system, then Novell's IPX protocol is running over the network. Are there also some Macintosh computers connected to form an AppleTalk network? Then the AppleTalk protocol is also running on the LAN. Is the LAN linked to a minicomputer running UNIX? If it is, then the TCP/IP suite of protocols is also running over the LAN. Network printers must be able to recognize different protocols and respond appropriately.

Context Switching

A network printer receives print jobs that require different fonts, forms, logos, and overlays. When it switches from one job to another, it needs the ability to retain the state of an emulation during its context switching so that the fonts, forms, logos, and overlays need not be downloaded once again.

Bi-Directional Communications

Some printer vendors, such as Hewlett-Packard, already offer bi-directional communications. This means that the printer and file server can communicate information back and forth. The file server can receive data that can be used in management reports. If a printer error occurs, the network printer can use bi-directional communications to transmit a message that, for example, it is out of paper.

Fax

Some network printers now offer a built-in facsimile (fax) feature. Faxes are printed out as they are received.

Enhanced Resolution

Many of the newer network printers now offer 600 dots per inch (dpi) resolution, four times better resolution than the 300 dpi of the first generation of laser printers. Although costly in comparison to black and white printers, color printers are gaining in popularity.

Asynchronous Communications Servers

For users on local area networks to access external computers and for traveling users to access the LAN, the answer often is an asynchronous communications server. Dial-in service by these servers enables a large number of remote users to dial into the network and connect as if they were local users. Dial-out service enables local users of the LAN to share communications resources such as modems; it is a far more efficient way of handling this function than to provide each user with a modem that sits idle for a significant part of the day. Figure 3.3 illustrates how a communications server is linked to a LAN as well as to several modems.

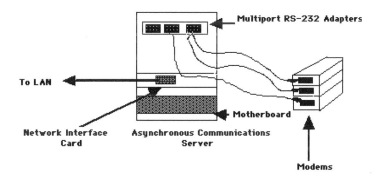

FIGURE 3.3.

An asynchronous communications server in action.

There are a number of questions that can be asked to help determine the appropriate asynchronous communications server to purchase.

What software is running on the server? Is it compatible with the network operating system (NOS) on the LAN?

Communications software can differ widely. Microdyne, for example, has worked very closely with Novell to ensure that Microdyne's asynchronous communications server works smoothly with Novell's asynchronous communications server software specifications. A company that runs VINES or Windows NT on their LAN should make absolutely certain that the asynchronous communications server and server software they purchase will be completely compatible with their network operating system. NetWare Connect and Remote Access Service (RAS) in Windows NT are two examples.

How many modems can be supported by the server?

The anticipated amount of dial-in and dial-out service on the LAN will determine what communications server is appropriate. Many of these servers come with serial interfaces for a specific number of modems. CubixConnect from Cubix combines Novell's NetWare Connect software with Cubix's hardware platform to create a product with strong dial-up capabilities.

Is multiprocessing required for faster remote communications?

Some high-end asynchronous communications servers offer slots in their chassis so that circuit cards containing their own microprocessors can be installed. These cards need not steal CPU time from the communications server because they have their own processing power.

What modem speed and modem protocols are supported?

A company that has international branches containing LANs that need to be linked together to form a wide area network must consider the modem protocols running on its European modems. A company with European branches should consider buying modems that support the CCITT's set of V modem specifications.

Selecting File Servers

Network managers today are faced with so many choices for file servers that it is very difficult to narrow down the alternatives. The following are some questions that can be asked to help determine the appropriate file server for a particular company:

What kind of processing power is required?

If the current file server uses a 33 MHz Intel 80486 microprocessor and is straining to keep up with the processing requirements, a 100 MHz Intel 80486 microprocessor-based file server might prove adequate. More intensive I/O requirements might cause a network manager to consider an Intel Pentium-based file server for even greater microprocessing power. If a new file server is to be purchased, then the network manager would usually buy a file server that uses the best processor that his/her budget would allow. This is due to the price difference between low- and high-end processors being so small.

Is a superserver required?

Simply adding additional processing power might not be enough for a file server to handle network traffic. Superservers are file servers specifically optimized to handle very high levels of network traffic. Some vendors offer symmetrical processing with their superservers; this means that with the appropriate network operating system this hardware can divide processing demands among multiple processors to cut processing time. These processors are normally only required on larger LANs or LANs that require a very high resilience. Windows NT Server supports symmetric multiprocessing.

What kind of storage is available?

Does the file server vendor offer RAID or other fault tolerance systems?

Can the file server be upgraded to other fault tolerance systems in the future?

What kind of diagnostic software and network management software is included or available?

More and more vendors including Hewlett-Packard and Compaq offer software that enables users to diagnose any problems that might develop on their file servers. The ability to manage file servers is very important on larger networks.

What kind of expandability is available?

File servers vary widely in the number of slots available for adding circuit cards. They also vary in the amount of RAM that can be added. Can the main areas of the server be upgraded without the need to completely replace the machine?

What kind of support is provided?

Some vendors now offer free on-site maintenance as well as free technical support lines. How long can you afford to have a file server down?

Is the file server certified for the specific network operating system that will be running on it?

NetWare, as an example, does not run equally well on all file servers. Check to see if the vendor has received certification from the network operating system manufacturer.

What Have You Learned?

1. Network interface cards are much easier to install if they are software configurable.
2. Wiring hubs centralize cabling management and control functions.
3. Intelligent hubs make it possible to manage and control all hub elements from a single console. They are more resilient than dumb hubs.
4. Network managers with large LANs are often attracted to the 8G capacity offered by digital audio tape as a backup medium.
5. Redundant arrays of inexpensive disks (RAID) provide network fault tolerance as well as improved I/O performance.
6. An on-line UPS conditions and filters power while remaining ready to provide backup battery power should electrical power fail.
7. Network printers with direct connections to a LAN can enjoy the enhanced data throughput of over 500,000 bytes per second.
8. Superservers are file servers with their architecture, hardware, and software optimized to handle the heaviest network traffic.

Quiz for Chapter 3

1. A combo card is a

   a. discount on a hamburger and french fries.

   b. an NIC with multiple interfaces.

   c. an card designed for a wiring hub.

   d. an NIC that runs at two different speeds.

2. The first network topology to offer the centralized wiring control of a wiring hub was

   a. LocalTalk

   b. 10Base2

   c. 10BaseT

   d. Token Ring

3. Intelligent hubs are intelligent because

   a. they can be trained very much like a dog.

   b. they have intelligence built-in.

   c. they are more expensive.

   d. they alert network managers if intruders try to break into the LAN.

4. Switching hubs provide nodes with a dedicated bandwidth by using techniques very similar to those used by a

   a. pbx

   b. tv

   c. microwave

   d. automobile

5. A major advantage of RAID is

   a. the elimination of computer bugs.

   b. its low price.

   c. improved I/O performance.

   d. its compatibility with SNA.

6. The most popular backup tape for LANs is still

   a. 4mm DAT

   b. quarter-inch cartridge tape

   c. 8mm DAT

   d. half-inch cartridge tape

7. Very large blocks of data are best handled by

   a. RAID 1

   b. RAID 2

   c. RAID 3

   d. RAID 5

8. Small files are best handled by

   a. RAID 5

   b. RAID 4

   c. RAID 3

   d. RAID 0

9. The minimum duty grade for a network printer with heavy LAN traffic is probably

   a. 15,000 pages/minute

   b. 25,000 pages/minute

   c. 75,000 pages/minute

   d. 150,000 pages/minute

10. Directly connecting a printer to a network can result in data throughput of over

a. 5,000 bytes/second

b. 100,000 bytes/second

c. 150,000 bytes/second

d. 500,000 bytes/second

11. For remote users to communicate with a corporate LAN as a LAN node, the communications server on the LAN needs to have

a. dial-out service

b. dial-in service

c. dine-in service

d. remote node service

A Guide to Network Software

About This Chapter

Many companies have found that installing a LAN also meant selecting new software written specifically for their network. Fortunately, MS-DOS and OS/2 have provided some uniformity in network software. Because the network hardware and software offered by IBM, Artisoft, and Microsoft all adhere to DOS standards, software publishers have found it fairly easy to write generic network editions of their products which work on almost any DOS-based network.

In this chapter, you examine how all versions of MS-DOS since version 3.1 provide network features (such as record locking) and what options companies have if their single-user software cannot be upgraded to at least DOS 3.1 standards. You survey the most desirable features found in word processing programs, spreadsheets, database managers, and accounting programs, and see how they function in a network environment.

Electronic messaging is more than electronic mail (e-mail) transmission; it also includes the use of network-based facsimile (fax) machines, many of which work in conjunction with network e-mail systems. You take a close look at several different electronic messaging systems that are available for the leading LANs, including some network fax applications.

Because there is an industry movement toward incorporating CCITT standards in electronic mail packages (in order to facilitate internetwork connectivity), you examine the CCITT's X.400 set of recommendations. You also look at Novell's Message Handling System (MHS), a product that network software companies and electronic messaging companies are licensing to provide e-mail services comparable to many offered by the CCITT X.400 set of recommendations. You examine the effects on electronic messaging of the new CCITT X.500 set of recommendations—which provide for the creation of a global mail directory of users.

MS-DOS

As Figure 4.1 shows, MS-DOS resides in the Presentation layer of the OSI model, along with the Redirector program. It acts as an interface between the application programs and the NETBIOS (which resides between the Presentation and Session layers).

FIGURE 4.1.

MS-DOS and the OSI Model.

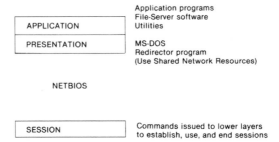

Under network conditions, MS-DOS provides multi-user access to files through its SHARE program. SHARE enables the programmer to specify that the first workstation to use a file has certain levels of access, while subsequent users have different levels of access.

For example, a crucial accounting data file, used by several different workstations, could be designated as read-write for the first user to request it. While this user continues to write to this file, other users (under SHARE's Read-Write with deny-write sharing mode) can only read the file.

MS-DOS versions 3.1 and later also have a byte-locking function—which enables a programmer to write a program so that a range of bytes is locked, and other users cannot write to this area until the first user "unlocks" the area. The result of the SHARE program's different access rights and MS-DOS's byte-locking is that a file will not be destroyed by two users simultaneously writing over each other's data.

Programs written prior to the release of MS-DOS version 3.1 are unable to utilize this multi-user feature. Although they can be installed on a network so that one user is allowed to write to a file while other users can only read it, such manipulation is of limited value in most modern office environments. This is because the only alternative with DOS 2.x versions is to write multiple copies of the file to different directories and have different people use different versions of the file (a cumbersome and confusing approach). With version 3.1's record locking, different users can take turns accessing the same record. In addition to MS-DOS's multi-user capabilities, it allows use of the Redirector program, and programmers have begun to utilize this capability. The Redirector acts as a "traffic cop," directing requests for shared network resources, and it is used by many network programs. As MS-DOS has significantly improved through to its current version 6.2 most companies would see performance improvements by moving to this newer version.

Client/Server Applications

The introduction of OS/2 in 1987 and Windows NT in 1993 heralded a new level of distributed network computing. Before these products, most LAN file servers handled a workstation's database query by sending the entire database file across the network to that workstation. When the workstation completed sorting the database (and making whatever changes it needed to make), it returned the information to the file server.

There are several problems associated with this traditional LAN approach to sharing a database program and its files. Network congestion increases as more and more workstations request that the program and its files be sent, and then send information back to the file server. Network overhead also can become a problem with this approach, because a database program may need to create several different processes to permit multi-user operations. With so many files traveling through the network, data integrity also may be an issue.

More and more network applications, particularly database applications that have very large files, use a client/server architecture. Running on a file server, these programs provide database management service to applications running on network workstations.

When a workstation queries a database under a client/server architecture, a *back-end* program receives the request, finds where the desired information resides on the database, then forwards only the specific information requested—not the entire database file—back to the workstation (which does its own processing). The end user's *front-end* application program uses APIs to make these queries and requests in a manner transparent to the user. It does not matter where the database is physically located. This client/server approach of having an application program access a "back-end" server is not limited to databases. Several different types of client "front-end" applications (spreadsheets, accounting programs, project management programs, and so on) can access the "back-end" server (in this case, an application server).

The "front-end" application program processes the information it requested and displays it on the screen. Meanwhile, the "back-end" server program maintains the database's integrity and ensures that the network functions with optimum efficiency.

●
Client/Server applications include a front-end client program and a back-end server program.

Network Software and the Law

Most single-user software packages specify that the program may only be used on a single machine and/or by one user at a time. Using such programs under network conditions is clearly illegal. Therefore, a major consideration in selecting network software is the software vendor's policy toward network use of its product.

Many companies have developed special network versions of their products; these are licensed for specific sizes of user groups. A network supervisor might select an application and then license a certain number of copies to run on the network. The customer pays for the initial package, and then a per-user fee. Beyond the basic program, the application may supply some extra network features (such as workgroup editing or multiuser document creation) that make it advantageous for a customer to purchase this edition.

For a negotiated fee, other companies provide a site-licensing agreement specifying that the product may be used at that site by an unlimited number of users.

Unfortunately, many major software companies simply offer discounts if their single-user products are purchased in large volumes. This solution is not acceptable for most companies that use LANs; it is far too expensive, even with substantial discounts.

> Most single-user software is licensed for one user and/or one machine. To use software on a network, it is necessary to buy a network version of a program, sign a site licensing agreement, or negotiate a volume purchase from the software manufacturer.

Word Processing Software

Word processing is probably the most common application that users require in their daily jobs. This section discusses how word processing programs fit into the network picture.

Why Use a Network Version?

Most network users have already developed a fondness for a particular word processing program, and prefer to continue using it. There are various problems, however, with everyone using a pet word processing program and then using the network file server for document storage:

> Network versions of word processing programs provide some assurances of file compatibility, printer compatibility, and a standardized appearance for company documents.

- Not all word processing files are compatible with one another.
- Because different programs have varying formatting capabilities, it is difficult to achieve uniformity within a company. Bill's proposals might look completely different from Janet's, and when they work on a document together (and try to exchange data files), it might be impossible for either of them to determine what the final document will look like.
- Various program versions offer varying features. If two employees are using two versions of Ami Pro, only one of them might be able to use specific functions in a later version. This may lead to difficulties in sharing the data file.

● Different versions of the same program also might contain slightly different printer drivers, and these could create some unpleasant printing surprises.

● Single-user word processing programs do not offer file-locking capabilities. This feature is extremely important on a network, because it means that several individuals can use the same word processing program without worrying about destroying a particular document file inadvertently.

Word Processing Features

While there are hundreds of word processing features available on some of the major network versions, here you will concentrate on those features of particular value to network users. Assume that a company with a LAN prints dozens of types of documents, including some material on pre-existing forms. Furthermore, the company has several hundred customers with which it wishes to communicate on a regular basis. To achieve these word processing objectives, a company would have to examine programs that offer certain formatting, editing, and file-managing features—and a number of utility programs. Let's look at some important formatting features.

Seeing Is Believing

One feature that distinguishes some word processing programs is the ability to display information exactly as it will appear when printed. This *what-you-see-is-what-you-get (WYSIWYG)* feature is particularly important in a network program, because network users frequently share laser printers as well as software.

Documents containing high-quality graphics can take a long time to print even on a high-performance network printer. Using WYSIWYG enables a user to get a preview of the document before it is printed, errors in the document can be seen before printing using this ability. Products such as Lotus Ami Pro and Microsoft Word for Windows have the WYSIWYG functionality.

Style Sheets

Companies large enough to support a LAN usually require specific formats for their various types of documents. A company might stipulate, for example, that all top-level headings in its proposals be uppercase and boldface, and all subheadings be lowercase and underlined. Company policy might also dictate that all memos use a specific font, with the headings in boldface. Research reports might require still another company-dictated format, with footnotes placed at the bottom of the page.

Most major word processing programs offer several styles for creating footnotes, headings, and subheadings. A network user writing a letter, memo, report, or proposal selects the

●
Style sheets enable word processing users to format documents after writing them, by linking the document to a particular set of style specifications.

appropriate style sheet, and the word processor automatically formats it correctly. This feature is especially valuable on a network, because it ensures that all company correspondence and reports are uniform in style and format.

Forms Processing

One frustrating aspect of using a word processing program instead of a typewriter is the difficulty of printing information precisely where a standard form requires it. This ability to define and print fields anywhere on a pre-existing form is known as *forms processing*; it is particularly valuable on a company network in which several different forms are used on a regular basis.

Certain word processing programs can design forms and then place information into these forms.

Editing Multiple Documents

A LAN user might need to view multiple documents simultaneously in order to compare certain passages. Most network word processing programs (such as Ami Pro and Word for Windows) enable users to view and edit different documents simultaneously as they are displayed in screen windows; Word enables the user to open as many documents as they want dependent only on the amount of free RAM in their PC. Other programs (such as WordPerfect for DOS) enable a user to load two documents and then switch back and forth between them; the Windows version of Word Perfect offers simultaneous viewing of more than one document.

Mail Merge

Word processing programs can merge information found in a database program (names, addresses, and so on) with a letter to produce individualized form letters.

One of the major word processing functions on a local area network is the mail merge. Companies frequently merge customer information (name, address, and so on) contained in database files with a form letter produced on the word processing program. Beyond that, the merge often permits individualized information to be inserted within the letter if certain conditions are met. Widget Company might write a form letter to all its customers, for instance, but it might include a paragraph about an upcoming Megawidget Seminar only in those letters addressed to customers who recently purchased this product.

If mail merging is to be a major network function, the network administrator must address the critical question of what form the customer data will take—and how easily this information can be merged with a particular word processing program. Most word processing programs offer the capability to merge with several types of files, including dBASE, ASCII, and ODBC formats.

Program File Formats

Effective mail merging requires complete compatibility between the word processing program and the database's customer files. If data communication is a major network concern, it is equally important to determine the file formats a word processor produces. A company might have its LAN connected through a gateway PC to its mainframe computer. It also might have its LAN connected with remote branch locations. Since PC communications programs are usually designed to transmit ASCII files without word processing control codes, it is important to consider which word processing file formats are available.

Most major word processing programs today can produce standard ASCII files, and can import the ASCII files produced by other word processing programs. Most word processors can also import files created in other word processors or graphics packages. For example, Word for Windows can import documents created in ASCII, WordPerfect for Windows, Word for Macintosh, and various other formats. If network users wish to incorporate Lotus 1-2-3 worksheets into their word processing documents, most word processing programs can read Lotus files directly.

●
Today's word processing programs are designed to import and export data in a variety of different formats.

Printer Support

Because software programs require printer drivers in order to print documents, a company with incompatible printers offers a real challenge for a network administrator; proliferation of microcomputers and accessories in the company may have resulted in serious incompatibility problems. In such a case, a principal advantage that a LAN offers is the capability to share valuable resources such as laser printers. Perhaps the administrator's most basic question, when selecting a word processing program for the network, is: "Does the program support all our printers?"

Under DOS, WordPerfect and Word are particularly strong in this area. Because network programs normally are installed to run with a specific printer, the administrator usually writes batch files under DOS that enable a user to access the word processing program along with the specific printer driver needed. When a novice network user accesses the network version of Word or WordPerfect (for example), usually the word processing program is already configured for the printer that it needs; the user does not have to specify the printer.

Operating systems like Windows and OS/2 have printer support built into them at a lower level than the application. This means that a network administrator can install the operating system with the correct printer drivers for the network printers installed. Then any application that runs on the operating system can print to the network printers. Having the printer drivers built into the operating system rather than the word processor means that the user or administrator only has to configure the printer once for all applications rather than for each application.

●
To use all the features of a laser printer, a word processing program should have a printer driver specifically written for that printer or take advantage of the built-in printer drivers of the operating system like Windows or OS/2.

Laser printers have assumed a major role on most LANs, which is a prime consideration in the selection of a word processing program for a network. Does the program support the laser printer's proportionally spaced fonts? Proportional spacing eliminates those gaping spaces found in most documents when a word processing program justifies the left and right margins.

For international companies with LANs, a second criteria for word processing programs is whether or not users must write in other languages. Both WordPerfect for Windows and Word for Windows come in a variety of languages including editions in French, German, Spanish, Finnish, Swedish, Norwegian, Dutch, and Danish.

If network users need to print in any foreign language, it is imperative that the administrator select a laser printer that can use downloaded fonts (such as the Hewlett-Packard LaserJet 4si). The network printer also needs this capability if its users want to print special mathematical symbols and other specific characters.

Other Desirable Word Processing Features

●
Among the more advanced word processing features are macros, mathematical functions, multiple columns, and graphics capabilities.

All the major networkable word processing programs offer the standard, expected features—such as the capabilities to search and replace text, move and replace block paragraphs, and format text. Other word processing features are not standard but might be desirable on a LAN; these include macros, glossaries, mathematical functions, dictionaries, and keyword searches of documents.

Some programs can produce macros—lists of instructions the program performs when a specific combination of keys is pressed. For example, if a company required documents to be formatted in a way that involved several complicated steps, a network administrator could write a macro that executed these steps with a single keystroke enabling the novice user to accomplish the formatting without having to learn the entire procedure.

Many companies use letters made up of a series of form paragraphs that are organized around a customer's individual request. For example, a customer who wanted to know about the availability of a Superwidget and the training classes offered might receive a letter with paragraphs describing the company, the Superwidget, and the training classes available, as well as a standard concluding paragraph offering immediate service. Some programs (such as Microsoft Word) provide glossaries that can be written and then stored. A network user who needs to insert a paragraph about the Superwidget's specifications checks the list of glossaries, and selects the appropriate Superwidget glossary entry. This material (which can range from one paragraph to several pages) is then inserted into the letter at the desired location.

Using mathematical functions can save network users valuable time. A salesperson can draw up a contract, have the word processing program line up the numbers in appropriate columns, and perform all the mathematical operations before providing the final cost to the customer on the appropriate contract line.

Also valuable is the inclusion of a dictionary, and even a thesaurus. Programs such as Microsoft Word and WordPerfect offer sophisticated dictionaries that help guide spelling accuracy. If a word processing program does not offer an internal dictionary, the administrator should determine whether the program's files can be read by one of the major dictionary/thesaurus programs on the market (such as those from Random House and American Heritage).

Because of the sheer number of document files found on many LANs, the capability of identifying documents by certain keywords can be an advantageous feature. A company routinely uses its word processing document summary screen to list the document's recipient (ABC Supply Company), the type of correspondence (sales order confirmation), and the salesperson involved (Frank Wilson). These include enabling each user to create a customized dictionary, as well as public and private document files. It is possible to create a document library and search it for a list of correspondence that matches specified criteria.

I have not discussed other significant word processing features; these capabilities—which include producing columns side-by-side and incorporating text and graphics on the same page—are related more closely to desktop publishing, which will be discussed shortly. The network administrator should, however, become familiar with these particular features of word processing, because desktop publishing is becoming a major network function for many companies.

Spreadsheets for Networks

Spreadsheet programs are ideal for creating and maintaining budgets, forecasting sales, performing financial analyses, and thousands of other jobs involving mathematical calculations. For network use, network administrators often provide services to make the spreadsheet program easier to use.

Many network administrators create spreadsheet templates for different types of users; salespeople might have a bid form, while financial analysts might have a budget form. These templates can be in a public area of the file server, so that everyone can use them. Network users who need to share the information in their completed spreadsheet with other network users can place a copy of their data in the shared directory.

⬤ Spreadsheets can be customized and templates created for users who need not understand the underlying formulas contained within these templates.

Macros for Spreadsheets

Because network users' levels of sophistication vary so widely, network administrators can enable novices to use complicated spreadsheets (such as Excel, Lotus 1-2-3, or Quattro Pro) by writing macros—mini-programs that execute specific commands within a spreadsheet, so that a user can perform very complex operations by pressing a small number of keys, Alt+K, for example.

Financial and Mathematical Considerations

Some companies select a spreadsheet because of particular financial or mathematical functions. One such feature is goal seeking—which allows a user to name a target value and have the program calculate the variable value required to reach that goal. If a company wants to achieve a certain profit level, for example, the spreadsheet indicates the sales volume necessary to achieve this level. Many programs offer this highly desirable feature. Some programs have built-in functions to handle amortization and depreciation. A network of financial analysts would want to use a program that offered various built-in functions, including those for net present value, internal rate of return, payment, future value, present value, and others.

Database Management

●
Database programs on a network must have record locking as well as the ability to provide customized reports to meet the network users' range of needs.

While word processing might be the function used most often on a LAN, the LAN's very heart—and cost justification—is likely to be its *database management program*. An insurance office, for example, might have several agents accessing a central database to identify customers whose policies are about to come due. Similarly, a mail-order business might have several people processing phone orders, checking current inventory, and determining customer credit history—all dependent upon a central database program on a LAN.

Because many network users need to use the database program simultaneously, it is essential to select a program that has a network version. Network versions provide record locking, which permits several people to use the same file (such as a list of customers), as long as they don't try to modify the same record (a customer's history) simultaneously. The program permits only one user to revise a specific record at a time.

Most of the major network programs are relational database programs. This means that it is possible to create a number of files or tables and then produce reports that reveal the relationships among various fields. Microsoft Access is an example of this type of program. While today's database management programs have hundreds of features, we'll examine only those few which are essential for a network.

Customized Reports

Because a network must serve many different user needs, it is essential that the database management program have a sophisticated report generator that can create customized reports. Network administrators with unusual reporting needs might want to consider programs that can perform these functions:

- Create column-oriented or row-oriented reports
- Stamp reports with the time and date
- Provide custom borders and footers

Record and Field Limitations

Because of the scope of many network database management files, it is imperative that the network administrator determine the maximum number of records and fields that might be needed, and determine unusual field requirements so the company does not outgrow the program. For example, a salesperson who wants to keep detailed records of conversations with each customer might want a memo field capable of holding an entire page of comments.

Procedural, Programming, and Query Languages

Some companies might find that even the most sophisticated database program cannot meet their needs. In such cases, it is essential that the program offer programming interfaces; then database information can be manipulated by a customized program.

Some programs permit data tables to be manipulated from C programs. In their network versions, many of these programs offer procedural language capabilities. This means they permit the writing of short programs within the database itself.

Many network users do not need a programming or procedural language so much as they need the ability to query the database—to ask complicated questions based upon data relationships. A police department with a network database program containing the characteristics of thousands of criminals might ask to see a list of all the male burglars between the ages of 20 and 35 who are left-handed, have red hair, and walk with a limp. A query language would permit the user to phrase this question in English.

IBM has made it clear that it supports its Structured Query Language (SQL) as the future standard for relational database programs. Companies that wish to install network software consistent with this language— and want their future minicomputer and microcomputer network software to have file compatibility—would be wise to look at programs that support SQL. Many of the leading relational database management systems (RDBMS) support SQL.

> ●
> Databases with programming interfaces make it possible to create customized programs for the company's business.

Microsoft SQL Server

Microsoft SQL Server is one of the leading LAN relational databases. SQL Server has earned a strong reputation for performance, reliability and usability, making it one of the main Database Management Systems (DBMS) for major LAN-based database applications. SQL Server runs on a wide variety of Intel and RISC-based hardware systems because it runs on the Windows NT operating system, from PCs to multiprocessor superservers, providing scalability to meet the growing needs of the LAN Community.

Some of the features of SQL Server include:

● An efficient multi-threaded engine that helps ensure high transaction throughput and quick response time

- Broad network support across a variety of platforms
- Scalability across processors
- Transaction recovery to correct database problems in the event of system failure
- Integrated security to both the network and the database
- Operates with all popular networks using native protocols, including NetWare, Windows and Windows NT, Banyan VINES, AppleTalk, TCP/IP-based networks, PATHWORKS, and Microsoft LAN Manager

●
Network accounting programs must have record locking capabilities, as well as a set of integrated modules that provide adequate network security.

Network Accounting Software

Just as a database program would lose most of its value on a network without record-locking capability, an accounting program must also enable several users to access the same module simultaneously. A large company with hundreds of payments arriving the first week of each month might need several accounts receivable clerks to update its accounting program. While not all these clerks would need to examine the same customer record at the same time, they all would need to be able to use the Accounts Receivable module. Similarly, a computerized retail store must have an accounting program that enables several clerks to perform order entry (or point-of-sale processing) as the program instantly updates the store's inventory information.

In addition to record-locking capabilities, the network administrator and company accountant should consider a number of other accounting program features. We examine some of the more pressing issues in the following sections.

The Scope of Integrated Accounting Modules

Network accounting programs offer a variety of integrated modules. This means that a customer chooses whether such program modules as Order Entry, Point-of-Sale, Fixed Assets, and Job Costing are needed to supplement the standard General Ledger, Accounts Receivable, Accounts Payable, and Payroll modules.

Many network programs offer integrated modules for specific industries. PROLOGIC, for example, links its financial modules and its distribution modules through Accounts Receivable and Accounts Payable. Figure 4.2 shows the relationships between integrated modules.

As the figure shows, this relationship can be quite complex. A wholesale distributor might have several different prices for various customers. The Customer Order Processing module creates an invoice (using information from the Bill of Materials and Inventory modules) and sends the invoice to the Accounts Receivable module (where a record of the customer's invoice amount is maintained, along with any payments made).

A network administrator who needs specialized accounting modules may have to compromise some basic accounting program features in order to enjoy the advantages of integrating specialized information into the General Ledger.

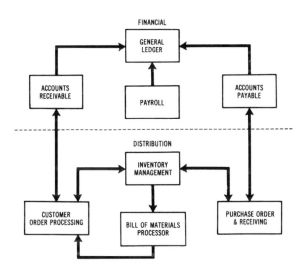

FIGURE 4.2

Data flow within a financial and distribution system. (Courtesy of PROLOGIC Management Systems, Inc.)

Program Security

Because of the nature of accounting, simple network security (such as a login password) is not sufficient. Most accounting departments need different security levels within a module. A payroll clerk might need a certain level of security access to produce a payroll—but definitely not a level that would allow unauthorized personnel to change pay rates or view confidential salary information.

Many of the more sophisticated network accounting packages (such as PROLOGIC) enable the network administrator to limit access to portions of a particular module. An employee might be able to enter inventory when it is received, but not see the screen listing the actual cost of the items; some companies don't want their employees to know what their profit margin is.

Closely related to this security issue is the accounting program's ability to produce a clear audit trail of all transactions. Most of the better programs produce a report listing all inventory transactions, for example. An employee cannot simply reduce an item's inventory total by one and then take the item home. The audit trail report will identify the employee from the password used when he or she logged onto the system, and indicate that on a certain date at a certain time, the employee reduced the inventory value by the specified amount.

Specific Accounting Requirements

While many companies keep track of their inventories using a FIFO approach (first in, first out) or a LIFO approach (last in, first out), most accounting programs don't compute inventory in this fashion. Instead, they use a weighted average approach; the value of inventory is totaled and then divided by the number of items, with some items "counting heavier" than others. Some powerful programs (such as Solomon) let the network administrator and accountant specify which type of cost method to use: LIFO, FIFO, average cost, specific identification, standard, or a user-defined approach.

Companies often have specific field requirements. They may need a 12-digit general ledger account number, for example, or inventory part numbers of 14 digits. The network administrator and accountant should use their present accounting reports as a model, and ask prospective software vendors to provide a demonstration that proves their programs can meet such requirements. The demonstration should also provide evidence of how easy it is to enter information and move from one menu screen to another. Figure 4.3 illustrates the amount of information provided on typical menu screens in the Solomon IV accounting program.

FIGURE 4.3.

Typical Inventory Screens. (Portions of this work have been copyrighted by Solomon Software, Inc., and have been used in this work with the consent of Solomon Software, Inc.)

```
01-82-0009          INVENTORY MENU          Screen 10.00

     DATA ENTRY              PROCESSES
01 Receipts              50 Compute Cost of Goods Sold
02 Sales                 51 Revise Sales Price
03 Adjustments
04 Transfers                OTHER
                         90 Reports
     INQUIRY             95 Inventory Setup
20 Inventory Items       99 Master Menu

     MAINTENANCE
25 Inventory
26 Sales Price
27 Unit Conversion
28 Product Class
29 Price Level
30 Inventory Substitute

          Enter Number of Selection: _
```

```
01-82-0009          INVENTORY INQUIRY          Screen 10.20

  Inventory ID     Inv Acct Sub     COGS Acct Sub

               Inventory Description

Prod Class Id _____  Suplr 2 _____  Qty On Hand _____
Stock Item(Y,N) _____  Item 2 _____  Qty Uncost _____
Val Mthd(F,L,A,S,T,U) ____  Ord Point _____  Per Beg Bal _____
Repl Mthd(Q,C,O) _____  Reord Qty _____  Inv Bal _____
Comp Sales(Y,N) _____  Max On Hand _____  PTD Qty _____
Disc Pricing(D,P) _____  Std Cost _____  PTD Sales _____
Stock Unit _____  Lst Cost _____  PTD Gross _____
Base Price _____  Avg Cost _____  YTD Qty _____
Revised Base _____  Qty On PO _____  YTD Sales _____
Deft Whse-Loc _____  Qty On BO _____  YTD COGS _____
Weight _____  Qty On SO _____  Pr YTD Qty _____
                                            Pr YTD Sales _____
                                            Pr YTD COGS _____
```

Accounting Report Capabilities

Many accounting programs offer dozens of standard reports, but what happens if a company needs a certain report that doesn't follow the conventional pattern? Some companies offer built-in financial report writers that permit some choice in selecting which lines are printed in a balance sheet.

What if a company needs a report comprised of information from two or three modules? There are two possible solutions to this dilemma. One solution is to pay thousands of dollars for a customized program. Another option is to buy an accounting program report generator. This program can generate reports from various files, and then perform mathematical operations within the reports.

Customizing Accounting Programs

It's unlikely that one program will satisfy all the accounting needs of a company. Some programs permit user customization. Others require the purchase of a source code or provide a customizing service to users at standard programming rates. Open Systems Accounting Software permits its users to customize menus (which can include rewriting menu entries and changing the order of a menu). If more elaborate programming changes are needed, Open Systems makes the source code available. The company also publishes a list of software developers familiar with its source code.

Other Features

Since the implementation of an accounting program on a network is supposed to make the accounting more efficient, a number of program features that can help achieve this goal are worth considering:

- Automatic (rather than manual) handling of recurring entries can help reduce errors.
- Because a network frequently adds users, a feature that provides on-line help screens can reduce training time and make new users more productive.
- Because networks are as prone to power failure as single-user systems, some accounting programs provide frequent backups, and even update their master file with each transaction. This approach ensures accurate on-line data queries, and minimizes data loss in the event of power failure.

Electronic Messaging on LANs

Today, electronic messaging means much more than simply one network user sending a note to one or more other users. Many electronic messaging programs also include the ability to send mail from one network to another—or even around the world. Often these programs also have the ability to maintain calendars for everyone on the network, schedule meetings, and even send phone messages automatically. More than simply a paperless office mail system, today's electronic messaging programs are designed to handle virtually all intraoffice and interoffice communications, and to link network users with each other and with the rest of the world.

●
Electronic messaging includes more than just electronic mail or *e-mail.* It includes gateways to other networks and fax machines, as well as numerous scheduling and organizing features.

CCITT X.400

In Chapter 2, I mentioned the *International Standards Organization (ISO)* and its *Open Systems Interconnect (OSI) model*, designed to promote a set of standards for internetwork communications. The OSI model designates the Application layer (layer 7) as the location for a *Message Handling System (MHS)*. The purpose of the MHS is to provide a standard for electronic messaging, so that different computer networks can communicate regardless of differences in their operating system environments.

In developing its model, the ISO used a set of standards from the *Consultative Committee for Telephony and Telegraphy (CCITT)*. These evolving standards are usually referred to as the CCITT X.400 set of recommendations; Table 4.1 reflects their scope.

Table 4.1. The CCITT X.400 Recommendations

Standard	Recommendation
X.400	System model and service elements
X.401	Basic service elements and optional user interfaces
X.408	Encoded Information and Conversion Rules
X.409	Presentation transfer syntax and notation
X.410	Remote operations and reliable transfer system
X.411	Message transfer layer
X.420	Interpersonal messaging user-agent layer
X.430	Access protocol for teletex terminals

While much of this material is too complex to cover in this book, it is important that we look at the basic building blocks of an X.400-compliant system, because virtually all LAN manufacturers have announced support for these international standards.

Message Handling

● An X.400 message handling system includes user agents, message transfer agents, and a message transfer system.

An X.400-compliant MHS includes various elements, each with specific functions. These are the basic three elements.

● The user agent (UA) is the software part of the MHS that provides the interface or connection between network user and MHS, enabling the user to retrieve and send messages.

● The UA interacts with a message transfer system (MTS)—software that operates in support of the network users, providing the screen display they see.

● The message transfer agents (MTAs) consist of the messages sent by users, plus the commands that provide a number of store-and-forward services—a "post office." Sometimes they store messages until a requested delivery time and date. Other times they may have to convert the message into a form that a destination user can understand.

Figure 4.4 illustrates how these elements are related within the structure of the MHS.

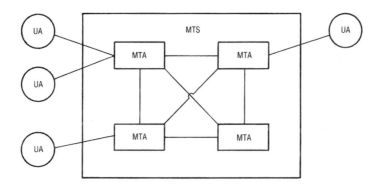

FIGURE 4.4.
A message handling system.

The MHS provides, on request, a variety of network and internetwork services that enhance electronic communications. These include notice of verified delivery or nondelivery (with an explanation), time and date stamps for submission as well as delivery, multidestination deliveries, alternate recipients, and even different grades of delivery service (including non-urgent, normal, and urgent).

The P1, P2, and P3 Protocols

As part of its X.400 recommendations, CCITT has developed three key protocols, or sets of standards. These set rules for routing information, specify services the user can request, and change the parameters of MTAs as needed.

Protocol P1 (defined in the X.411 recommendation) provides rules for routing information between two MTAs. These rules take the form of formatting specifications to be followed in packaging information. The "envelope" for the information consists of the data to be sent, plus several fields that provide such important control elements as the following:

● A *message identifier*, which provides unique identification for where this message originated, as well as the name of the user sending the message.

● A description of how this information should be displayed.

●
The P1 protocol provides rules for routing information between two MTAs.
The P2 protocol defines the types of services requested.
The P3 protocol provides rules for changing existing parameters for electronic mail routing and delivery.

● Information describing the destination user and this user's address.

● Delivery instructions, and instructions for any return receipt information required.

Notice that the type of information defined in Protocol P1 is very similar to the information that the post office requires when you request any kind of special service.

Protocol P2 (defined in the X.420 recommendation) enables users to request particular services, such as the following:

● Restricting the sending of certain messages to authorized users.

● Specifying the types of notification required of the request's recipient (for example, an immediate reply to a message).

● Providing subject information (and even cross-filing data), making it easier for companies that receive large volumes of messages.

Protocol P3 has been defined in the X.410 recommendation. Perhaps the easiest way to understand this set of standards is to think of it as a set of rules for a user or user agent to follow when talking to the MTA after a message has been transmitted. Under Protocol P3, for example, a user can change existing parameters and conditions to respond to needs such as these:

● The need for a password.

● A need to alter the maximum size permitted in a message.

● The need for a test (before the actual delivery takes place) to see if a message can be delivered.

●
The CCITT X.500 set of recommendations facilitate worldwide electronic mail by providing the basis for a common directory.

CCITT X.500

One major limitation of CCITT's X.400 set of recommendations is that they do not solve the problem of incompatible post-office-box addresses in the electronic mail services of different networks. The X.500 recommendations respond to this problem by providing a standard for a global directory of electronic mail users.

Once fully implemented, the X.500 set of recommendations will have a major impact on worldwide electronic messaging. In the not-too-distant future, a user on a NetWare network in St. Louis will be able to send a message to a user on an IBM mainframe computer in Paris, as routinely as we now drop a letter into our mailbox and raise the flag to indicate that we want the letter picked up and delivered.

The X.500 uses a hierarchical directory structure. Users access the X.500 directory through a directory user agent. This special UA communicates with the directory by using the *directory access protocol.*

Message Handling Service (MHS)

> **Note:** As used in this section only, MHS will refer to a specific messaging program from Action Technologies, and not to the CCITT's term "MHS" (as used in the X.400 set of recommendations). This is the only section of the book that will discuss the MHS program.

● Message Handling Service (MHS) provides X.400-like control information and a way to connect different electronic mail systems together.

In October 1986, Action Technologies began offering its *Message Handling Service (MHS)* program to developers; beginning in early 1988 with v2.1, Novell began bundling MHS with NetWare without charge. Today, Novell owns Action Technologies' MHS, and is actively soliciting other vendors to write to this interface. Basic MHS is provided in both Netware 3.12 and 4.1.

When a user requests that a message be sent, MHS takes this message and places it in an "envelope" containing X.400-like control information. A *message control block (MCB)* accompanies the message; it is an 18-line ASCII file that provides such information as the desired destination, a date/time stamp, the priority requested, and return notification requirements. Because a three-part MHS message consists of a header, the text or message itself, and an associated parcel (which can consist of any binary encoded data), messages can be sent along with lengthy reports or data files.

Other X.400-like services include the following:

- Management of access to user agents
- Nondelivery alert
- Content type
- Delivery notification
- Multidestinations
- Relay and forward message
- Workgroup addressing
- Dead-letter notification

Just as important, MHS provides gateways to other networks, and even converts messages to the format appropriate for these networks. Because MHS is fully compatible with X.400 recommendations, its store-and-forward method of operation means that messages can be sent with delivery dates and times. Companies can schedule noncritical reports for night delivery and even schedule electronic document interchange (EDI)—a process in which information can be transmitted electronically, and then placed in a form running on another computer.

● MHS provides store-and-forward service, which means messages can be sent from one network to another with scheduled delivery dates and times.

MHS is a utility program that virtually no network users ever see or use directly. It is a program that enables programmers to develop the application programs (and electronic mail/scheduling programs) that will work in conjunction with it. Because different application programs share this common interface, it is reasonable to foresee a time—not too far in the future—when all programs will use MHS to communicate directly with other programs on different networks.

As an example, a network supervisor at Widget Company's branch in Phoenix might schedule an accounting program to produce a management report that reflects sales and profits for that day. This report could be scheduled to be run each evening and then transmitted at a certain time to the company's New York headquarters so that it could be an agenda item for an 8 a.m. executive meeting. Similarly, this same report could be scheduled to be produced at night, and then sent immediately to a long list of company managers worldwide. Because MHS keeps workgroup addresses on file, mailing reports to distribution lists is very easy.

Finally, because MHS messages can start executable programs, it also is possible in our example to have one hundred sales branches of The Widget Company compile sales reports at night and then submit them at scheduled intervals to the corporate New York headquarters. At headquarters, the information is received automatically and then transmitted to a database program. The database is scheduled to compile all this data at a certain time and then produce a report with accompanying graphics. Assuming a printer does not suffer a paper jam, this entire scenario can take place without human intervention.

Simple Mail Transfer Protocol (SMTP)

The Simple Mail Transfer Protocol (SMTP) was designed for the Department of Defense as a simple, easy-to-use mail system that could be used to transmit mail from one network using the TCP/IP suite of protocols to another network using the same suite of protocols.

Simple Mail Transfer Protocol (SMTP) was developed for the US Department of Defense as a simple, easy-to-use mail system for the Internet. SMTP is part of the suite of protocols known as Transmission Control Protocol/Internet Protocol (TCP/IP), that now runs on a wide range of networks—including those using UNIX or NetWare as their network operating systems.

SMTP often is used to transfer mail between two network workstations connecting remotely. What makes SMTP so easy is that there are only a few commands to type. A list follows:

HELO—A command to identify the sender to the receiver. This is the first command issued during a SMTP session.

MAIL—This command initiates the mail transaction so that data is delivered to a specific network mailbox.

RECPT—The Recipient command indicates the recipient of the mail message.

DATA—This command indicates that the lines of text to come are data.

SEND—This causes mail to be sent immediately and is often used when someone wants to send a page of data at a time.

SOML—This command can be translated as "send and mail." If a user is logged in, a message is sent to the user's screen. If the user is not logged in, the message is sent as mail to the user's mailbox.

RSET—The Reset command aborts a mail transaction.

VRFY—The Verify command checks to ensure that the user has a mailbox on the receiving system.

EXPN—The Expand command indicates that a message is to be sent to a mailing list, and not to an individual user.

HELP—This command results in a message being displayed.

NOOP—The No Operation command doesn't really do anything, except cause the mail server to send an "OK" in reply. This is useful for verifying the connection.

QUIT—The Quit command tells the mail server to issue an "OK" reply and close the channel.

TURN—The Turn Around command "turns around" communications so that sender becomes the receiver, and vice versa.

The cc:Mail Program

The cc:Mail program is one of the leading network e-mail programs. It offers a number of major features—including the ability to attach files, send graphics, create distribution lists, and send copies to other network users. An examination of some of its major features reveals how companies use e-mail on networks.

Reading Your Mail

Let's assume that Carol Jackson works for a company running cc:Mail on its LAN. Carol has logged in from her DOS-based workstation. Her login script executed a batch file that brought up the cc:Mail Main menu (illustrated in Figure 4.5).

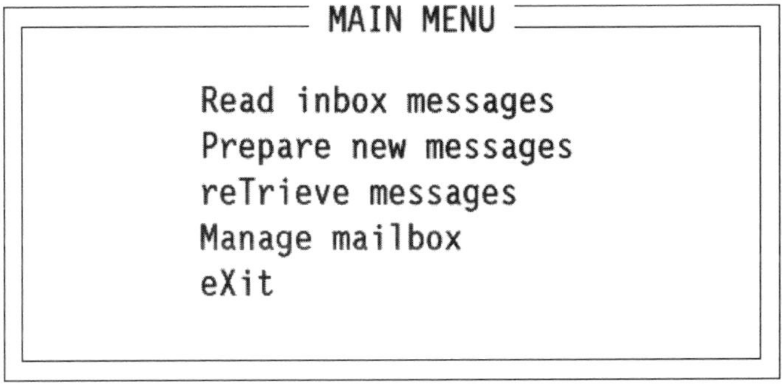

```
═══════════════ MAIN MENU ═══════════════

          Read inbox messages
          Prepare new messages
          reTrieve messages
          Manage mailbox
          eXit
```

FIGURE 4.5.
The cc:Mail Main Menu.

The Inbox, shown in Figure 4.6, is the place where you receive messages from other cc:Mail users. Carol currently has four messages in her Inbox; as she opens and reads each message, the "New" counter will decrease by one each time.

FIGURE 4.6.

The cc:Mail Inbox shows messages from other users.

```
Inbox
4    Joe Blow         1/13/92      435t      Expense Report
3    Jack Smith       1/10/92     1044t      PR release
2    Mary Madrid      1/10/92     2400t      Product description
1    Bill Harris      1/09/92    12323       Market analysis




↑ ↓ and ENTER to display message.   F5 and F6 to select.   ESC to end
```

As Carol files some of these messages, the folder count adjusts to include the new folders she creates. The program permits a user to have up to 200 folders at any time. If Carol simply does not want to deal with one of the new messages in her Inbox, she can leave it there, and it remains as part of the total.

The cc:Mail program provides bulletin boards—accessible to all users—where they may read and post messages, but only the administrator may delete them. Carol could read a bulletin board message and then copy it to a personal folder for her own personal copy.

Joe Blow happens to be Carol's boss, so she selects his message and press Enter. Figure 4.7 illustrates how cc:Mail displays a message under DOS. After Carol has read her message, she presses Enter to bring up an Action menu (Figure 4.8), which appears over the message text.

FIGURE 4.7.

Reading a message in cc:Mail.

```
[4] From: Joe Blow  1/13/92  7:25PM (432 bytes: 101n)
To: Carol Jackson
Subject: Expense Report

--------------------Message Contents--------------------

    Carol:

    I'm really concerned about the expense report
    you handed in for your Dallas trip. I realize
    that Consolidated Widgets is our biggest
    distributor in the southwest, but I can't imagine
    spending $200 on a lunch. Check that figure and
    please get back to me today.

    Joe


Window: 1-24   Lines:10   ↑ ↓ ← →   Help: F1   End:ENTER
```

```
╔══════════════════ ACTION MENU ══════════════════╗
║                                                  ║
║   display Next message    │   Move to folder     ║
║   display Item            │   Copy to folder     ║
║   attach new iTems        │   Forward mesage     ║
║   Return to main menu     │   replY to message   ║
║                           │   Print message      ║
║                           │   Write to ascii file║
║                           │   archiVe message    ║
║                           │   Delete message     ║
║                                                  ║
╚══════════════════════════════════════════════════╝
```

FIGURE 4.8.

The Action Menu.

Replying to a Message

Assume that Carol wants to reply immediately, and let Joe know that there's a mistake in her expense account report. She selects "replY to message," and sees a screen similar to that displayed in Figure 4.9.

While replying, Carol can use the resources of cc:Mail's text editor. She can enter up to 20,000 characters in a text item, and use word processing features such as word wrap, re-formatting, block movement of text, text finding and replacing, ASCII file creating, and printing to most standard printers.

```
     From: Carol Jackson
     To: Joe Blow
     Subject: Correction to Expense Report

     --------------------Message Contents--------------------

     Joe:

     I've looked over the expense report, and you're right,
     Consolidated Widget may be my bigget distributor,
     but the lunch in Dallas ran $20 and not $200. Believe
     it or not, $20 still buys a hamburger feast in Texas.

     Hope this clears up any questions or concerns you
     have about the report.




     L:10  C:37  %Full:0  Highlight (   ): Alt+F1  Help:F1  END:F10
```

FIGURE 4.9.

Writing a quick reply.

Once Carol has completed her message, she can press the F10 key to bring up the Send menu (displayed in Figure 4.10).

If Carol had wanted to send a copy to another user, or even send a blind copy to another user, she could have selected the Address menu. Figure 4.11 illustrates the other options available here, including requesting a receipt.

FIGURE 4.10.
The Send Menu.

```
╔═══════════════════ SEND MENU ═══════════════════╗
║  ┌─────────────────────────────────────────────┐ ║
║  │  Send message                               │ ║
║  │  attach copy of dos File                    │ ║
║  │  attach new iTems                           │ ║
║  │  display Message                            │ ║
║  │  edit sUbject                               │ ║
║  │  Address message                            │ ║
║  │  display Next message                       │ ║
║  │  Return to main menu                        │ ║
║  └─────────────────────────────────────────────┘ ║
╚═════════════════════════════════════════════════╝
```

One of the options available under cc:Mail's Main menu is "Prepare new messages." The screen for writing new messages looks exactly like the screen displayed earlier for replying to messages. When Carol creates a new message, she has the option of including any kind of file with the message—as well as copying the message to a personal folder so she can keep the material on file with other related items. She also can send her communication to public mailing lists (available to all cc:Mail users), or to one of her own mailing lists.

FIGURE 4.11.
The Address Menu.

```
╔═══════════════════ ADDRESS MENU ═══════════════════╗
║                                                    ║
║  eNd addressing          │  Copy to person         ║
║  Address to person       │  copy to mailing List   ║
║  address to Mailing list │  Blind copy to person   ║
║  address to bboard/Folder│  reQuest receipt        ║
║  Return to main menu     │  Delete address list    ║
║                                                    ║
╚════════════════════════════════════════════════════╝
```

Notice how practical this feature is for a department such as Human Resources; they might need to communicate with employees by position (all managers), by payroll designation (all non-exempt employees), or by department or hire date.

Similarly, the bulletin board option under cc:Mail permits companies to post general announcements, job vacancies, and other company-wide information, without having to mail notices physically to everyone.

Attaching Files to Your Mail

Any type of DOS file may be attached to a cc:Mail communication—even an executable program (.COM or .EXE), as long as it isn't copy-protected. By selecting the attach copy of DOS File option from the Send menu, Carol sees a screen similar to the one displayed in Figure 4.12.

Notice that the directory shows a variety of different files, including electronic spreadsheets and picture files. By selecting "attach new iTems" from the Send menu, Carol is provided with additional options for attaching material, as shown in Figure 4.13.

```
From: Frank Lorrison
To: Mary Worth
Subject: Spreadsheet file
----------------------Message Contents--------------------

Attach copy of dos file: H:\____

BUDGET.WKS     ORGANIZ.PIC     SALES.CAL     FORECAST.CAL
```

FIGURE 4.12.

Attaching a DOS file.

```
↑ ↓ ← → to move highlight or type filename. ENTER to select. Esc to cancel
```

Up to 20 different items may be attached to a communication, and each item can be given a title, such as "Agenda for Annual Retreat" for a text item, or "Map showing directions to annual retreat" for a graphics item.

```
┌────────────── ATTACH MENU ──────────────┐
│ ┌──────────────────────────────────────┐ │
│ │                                      │ │
│ │   attach Text item                   │ │
│ │   attach Graphics item               │ │
│ │   attach copy of dos File            │ │
│ │   attach Snapshots                   │ │
│ │   attach bboard/folder Msgs          │ │
│ │   eNd attaching                      │ │
│ │                                      │ │
│ └──────────────────────────────────────┘ │
└──────────────────────────────────────────┘
```

FIGURE 4.13.

Attaching an item to a message.

Viewing the Mail Directory of cc:Mail

One of the NetWare network supervisor's responsibilities under cc:Mail is to manage the network mail directory (see Figure 4.14). The network supervisor accesses the cc:Mail directory by typing **MAIL** and providing the correct password.

> **Note:** When I talk about e-mail programs running at different sites, familiar terms take on different meanings. The term post office refers to a network mail hub, and not to a government postal facility; mailbox refers to the computer storage used for e-mail, and not to a receptacle for letters.

FIGURE 4.14.

*Network mail
directory.*

```
 ┌──── Name ──────── Loc ── Last Checked In ─────── Comments ──┐
 │                                                              │
 │  Albert, Charles    L    1/13/92    2:54PM      VP Sales     │
 │  Bush, George       L    1/13/92    9:00AM      President    │
 │  DeBaugh, Francis    R    1/13/92    7:01AM      Miami        │
 │  Jackson, Andrew    r                           Phoenix      │
 │  Peoples, Paul      L    1/13/92   10:09AM      Sales        │
 │  TUCSONPOST         P    1/13/92    1:04PM      Tucson PO    │
 │  Zaslow, Ziggy      L    1/10/92    3:45PM      Accounting   │
 │                                                              │
 └──────────────────────────────────────────────────────────────┘
```

As Figure 4.14 illustrates, the location status of a mailbox is identified as follows:

L   local user

R   remote (stand-alone) user

r   remote network user on another post office

0   (letter O, not zero) remote post office that connects directly to yours

P   remote post office that can be accessed through another remote post office

Remote users have mailboxes in the network post office, just as local network users do; unfortunately, these remote users must access their mailboxes from outside the LAN. For direct access, they can use a stand-alone PC running cc:Mail Remote software, or they can access their post offices indirectly from another post office. These remote users can send and receive messages, but cannot use the local bulletin boards.

When a cc:Mail Remote user directly accesses a cc:Mail post office, the post office checks to see if the user has a mailbox at that particular post office. If the user is not listed in the mail directory, he or she can send messages to specific mailboxes but cannot receive mail.

Other post offices running the cc:Mail Dialin utility program can directly access a remote post office if it is running cc:Mail Gateway. The cc:Mail administrator must provide these remote users with a post office name, and a telephone number to which the cc:Mail Dialin utility program is connected.

Because you may need to see the mailbox address for remote users, you can use the right arrow key to move to the right of the "Comments" column, and see a screen that resembles Figure 4.15.

FIGURE 4.15.

*Viewing cc:Mail
addresses.*

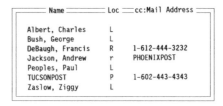

Compiling and Analyzing Mailbox Statistics

The cc:Mail program provides several vital utility programs to help the administrator manage a network's electronic mail efficiently. A directory function of the cc:Mail Chkstat program provides a listing of information on each individual mailbox, including the mailbox name, the location, the time the user last checked in, and any general comments. The list looks like this:

```
Mailbox Name Locn   Last Checked In     Comments

Alpert, Harmon    L    01/13/92 2:15pm     Sales Mgr
Boris, Barbara    R    01/13/92 10:00am    LA Office
Smith, Sylvester  L    01/10/92 10:53am    Account Exec
```

A *Users* function of the Chkstat utility program provides detailed information on the mailbox users—including mailbox name, location, USR file number, and the number of bytes in the file. Because remote users and post offices have a remote post office as their cc:Mail address for indirect access, they do not have an individual user file number, hence no file bytes appear when these users are listed. Chkstat provides a list that looks like this:

```
                        USR         File

Mailbox Name         Locn    File #    Bytes

Alpert, Harmon        L      00007     672
Boris, Barbara        R      00003
Smith, Sylvester      L      00010     1074
```

The *Messages* function of the cc:Mail Chkstat utility program provides the administrator with information (arranged by mailbox and by bulletin board) on how messages are dispersed on the mail system. It is possible to examine the total number of stored messages. The Messages function produces a report that looks like this:

```
cc:Mail Post Office: LOCALPOST
    Message Statistics 01/13/92

Number of stored messages        50
Total bytes in messages       143356
Total bytes remaining         272772
Reclaimable bytes              16772
Additional bytes              512000
```

The Messages function can also provide detailed statistics on the distribution of messages for individual mailboxes, including how many messages (in bytes) are shared, and how many are not shared (unique to a particular mailbox or bulletin board).

An administrator could also request reports regarding specific groups of messages—including (for example) information on the messages in Carol Jackson's mailbox, dated on or before January 10, that have already been read.

● The Chkstat utility program provides the cc:Mail administrator with detailed statistics on individual mailbox usage, as well as total post office usage.

The cc:Mail program has gateways to a number of other e-mail programs, including those running on IBM mainframes and DEC computers.

Gateways from cc:Mail to the Rest of the World

The cc:Mail program provides a number of gateway connections to other computer mail systems. These include cc:Mail ProfsLINK providing electronic mail exchange between a NetWare LAN running cc:Mail and any VM computer running IBM Professional Office System (PROFS). Users on this IBM mainframe system may also send mail to cc:Mail users on the local area network.

There is also a cc:Mail DEClink program to link a NetWare LAN to a DEC computer. Using this link, All-in-1 and VAXmail users can communicate directly with LAN users.

Other major cc:Mail gateways for interconnectivity of electronic mail include cc:Mail for the Macintosh and cc:Mail FAXlink. The cc:Mail for the Macintosh program provides a convenient way to transfer Macintosh and IBM PC files back and forth between networks: these files are placed in cc:Mail envelopes that use the same format on both computers. The cc:Mail FAXlink program permits PC and Macintosh users to create, send, receive, and view text and graphics messages electronically, to and from facsimile machines. Fax messages can be viewed prior to printing, replying, forwarding, or storing in electronic files. Only one facsimile board is required for each network.

A license for Microsoft Mail comes with Windows for Workgroups and the Microsoft Office suites.

Microsoft Mail

Microsoft also provides one of the largest e-mail systems to date. This is the Microsoft Mail product.

Before you can use Microsoft Mail the Network Manager sets up a *Workgroup Post Office* (WPO). This post office is usually located on a shared directory on a user's PC or on a network drive. The post office is accessed via a Mail application that runs on each workstation. In addition, the person setting up the post Office also becomes the Post Office Manager. The Post Office Managers responsibility is to

- Add or remove names from the post office
- Modify users accounts (change passwords and so on)
- Manage the disk space where the post office is stored
- Manage the mail system files

Figure 4.16 shows the post office manager manipulating post office users.

Once the post office is created and all the users have been added, a mail user may send a note to another user very easily. The user chooses the recipient from the post office list (Figure 4.17).

The user then addresses and types the note, attaching files if required (Figure 4.18).

Then when the user presses the 'send' key the mail is sent to the post office for collection by the other user. The MS Mail product contains identical functionality to that already covered in the cc:Mail section including the reply facility (Figure 4.19).

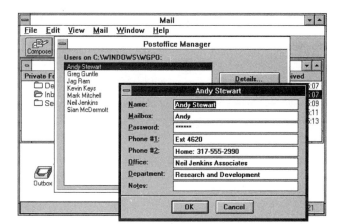

FIGURE 4.16.

Changing post office users under MS Mail.

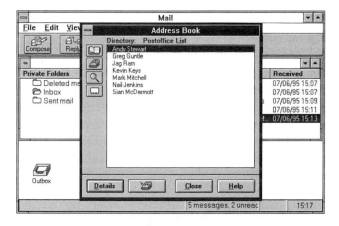

FIGURE 4.17

Choosing a person to send mail to.

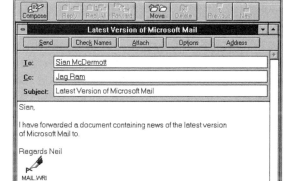

FIGURE 4.18.

Typing a mail note and attaching files under MS Mail.

FIGURE 4.19.

The Reply facility under MS Mail.

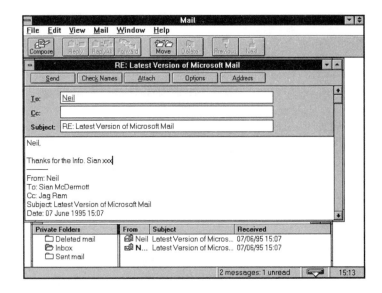

As you can see from Figure 4.20, MS Mail uses icons to indicate the status of mail that has arrived. In the Inbox mail is marked in the 'From' section with unopened envelopes for new mail, open envelopes for mail that has been read, an exclamation mark for urgent mail, and a paper clip for mail that has a file attached. Using this type of interface, it is easy to identify the different types of mail that you have received.

FIGURE 4.20.

The different mail types in MS Mail.

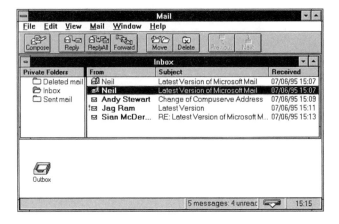

Selecting the Electronic Messaging System

One major issue when selecting an e-mail system is compatibility. Does the program work on all the different networks you have? Does it work on the gateways to your company's minicomputers and mainframes? Some of these programs may not offer Macintosh versions at this time, is this a requirement?

The gateways will not do much good, however, if the electronic messaging system does not have the features your company needs. The description of some of cc:Mail's features was intended to make you aware of what one of the top-selling e-mail programs offers for LANs. The following list summarizes many of the features that may prove necessary if your company's electronic messaging is to be effective.

●
Make sure that the electronic messaging system you select contains both the features you need now and those that you may need in the future.

- Connects to other networks' electronic mail
- Sends to distribution lists or multiple distribution lists
- Places restrictions on users' sending and receiving of mail
- Automatically files messages that are sent or received
- Provides on-line help
- Automatically bills users who send mail
- Uploads files to accompany messages sent
- Prioritizes messages
- Permits enclosures in the form of files
- Permits attachment of related documents

Network Groupware Software

One major new type of network software is known as *groupware*. In its simplest form, groupware is a type of software that allows people or workgroups to integrate their working environment and knowledge with computer applications to improve their overall effectiveness.

Typically, groupware is centered around documents. Several users may work on the same document and observe each other's suggestions. Computer Associates' ForComment, for example, enables authors to supply annotations and suggested revisions to a document. These notes are collated automatically, on a line-by-line basis; the original author can view each suggested revision, and then accept it with a single keystroke. The software maintains an audit log that records all suggestions and changes.

Group Technologies' Aspect is a program that permits several authors to work simultaneously on the same document. When one user makes a change, all users' copies of this document change to reflect the recommendation.

While groupware lends itself very easily to word processing applications, it can be used with a variety of different types of programs. SoftSolutions Technology Corporation, for example, publishes a program called SoftSolutions Global—which enables users of a LAN or a WAN (wide area network) to access, manage, and combine spreadsheets or documents produced with other applications, across several LANs or WANs.

One vital requirement for many groupware packages is the ability to share information across a distributed platform that includes several different network operating systems. Some users of a company's UNIX network might need to exchange or replicate information from a document found on a LAN Manager or NetWare network.

Lotus' Notes is a PC-based document database management system that allows people to share, track, discuss, and pass information across several different platforms.

The Notes program illustrates how groupware programs replicate a document so it can be edited and revised simultaneously on several different platforms. A Notes domain consists of up to 10,000 network users. Each domain has its own Name and Address Book, which defines the domain's structure. Each Notes server communicates with another Notes server by creating a Connection Document (which handles replication of a document by prioritizing when a particular database should be replicated). Figure 4.21 shows an example of the Notes Desktop environment.

FIGURE 4.21.

An example of the Notes Working Desktop.

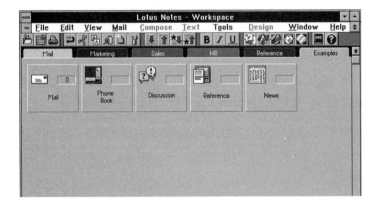

A network manager can determine whether Notes replication takes place in a bi-directional or unidirectional way. When two servers exchange information in a *bi-directional replication mode*, both servers' databases are updated to reflect changes to the same document made by users on both networks. The Notes program uses a time-stamp feature to determine the latest version of a document that has been undergoing a number of changes.

Notes has its own application development language, including a GUI front-end, a macro language, and its own database structure. Finally, Lotus Notes can run a variety of platforms including Macintosh, OS/2, UNIX, and Windows.

Facsimile Servers on a Network

While electronic messaging software has become very popular, the link between these e-mail systems and facsimile machines is relatively new. A facsimile (fax) server can be used to transmit fax messages from different network workstations, as well as to receive messages and forward them to the appropriate workstation. One approach to using a fax server is to route messages to a fax queue: the fax server polls the file server, extracts a document from the queue (along with control information, such as the name and phone number of the destination user) and then transmits the fax message.

Some fax servers work in conjunction with e-mail systems. An e-mail user specifies that the message is to be sent to the receiver via fax transmission. This approach can be very efficient, because the fax server can take advantage of the e-mail's features (such as its global user directory). Messages can even be faxed to distribution lists created on the e-mail system.

What Have You Learned?

1. MS-DOS versions 3.1 and later permit multi-user operations on a LAN because they permit byte-locking.

2. Single-user software often lacks the record-locking feature desirable on a LAN. Using such a program on a network for multiple users also violates its licensing agreement.

3. Document-oriented word processing programs offer many advantages over page-oriented programs.

4. A query language can make it much easier to use a powerful database management program.

5. Network accounting programs often consist of a number of sophisticated integrated modules.

6. Some software vendors encourage customers to customize their packages to meet individual needs.

7. Groupware software enables several users to work on the same project at the same time, and see one another's comments.

8. An electronic messaging system can encompass far more than just basic e-mail. It can include gateways to other networks and facsimile machines, as well as scheduling and organizing functions.

9. An X.400 message handling system includes user agents, message transfer agents, and a message transfer system.

10. Protocol P1 provides rules for routing information between two MTAs. Protocol P2 describes types of user services requested. Protocol P3 provides standards for changing existing mail parameters.

11. The CCITT X.400 recommendations cover electronic messaging, while the X.500 recommendations cover a worldwide common directory.

Quiz for Chapter 4

1. For multi-user operations, use a version of MS-DOS that is at least

    a. 3.0

    b. 2.1

    c. 3.1

    d. 1.1

2. The program that acts as a "traffic cop" to direct requests for shared network resources is called

    a. Master Manager.

    b. IBM PC Traffic Manager.

    c. the Director.

    d. the Redirector.

3. A single Notes domain can handle

    a. 10,000 users.

    b. 100 users.

    c. 1,000 users.

    d. 1 million users.

4. Writing a customized form letter using a list of names and addresses is a function known as

    a. the "Dear John" letter.

    b. boilerplate.

    c. mail merge.

    d. "shopping list" processing.

5. A series of form paragraphs linked together is a word processing function known as

    a. mail merge.

    b. boilerplate.

    c. mail link.

    d. paragraph meld.

6. A feature that enables an electronic spreadsheet user to program several spreadsheet functions so that they may be performed with a couple of keystrokes is known as a

    a. micro.

    b. macro.

    c. BASIC interface.

    d. firmware chip.

7. A spreadsheet feature that allows a user to name a target value and have the program calculate the variable value required to reach that goal is known as

    a. circular reasoning.

    b. target variables.

    c. micro justification.

    d. goal seeking.

8. As a query language, IBM supports

    a. Clout

    b. SQL

    c. ADL

    d. QUESTION.c

9. Electronic mail and the CCITT X.400 set of recommendations would be handled by which layer of the OSI model?

    a. Network

    b. Presentation

    c. Application

    d. Data Link

10. Which item is not part of an X.400 message handling system?

    a. A file server

    b. A user agent

    c. A message transfer agent

    d. A message transfer system

11. The basic approach of the MHS program is

    a. first-in-first-out

    b. store-and-forward

    c. list-in-first-out

    d. transfer-and-process

12. A request for an immediate reply to a message is described by which protocol under X.400?

    a. P1

    b. P2

    c. P3

    d. P4

13. Standards for a worldwide common directory are provided in

    a. X.300

    b. X.400

    c. X.500

    d. X.600

14. The Chkstat utility program, providing detailed information on mailbox users, is available with

    a. Lotus Ami Pro

    b. The Network Courier

    c. cc:Mail

    d. DOOM 2

Network Management and Control

About This Chapter

The network manager has overall responsibility for a local area network. In this chapter, you examine many of the network manager's most important functions. Whenever possible, you examine some of the actual management programs a network manager uses to manage and control a LAN. Finally, you look at a protocol analyzer, one of the essential tools a network manager uses to analyze a network to determine why it is not running at maximum efficiency.

Five Functional Areas of LAN Management

The five functional areas of network management are configuration management, fault management, performance management, security management, and accounting management. You examine each of these key areas to see how a network manager spends a typical day.

Configuration Management

Configuration management consists of keeping track of what devices are attached to a network, and maintaining this information in a database for quick retrieval. The database can contain valuable information about the device, including any hardware attached and the type of software installed. This type of information is often produced by an automated network inventory program; the information such a program can retrieve and store about each workstation includes the following:

> The five key functional areas associated with LAN management are configuration fault management, performance, security, and accounting management.

> Configuration management enables a network manager to track devices on a network.

- The amount of RAM installed in this workstation.
- The microprocessor installed (Intel 80386, Intel 80486, Pentium, and so on).
- The coprocessor (if any) installed.
- The type of network interface card installed.
- The type of video interface card installed (VGA, SVGA, and so on).
- The operating system running and its version.
- The application programs and their version numbers.

Among the more popular network inventory programs are Magee Enterprises' Network H.Q., Intel's LANdesk, Brightwork Development's LAN Automatic Inventory, Horizons Technology's LAN Auditor, and Novell's ManageWise. Some network inventory programs permit a network supervisor to add information and even create additional fields. Figure 5.1 illustrates a sample hardware documentation sheet created by a network manager who wanted to be able to retrieve this information.

FIGURE 5.1.

A hardware documentation sheet.

Hardware Network Documentation

```
Type of Equipment:_____
Serial Number:_____
Location:_____
Date Purchased:_____
Warranty Expiration Date:_____
Vendor:_____  Contact:_____
Telephone:_____

Service Contract #:_____
Vendor:_____  Contact:_____
Telephone:_____

Problems:

Date     Problem          Solution
```

By using this format to keep vital information on all workstations, interface boards, printers, and other devices, the network supervisor is able to organize network resources more efficiently. Figure 5.2 illustrates a software documentation sheet, a similar profile that can be maintained for all software installed on the network.

An advantage of maintaining a network inventory in a database is that a manager can create network configuration reports for planning purposes. How many workstations, for example, are still using Intel 80386SX microprocessors? These machines will not be able to take advantage of Microsoft's Windows NT. How many machines only have 1MB of RAM installed? These machines will have to be upgraded to at least 4MB of RAM to take full advantage of Windows software. A network manager might also be interested in learning how many workstations are still running MS-DOS 5.0. What would it cost to upgrade these workstations to MS-DOS 6.2 in order to provide them with data compression capabilities?

FIGURE 5.2.

A software documentation sheet.

```
                   Software Network Documentation

Name of Program:_____ DOS Version:_____
Publisher:_____ Tel:_____

Purchased From:_____ Tel:_____
Date Purchased:_____
Warranty Expires:_____

System Requirements:
  RAM Required: _____
  Hard Disk/Floppies:_____

Software Maintenance/Support:
  Vendor:_____
  Telephone:_____

Problems:

Date      Problem          Solution
```

Another important function of inventory software is to provide the information needed to solve network problems. In many companies with large local area networks, a network user who is having trouble running a particular program can call a network help desk and request help. The *help desk* specialist can use information provided by the network inventory software (in the *configuration database*) to examine the user's hardware and software configuration. The specialist might determine (for example) that a RAM shortage is causing the user's machine to lock up when a graphic file is loaded into a WordPerfect program.

Another user might be having a problem with a certain program because of its incompatibility with the version of MS-DOS running on the workstation. The network inventory program can help the supervisor isolate this problem.

LAN configuration programs can also provide a network manager with information about the status of all network devices, including bridges and routers. Some programs provide this information in a graphical format. (For example, the network supervisor's screen might show a device displayed in red to indicate that it is either turned off or malfunctioning.)

Fault Management

Fault management is the network management function concerned with documenting and reporting network errors. A network manager needs to know how many bad packets are being produced, how many times packets must be retransmitted on an Ethernet network, whether a workstation is transmitting a beacon signal on a token ring network, and so on.

The Frye Utilities for Networks includes the NetWare Early Warning System, an example of how a network manager can use specialized software for fault management. A network

●
Documenting and reporting network management is the function of fault management.

manager might set the program's thresholds so that it issues an alert under the following conditions:

● The file server does not respond.
● The file server's utilization reaches a certain percentage of capacity.
● Packets are discarded because they have crossed over 16 routers.
● A printer is off-line.

The program can be instructed to notify the network manager in a number of different ways. One method would consist of displaying a 25th-line message on the network manager's monitor. A second method might transmit an electronic mail message automatically. If an electronic mail program with a *notify* feature (such as cc:Mail or Novell Groupwise) is installed on the network, the network manager hears a beep and sees a message displayed—indicating that an e-mail message has just been received.

If a Hayes-compatible modem is available to the network, the Frye Utilities NetWare Early Warning System program can be instructed to transmit a pager message (for people who are rarely in their offices). The program can also be instructed to send a facsimile message (fax), but perhaps its most unusual option (assuming the proper hardware is installed) is to provide incoming and outgoing voice notification.

With these options installed, a network manager can call the LAN and receive a voice update concerning error conditions. The outgoing voice notification option enables the program to call a number and send a voice message. (Imagine the reaction of a network manager who receives a call at home at 3 a.m. from the LAN, and hears a digitized voice describe network error conditions.)

Fault management is a very useful way of preventing problems on networks as you can use it to track and resolve many easily avoided repetitive problems.

Performance management is concerned with ensuring that a network is performing efficiently.

Performance Management

One of a network manager's major responsibilities is to ensure a network's *efficient performance*, and that its service is not deteriorating. Because new and occasional users may have trouble with such routine network functions as the login (for example), network supervisors must help them by establishing routines to follow. In the case of IBM's network software, such routines are customized batch files that need be written only once. Novell's NetWare includes login scripts; though these may take only a few minutes for a supervisor to write, they can save novices hours, and eliminate a good deal of frustration.

Another area of network efficiency that needs to be monitored by the network supervisor is *network traffic* statistics. By examining printer usage statistics, for example, the supervisor might determine that certain log reports need to be spooled and printed after peak hours. Heavy usage of certain accounting programs that place a premium on file server access can slow the entire network. The supervisor might decide to add a separate file server for the accounting department in order to speed up the rest of the network.

Several companies, including Network General, Hewlett-Packard, Spider Systems, and Novell, offer network analyzers. Network General's *Watchdog* is an example of software (and hardware) a network manager can use to ensure that a network performs efficiently. The workstation into which this software is loaded includes a network interface card that allows the workstation to capture real-time network data. The Watchdog provides detailed statistical information about network traffic patterns. This information can be displayed graphically, so that the network manager can view which workstations are generating the most traffic.

The Watchdog can report which workstations are generating packets with the most errors (a sign that the workstation might have a defective network interface card). The network manager can also monitor the traffic between a file server and print server—or between two workstations—to examine potential bottlenecks that might be causing network traffic congestion.

One advantage of gathering network traffic statistics when the network is performing efficiently is that it provides a benchmark the manager can use to discover why a network suddenly begins to operate sluggishly. The Watchdog also has a cable test function that enables the network manager to check a network segment to see if there is a cabling problem. Microtest's Compass has similar features and functionality.

Security Management

Another major network management function is security. A network manager must keep a network secure from unauthorized access, as well as from invasion by computer viruses. Protecting a network from unauthorized users means limiting the access of a company's own network users, as well as eliminating network access by non-employees.

Limiting a Company's Own Network Users

A network manager can use features found in most network operating systems (such as NetWare) to limit access by network users to the company's most important directories and files. A directory can be "hidden" so that it does not show up when a user issues a DIR command. Also, if the manager of a NetWare LAN does not give a user read and file scan rights to a particular network directory, the user will not see any files in that directory when issuing a DIR command. Similarly, a network manager can limit the rights of users to a specific file within a directory.

The network manager can require passwords for users when they log into a network and a specific file server. This means that a user can be restricted from accessing a particular file server, while retaining access to a different file server. Some additional ways the network manager can enhance password protection when users log into the network are the following:

● Prevent users from placing their passwords in a batch file for automatic login per company policy that this is not allowed. (Batch files can be viewed by unauthorized users.)

● Security management includes protecting a network from unauthorized access, both from network and non-network users.

● Network users' access can be limited by password protection, time restrictions, and restrictions on which workstations can be used to log into the network.

● Require the user's password to have a certain number of characters.

● Require the user to change a password at intervals (such as every 30 or 60 days).

● Prevent users from using the same password twice.

● Have a company policy that requires users' passwords containing random combinations of letters. (Passwords that represent the names of spouses, children, or pets are often too easy for outsiders to guess.)

● Prevent users from logging into the network from several different workstations concurrently.

● Restrict users from logging into the network during certain hours, and even during certain days of the week (Saturdays, Sundays, and so on).

● Some network operating systems (such as NetWare 3.x) encrypt passwords so that sophisticated users cannot examine the password file and learn users' passwords.

● Network managers must also be alert to prevent users from writing their passwords on scraps of paper and taping these notes to their computers or monitors because they are afraid they will forget them.

● Some users will log into the network and then leave their workstations unattended for extended periods of time. Unauthorized users can do enormous network damage if they take advantage of this situation.

● Network managers must be notified whenever an employee is terminated or voluntarily leaves the company, so that this person's network account can be disabled or eliminated.

● Temporary users should be assigned a network account with an expiration date, and with very limited access to sensitive network files.

Preventing Unauthorized Users from Dialing into a LAN

●
Remote users
logging into a
network create a
number of security
problems.

LAN security becomes even more difficult to maintain when users are permitted to log in from remote sites. Intruder detection provides one level of protection. This protection can be enhanced by limiting the number of unsuccessful login attempts before locking the user's account. After three (or perhaps five) unsuccessful login attempts, users might be required to contact the network manager to reset the account. This measure prevents unauthorized users from dialing in repeatedly and using a random password generator to try to break into a network.

Another effective way to prevent unauthorized users from logging into a LAN from a remote site is to use a *call-back modem*—which receives a call, requires a password, and then calls the user back after a random number of seconds. The call-back modem is programmed with a table containing a list of authorized users, their passwords, and their phone numbers.

Protecting a Network from Computer Viruses

Viruses are self-replicating bits of computer code that hide in computer programs (and often in RAM). They attach themselves to other programs, and accompany them when they are copied to other disks or onto a network. Once activated, these viruses can disrupt the programs to which they are attached. When they "hide" in RAM, viruses attach themselves to more and more programs as each one is executed.

A virus is particularly disruptive on a network; it can spread rapidly through a network's various directories and subdirectories potentially damaging data. The solution for many network managers is to install *preventive software* that checks for viruses before other software is executed; usually detecting a virus before it can do any damage. Many programs also destroy the virus once it is detected.

Central Point's Anti-Virus software serves as an example of how many of these programs function. It checks for viruses by verifying files' checksums, and checking for other file irregularities. A terminate-and-stay-resident (TSR) program loads into memory, and checks programs before they are executed. It notifies the user when a virus has been detected, names it, and then destroys it. The program is capable of removing viruses from infected files, boot sectors, and partition tables—without having to delete these files.

On many networks, only the LAN manager can load files onto the network. Often the network manager will test a program on a local workstation, and scan it for viruses before adding the program to the network. Users are normally prohibited from uploading files and programs directly from bulletin boards onto the network.

Accounting Management

Accounting management is the network function associated with allocating network costs to users and their departments. A network operating system such as NetWare provides the built-in capability to perform this task.

Under NetWare, a network manager can keep accurate track of when specific individuals use specific network resources (file servers, hard disks, or printers). This means that users can be charged for using a print server, a file server, and even a gateway.

Users can be charged for how many blocks of information they read from a file server, and how many blocks they write to a file server. Network managers can even vary the charge rates for connections, so that it is less expensive for users who log into the network during off hours. A network manager can set charge rates for service requests so that users who want to print during prime time will pay considerably more than users who are willing to print during the late afternoon or evening.

● A network must be protected from computer viruses that attach themselves to other programs and then spread to additional programs, disrupting their operation.

● Accounting management is the ability to allocate network costs to users and their departments.

Daily Network Management Chores

You have examined some of the broad functional areas of network management associated with LAN management; now you look at some of the day-to-day responsibilities associated with network management and control. These responsibilities include backing up file servers, maintaining the network user interface, troubleshooting network problems, and maintaining network hardware and software.

Backing Up File Servers

●
A network requires an effective file server backup system to ensure that valuable files are never destroyed.

A major chore for all network supervisors is to develop a carefully planned schedule for network *backups*. Some network areas, such as accounting, might require backups twice a day. The entire system, of course, should be backed up on a daily basis. Most software will time-stamp files, requiring backup only of those files that have been modified since the last backup.

The supervisor should perform backups of all files every week, and should perform incremental or full backups every day. They should also periodically place a backup in a safe off-site location.

Several companies, including Palindrome, Cheyenne Systems, and Emerald Systems offer backup software. Palindrome Corporation's The Network Archivist (TNA) and Cheyenne System's Arcserve serve as examples of specialized software that helps a network manager manage and control network backups. TNA enables a network manager to establish a backup schedule, indicate when tapes should be rotated, and schedule an unattended backup. The program maintains a backup history for each file, so the network manager can restore a specific version of a file. This feature is useful when a user needs an earlier version of a file that has been overwritten. The network manager can restore an individual file, a directory, or the entire file server. For larger networks, the Network Archivist can be used in conjunction with an 8mm tape drive.

Maintaining Network User Interfaces

The network manager must maintain the LAN's user interface whether it's under DOS, Windows or another operating system. With DOS this often means using a *menuing program* to create a common menu for network users, so that they do not need to know network commands to use the LAN.

The Saber menuing system serves as an excellent example of how a menuing program works. Each time the network manager adds an important program to the LAN, the new program can be added to the network's menu as well. A user who wants to use a word processing program, for example, can select the "Word Processing" menu option. A second menu is then displayed, offering WordPerfect 5.1, WordPerfect 5.0, and Word 5.0 as options. The user selects one of these programs, and presses Enter to load a copy of the chosen program from the network.

A network operating system lets you place users into groups, and the Saber menuing system can work with the operating system to display different menus to different groups. An Accounting department employee might see a menu displayed that lets him load the Accounts Payable, Accounts Receivable, or Payroll programs. A Drafting department employee might see an entirely different menu, which lets him load computer-assisted drawing and graphics programs. Finally, a temporary employee hired to perform word processing might see a menu that offers only the word processing option.

A menuing system can also be used to control network printing. A user can select the Print menu option and see several different printing options (Epson dot-matrix printer, Hewlett-Packard LaserJet 4, and so on). The user then can load a program and select the print option, knowing the document will be sent to the selected printer.

A menuing system can also be customized for an individual user's hardware, so that a user with a monochrome monitor loads a monochrome menu. The Saber menuing system even permits users to customize their own menus. A user who frequently loads a word processing program might want to place this option in the Main menu to avoid going through two different menus to select this program.

A menuing program such as the Saber system can be used by a network manager to prevent users from issuing DOS-level commands. Because a user cannot break out of the menu to a DOS prompt, the user is unable to download files, load programs from a local hard disk, or perform any one of a host of tasks that could compromise a network's security.

A menuing system can also be used to monitor and control the number of users who can run a program concurrently. The Saber system, for example, lets the network manager control the number of users able to access a program at any given time. The network manager can purchase a license for 15 users, for example, and then establish this limit in the menuing program. The 16th user who attempts to access this program is informed that the maximum number of users are currently running the program, and is then provided with a list of these users. A user who desperately needs to access this program can check to see if someone on this list has forgotten to log out of the network.

Menuing systems such as Saber for Windows are available for graphical user interfaces (GUI) such as Windows and OS/2. These products apply the same techniques as described above to the graphical environment. By modifying the various configuration files in the operating systems (WIN.INI and PROGMAN.INI within Windows for example), the network manager can restrict access to DOS and any other applications. Most organizations use this approach to restrict the windows environment.

Troubleshooting Network Problems

Many network managers spend a disproportionate amount of their time *troubleshooting* network problems. A user calls to report that she is unable to print, while a second user calls to complain that he is unable to use his mouse with a program. A third user might call to complain that he is unable to log into the network. The network manager

●
One way for a network manager to troubleshoot a user's problem is to use a program that makes it possible to take over remote control of that user's workstation.

diagnoses the user's problem by asking a series of questions—just as a doctor asks several questions to diagnose a patient's illness.

First, the network manager must determine whether the problem is hardware- or software-related. Is the problem limited to a single user's workstation, or is it a problem with the network program itself? Is the user's local network interface card defective, or is the network connector linking the workstation to the network loose?

Some network managers utilize a program such as Closeup, which enables them to "take over" a local workstation and view that workstation's screen from their own monitor. The network manager might take over the workstation of the user who complained about not being able to print, to see if the correct printer has been selected. The network manager might take over the workstation of the user unable to use his mouse so that the appropriate mouse can be installed (using the program's install option). In a later section, you will examine some of the network manager's major troubleshooting tools, including a protocol analyzer.

Maintaining Network Hardware and Software

●
Network mainte-
nance includes
updating software
as new versions are
released, creating
and updating
network documenta-
tion, replacing
defective equipment,
and periodically
checking network
cabling.

Network maintenance is a very important part of a network manager's daily responsibility. When a new release of a network application program appears, the network manager must install this software promptly, so that the software vendor can provide accurate technical support should it be needed. Another major maintenance chore for the network manager is to create and maintain network documentation. If a user's network interface card becomes defective, the network manager must have documentation available that shows when the card was installed, the card's serial number, and the warranty expiration date. If a file server goes down, the network manager must know whether it is covered by a 24-hour service contract or an 8–5 contract. Similarly, the network manager must keep accurate documentation on other network equipment (such as printers, bridges, routers, gateways, and tape backup units).

This type of critical information often can be placed in a *network log book* to provide clear audit trails of all network changes. Password changes, alterations in user access, software updates that have been installed, and program additions or deletions can be noted and dated. Such a log book should be kept under lock and key when not being used. Without such an administrative tool, the network represents a disaster waiting to happen.

The network manager should be able to access this information rapidly, so that the equipment's manufacturer or vendor can be called quickly. Technical support departments usually require the equipment's serial number, warranty expiration date, and detailed information about the LAN's topology—including the version number of the network operating system.

In order to reduce the number of calls from frustrated users, the network manager must provide users with accurate and easy-to-read *network documentation*. How can users direct a document to a specific printer? How can a user copy several network files from one directory to another directory? How can a user customize a Saber menu? These are the types of questions that must be answered in user documentation.

Periodically, a network manager must "walk the network" to check the LAN's cabling. Checking the cabling can determine whether connectors are coming loose, cabling is cracking or pinched, or hubs are operating properly.

Some network managers report they have to reset network devices such as hubs at least a couple of times a week to keep them operating efficiently. Because so many network devices now have diagnostic lights to indicate how they are performing, a network manager can quickly determine whether traffic is flowing smoothly—or whether access collisions are taking place or a channel is not operating properly. Because many modern file servers are running 24 hours a day, 7 days a week, a network manager will normally shut down a file server and then power it up again. This allows a server to go through its diagnostic routines and self test. This is very useful in determining if components are failing on the server.

The Network Supervisor's Tools

A network supervisor would be well advised to have a number of tools and materials on hand—including both straight and Phillips screwdrivers, as well as needle-nose and diagonal-cutters pliers. A volt-ohm meter or digital voltmeter is useful for cable testing.

When workstations suffer hardware failure, often it is because of a bad interface board, a defective floppy disk drive, or some bad memory chips. While large companies probably have in-house technicians to handle these problems, a network supervisor might find it expedient to keep some of these materials on-hand. They should also keep an ample supply of printer ribbons, printer paper, extra formatted tapes for file-server backups, toner cartridges for the network laser printer, and certainly a box (at least) of formatted floppy disks.

A Protocol Analyzer

A *protocol analyzer* provides the key to understanding why a network is not running at top efficiency. Protocol analyzers analyze the packets of information flowing across a network and provide very valuable statistics. While there are several major protocol analyzers on the market, I will focus on one of the major contenders: Network General Corporation's The Sniffer.

Attached to a network as if it were a workstation, the Sniffer listens to every transmission that goes by it. Although its major focus is the Data Link layer of the OSI model (discussed in Chapter 2), it displays information used by applications up to the Session layer.

The Sniffer is a self-contained computer—with its own network adapter card, hard disk, operating system, and software. If you exit from the Sniffer program, the machine becomes

●
A protocol analyzer analyzes the frames traveling across a network. It provides valuable information on the performance of the network's interface cards, file server, and software.

a standard DOS-based Compaq microcomputer or Toshiba Portable. While running the Sniffer, however, the machine has two major functions: to capture frames and to display information.

Because of the amount of information passing through a protocol analyzer, it is usually filtered by establishing parameters. The user may want to select by station address, protocol, or particular frame pattern.

The Sniffer uses a bar graphic to display traffic density as kilobytes per second, as frames per second, or as a percentage of the network's available bandwidth. Information can be displayed in linear form or logarithmic scale.

The Sniffer also displays traffic statistics through the use of counters that reveal the number of frames seen, the number of frames accepted, and the percentage of the capture buffer (the area in the Sniffer's memory that holds captured packets) in use.

For each station that is contributing to network traffic, the Sniffer is able to display (in real time) a count of frames per second or kilobytes per second. The machine also displays pair counts for each pair of workstations communicating information.

Figure 5.3 illustrates both a summary and a detailed display of an exchange between two stations. Notice that the Sniffer identifies the two stations communicating from its own name table; apparently user Dan is communicating with the NetWare SERVER. The conversation we are eavesdropping on consists of a response from the NetWare file server regarding its LOGIN file.

Notice also that this protocol analyzer provides some detailed file directory information about the file being accessed. We are able to observe the file's length, its creation date, the last access date, and the last update date/time.

As this brief discussion of the Sniffer illustrates, protocol analyzers have proven to be invaluable tools for network managers. With some practice, a network manager can read and analyze their reports with relative ease—revealing a good deal of information regarding the network's general health.

```
- - - - - - - - - -  Frame 31 - - - - - - - - - - - - - - -

SUMMARY Rel Time NW Util Destination Source  Summary
   31   2.9825  1.43%  SERVER      User Dan LC 802.2 size=46 bytes
                                            NS NetWare Request N=89 C=4 T=1
                                            CP C Open file LOGIN
- - - - - - - - - -  Frame 32 - - - - - - - - - - - - - - -

SUMMARY Rel Time NW Util Destination Source  Summary
   32   2.9860  1.57%  User Dan    SERVER   DLC 802.2 size=74 bytes
                                            ILS NetWare Reply N=89 C=4 T=0
                                            NCP R F=08F1 OK Opened
DLC:  ---- DLC Header ----
DLC:
DLC:  Frame 32 arrived at 13:58:56.7703 ; frame size is 88 (0058 hex) bytes.
DLC:  Destination: Station 02608C119421, User Dan
DLC:  Source     : Station 02608C217692, SERVER
DLC:  802.2 LLC length = 74
DLC:
INS:  ---- INS Header ----
INS:
INS:  Checksum = FFFF
INS:  Length = 74
INS:  Transport control = 00
INS:         0000 .... = Reserved
INS:         .... 0000 = Hop count
INS:  Packet type = 17 (Novell NetWare)
INS:
INS:  Dest  net = 00217692, host = 02608C119421, socket = 4001 (16385)
INS:  Source net = 00217692, host = 02608C217692, socket = 1105 (NetWare Server)
INS:
INS:  ---- Novell Advanced NetWare ----
INS:
INS:  Request type = 3333 (Reply)
INS:  Seq no=89  Connection no=4   Task no=0
INS:
NCP:  ---- Open File Reply ----
NCP:
NCP:  Request code = 76 (reply to frame 31)
NCP:
NCP:  Completion code = 00 (OK)
NCP:  Connection status flags = 00 (OK)
NCP:  File handle = 0AF6 AC08 AEOF
NCP:  File name = "LOGIN"
NCP:  File attribute flags = 00
NCP:         0... .... = File is not sharable
NCP:         .0.. .... = Not defined
NCP:         ..0. .... = Not changed since last archive
NCP:         ...0 .... = Not a subdirectory
NCP:         .... 0... = Not execute-only file
NCP:         .... .0.. = Not a system file
NCP:         .... ..0. = Not a hidden file
NCP:         .... ...0 = Read and write allowed
NCP:  File execute type = 00
NCP:  File length = 16
NCP:  Creation date       = 2-Dec-86
NCP:  Last access date    = 13-Feb-87
NCP:  Last update date/time = 2-Dec-86 16:08:54
NCP:
NCP:  [Normal end of NetWare "Open File Reply" packet.]
NCP:
```

Summary view
of a request to open a file

Summary and detail views
of the server's reply

Low-level source and destination data

Stations identified from The Sniffer's
name table

High-level source and destination data

The Sniffer points back to the query
for which this frame is the response

File's name and handle

Attribute flags decoded

File directory data

FIGURE 5.3.

*A report from The
Sniffer (reprinted with
the permission of
Network General
Corporation).*

What Have You Learned?

1. The five functional areas of network management are configuration management, fault management, performance management, security management, and accounting management.

2. Automated inventory programs are useful tools for configuration management.

3. Fault management includes documenting and reporting network errors.

4. Monitoring network traffic patterns and generating network statistics are important parts of performance management.

5. Network users can be restricted from using key directories and files.

6. Call-back modems are a way of protecting a network from remote users' unauthorized access.

7. Network users can be limited to using the network certain days of the week and certain hours.

8. Viruses are self-replicating bits of computer code that hide in certain programs and then disrupt their operation.

9. A menuing program can provide an easy-to-use network user interface.

10. Protocol analyzers are excellent troubleshooting devices that examine the contents of network packets.

11. A network manager's primary responsibility is to keep the network running efficiently.

Quiz for Chapter 5

1. _____ is not a functional area of network management.
   a. Configuration management
   b. Documentation management
   c. Performance management
   d. Security management

2. Automated inventory programs are a part of
   a. configuration management.
   b. performance management.
   c. security management.
   d. accounting management.

3. Keeping track of the number of bad packets is a function of
   a. performance management.
   b. fault management.
   c. security management.
   d. accounting management.

4. Network General's Watchdog is utilized by a network manager for
   a. accounting management.
   b. configuration management.
   c. security management.
   d. performance management.

5. Network security can be enhanced by all of the following except

    a. restricting users to certain days and hours.

    b. making users change their passwords at set intervals.

    c. giving everyone supervisor access.

    d. preventing users from repeating the same passwords.

6. Remote users to a LAN can be restricted by

    a. dial-up modems.

    b. call-back modems.

    c. asynchronous modems.

    d. synchronous modems.

7. Computer viruses can be found in all but

    a. boot sectors.

    b. partition tables.

    c. RAM.

    d. video cards.

8. Network accounting bills everything except

    a. file server blocks read.

    b. file server blocks written.

    c. local workstation disk space used.

    d. network connections.

9. A menuing system can provide all the following benefits except

    a. making a network perform more efficiently.

    b. making it easier to use the network.

    c. preventing users from seeing certain menu options.

    d. preventing users from reaching a DOS-level prompt.

10. A protocol analyzer can

    a. display traffic patterns in graphic form.

    b. summarize traffic between two stations.

    c. provide detailed data on traffic between two stations.

    d. perform all of the above.

Connectivity and the Enterprise Network

About This Chapter

The major problem many companies face is how to link their various computer networks. The Accounting department might have an Ethernet LAN that uses thin coaxial cabling, while PCs in the corporate offices may be linked via a 10BaseT LAN that uses twisted-pair wire. Manufacturing might be using an IBM mainframe computer, while Research & Development has a DEC minicomputer.

In this chapter you will examine how different LANs can be linked via *bridges* or *routers*. You will also look at how PC LANs can communicate via *gateways* to mainframes and minicomputers.

You will take a close look at this mainframe and minicomputer world and how information is handled there—including the most common protocols used.

Bridges

Bridges are devices that function at the Data Link layer of the OSI Model (a topic you learned about in Chapter 2). At this level, there is a concern with packets' source and destination addresses, but not with any higher-level protocols. Packets that have the same Data Link layer can travel through a bridge regardless of whether they use Novell's IPX protocol or the XNS protocol (which several major network operating systems use).

> Bridges are devices that connect LANs at the Data Link layer of the OSI model. They do not concern themselves with higher-level protocols.

●
The major function of a bridge is to forward and filter packets depending on their destination addresses.

A bridge keeps a table that lists the addresses of the microcomputers found on its LAN. It examines a packet to see if its destination address is found on this particular LAN. If the packet is addressed to a local microcomputer, the bridge *filters* it from the packets transmitted to the bridge, and redirects it to its final destination on the local LAN. Packets addressed to microcomputers not found on this local LAN are *forwarded* across the bridge, to the bridge on the other side. This bridge goes through the same process of determining whether this same packet needs to be filtered or forwarded to still another LAN.

Bridges are usually very fast because they do not need to do any reformatting. They simply read a destination address and make the decision to filter or forward the packet. Bridges can have different types of cabling interfaces so that, for example, an Ethernet LAN with thick coaxial cabling can be bridged to a second Ethernet LAN that uses twisted-pair wire.

Spanning Tree Bridges

●
A spanning tree approach to bridging multiple networks results in a single path from one LAN to the next.

A *spanning tree* bridge has been adopted as a standard by the IEEE 802.1 committee. The spanning tree method describes how to bridge multiple networks in which more than one loop might exist. The bridges "negotiate" among themselves to ensure that only one bridge port is available in each direction on a LAN, and that the path selected is the most efficient (given network traffic conditions). Figure 6.1 illustrates the spanning tree approach to bridging multiple networks.

Source Routing Bridges

●
Source routing bridges are utilized by IBM's Token Ring Network. A workstation determines the complete route a packet must take, and includes this information as part of the packet.

IBM's Token Ring Networks use a *source routing* approach when they are bridged. Each LAN ring is assigned a unique number. A workstation sends out an *all-routes broadcast frame*, and requests information on the address of the workstation that will receive the packet. Each ring adds its number to this all-routes broadcast frame and forwards it. The destination workstation receives this frame and sends it back to the transmitting microcomputer. This frame now includes a complete set of routing directions, including which rings must be crossed to reach the destination address.

Bridging Ethernet and Token Ring Networks

●
Because Ethernet and Token Ring packets have different structures, a bridge connecting these two networks must do more than simply forward and filter packets.

Some companies have both Ethernet and Token Ring LANs, and wish to link the two. As discussed in Chapter 2, these two networks use very different packet structures. An Ethernet packet has a maximum size of only 1,500 bytes; a 4 mbps (megabits per second) Token Ring packet might contain 4,000 bytes, while a packet from a 16 mbps Token Ring Network might have close to 18,000 bytes. To make matters even more complicated, a bridge connecting these very different environments must reconcile Ethernet's spanning tree approach to routing packets with the Token Ring Network's source routing approach.

A bridge connecting Token Ring and Ethernet networks must segment the large Token Ring packets into several smaller packets for transmission over Ethernet networks. When source routing information crosses an Ethernet bridge, it is stripped off so that the packet resembles a conventional Ethernet packet. IBM's 8209 bridge, for example, is designed to connect these two very different worlds. It operates in three different modes:

● Token Ring to Ethernet version 2
● Token Ring to IEEE 802.3 LANs
● A mode in which the bridge detects the type of LAN, and then switches to mode 1 or mode 2

Why Use a Bridge?

As long as you are connecting like networks at the data link level, a bridge will typically outperform a router. A bridge is also normally cheaper than a router.

A bridge is normally faster than a router because it filters every LAN packet and simply forwards packets rather than making intelligent routing decisions.

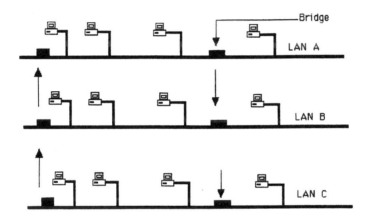

FIGURE 6.1.

The spanning tree algorithm determines the direction in which data flows to and from a network bridge.

Routers

Routers function at the Network layer of the OSI model and thus are protocol-specific. A router might route TCP/IP protocol packets, for example, or NetWare packets.

One major advantage of a router over a bridge is that it builds a *firewall* that protects one network from packets generated by another network, thereby reducing message traffic at the workstation level.

Bridges connect LANs so that they form one very large network. Connecting several Ethernet LANs via bridges, for example, results in every workstation on every connected LAN receiving all packets.

Naturally, traffic is very heavy on these connected LANs. If a network interface card goes bad on one workstation and begins generating thousands of bad packets (a *broadcast storm*)

●
Routers function at the Network layer of the OSI model and are protocol-specific.

it can congest all the bridged LANs. A router, on the other hand, is protocol-specific; it can be programmed to permit only those packets which match certain profiles.

Routers are much more sophisticated—and typically more expensive—than bridges. Before transmitting a packet to its destination, a router can analyze current traffic conditions and determine the best route for the packet to take. If traffic conditions change (for example, if a router down the road fails), the router can change its proposed route and redirect its packets over this revised path.

If it becomes necessary to link LANs that run different network operating systems which utilize different protocols, routers are required. For example, a company that has a NetWare LAN, a VINES LAN, and an IBM LAN Server network would need routers that understand these different protocols, so it could translate packets into the appropriate format before forwarding them to the destination network. Bridges operating at a far less sophisticated level would not be able to distinguish a VINES packet from a NetWare packet.

A second solution to this problem would be to have each of these three different LANs use a common protocol—such as the *Transmission Control Protocol/Internet Protocol* (known as the TCP/IP protocol)—on top of its file server protocol. Then install routers that only need to understand the TCP/IP protocol.

Why use a Router

A router operates at the Network layer of the OSI model. Routers only deal with protocols that have implemented Network layer addressing. The most common protocols are TCP/IP, Digital's Decnet, and Novell's NetWare.

Router networks can be linked with a large Wide Area Network (WAN) and the routers can determine multiple paths across the WAN, hence an internetwork made up of routers is more resilient than that of a bridged network. Sophisticated routers can select a specific path between networks that may be the cheapest or quickest. Therefore, in a good network design, considering best performance, management, and resilience, a router implementation is better than a bridge.

Connecting LANs to the Internet or CompuServe

There are many different ways of connecting a LAN to the Internet or CompuServe. Perhaps the simplest method is to attach an asynchronous communications server to the LAN running multiple modems with each modem dialing out to the Internet or CompuServe.

For larger numbers of users, a communications server connected to an X.25 leased line directly attached to an Internet provider may be beneficial.

For very heavy usage a router may be attached to the LAN directly linking it to the Internet provider at very high speed, normally 22 mbps.

Each user runs a communication program on their microcomputer which attaches the computer to the connection device whether it's the Async server, Comms server, or router. The communication program then links them through the connection device to the Internet or CompuServe. Popular programs for CompuServe include WinCIM and CompuServe Navigator, for the Internet: Netscape and Mosaic.

The World of Systems Network Architecture (SNA)

Any discussion of the mainframe world has to begin with IBM's set of specifications for distributed data processing networks. As Figure 6.2 illustrates, *Systems Network Architecture (SNA)* provides a model composed of network layers, very much like the OSI model you surveyed in Chapter 2. The data flow through this model is virtually identical to that of the OSI model, except that the frames use the Synchronous Data Link Control format (SDLC) rather than the High-Level Data Link Control (HDLC). As pointed out in Chapter 2, the SDLC frames contain some frames that are transmitted from one node to another throughout an SNA network.

IBM's NetView provides a centralized management system that performs diagnostics on SNA protocols, communication sessions, and network accounting procedures. It also displays network diagnostic alerts, and determines network component failures. NetView also has the capability of monitoring X.25 traffic in the SNA environment. IBM's X.25 SNA Interconnection program allows SNA networks to carry data under X.25 packet-switching protocols.

IBM's SNA contains several layers of protocols that are very similar to those of the OSI model discussed in the last chapter. SNA uses SDLC, a subset of HDLC.

TRANSACTION SERVICES	controls document exchange distributed database access
PRESENTATION SERVICES	formats data
DATA FLOW CONTROL	synchronous exchange of data
TRANSMISSION CONTROL	matches data exchange rate
PATH CONTROL	routes data packets between source and destination
DATA LINK CONTROL	transmits data between nodes
PHYSICAL	provides physical connections

FIGURE 6.2.

Systems Network Architecture (SNA).

● Asynchronous transmission sends data one byte at a time. Synchronous transmission uses frames that permit a stream of data.

Synchronous Versus Asynchronous Data Transmission

Data transmission in the microcomputer world has long taken the form of asynchronous transmission. Serial printers and modems are everyday reminders of how common this form of data communications really is. The SNA mainframe world uses the Synchronous Data Link Control (SDLC) protocol, a synchronous method of data transmission you learned about briefly in Chapter 2. As Figure 6.3 illustrates, asynchronous transmission is limited to sending characters a byte at a time with a start bit and a stop bit on either end, while the synchronous approach sends continuous information until the entire transmission is concluded.

FIGURE 6.3.

Asynchronous versus synchronous transmission.

Some older IBM mainframes use Binary Synchronous Communication (BSC), a protocol that is synchronous but is not SDLC. This protocol is character-oriented (rather than bit-oriented, as is SDLC); it assumes eight-bit characters. You focus your efforts on SDLC protocol machines in this chapter.

● Logical units (LUs) can represent end user workstations or application programs.

Logical Unit (LU)

Communication in an SNA network takes place between *logical units (LUs)*. Logical units can represent end users (as is the case with the firmware associated with IBM 3270 terminals) or application programs (such as an accounting program or database program). The application programs do not concern themselves with where the terminals are physically located but rather with the terminal's network name. SNA is capable of translating this network name into a corresponding address.

● Network-addressable units (NAUs) consist of logical units (LUs), physical units (PUs), and System Services Control Points (SSCPs).

Network-Addressable Units (NAUs)

SNA uses *network-addressable units (NAUs)* to perform a number of network management functions. These include handling the communications portions of application programs and providing network control. There are three types of network-addressable units. These NAUs can be logical units, *physical units (PUs)*, and *System Services Control Points (SSCPs)*. You examine the latter two types briefly before looking at an actual SNA network in operation.

A physical unit is not actually a physical device. It represents something tangible (a terminal or an intelligent controller, for example) to Systems Network Architecture—which deals (in effect) with this PU rather than with the device itself.

Finally, a System Services Control Point (SSCP) serves as the SNA network manager for a single SNA domain. It coordinates communications among network elements, makes sure the corresponding physical devices are active when two logical units wish to converse, and provides error-checking information.

The Path Control Network

Under SNA, the *Path Control Network* contains a path control layer and a data link control layer. This network is concerned with traffic flow, transmission priorities, and error recovery.

The Path Control Network is responsible for identifying the correct addresses of units that wish to converse, and then establishing a network path for their conversation.

> **Note:** Remember that all LUs, PUs, and even SSCPs have different network addresses under SNA.

●
The Path Control Network is responsible for identifying the addresses of devices that wish to converse on the network and then establishing a network path for their conversation.

Sessions

A *session* under SNA is a logical and physical path connecting two NAUs for data transmission. SNA thinks of its terminals, controllers, and front-end communication processors as *nodes*. Each of these hardware pieces has a corresponding PU. If a terminal wishes to communicate with a front-end communication processor, for example, the SSCP would establish a session between the two nodes. Two end users would establish an LU-LU session.

The SSCP controls the activating and deactivating of a session. An application program can maintain several different sessions with different terminals simultaneously under SNA. Figure 6.4 illustrates an example of the NAU elements found under SNA related to an IBM Mainframe.

●
A session consists of a logical and physical path connecting two NAUs for data transmission. NAUs can have multiple sessions.

LU 6.2

It is now possible to have transparent communication between two programs. IBM has added *Advanced Program-to-Program Communications (APPC)* to SNA, resulting in two new protocols (LU 6.2 and PU 2.1).

LU 6.2 enables a microcomputer running a program under an operating system such as Windows or OS/2 to communicate with a mainframe computer that runs under a different operating system—while still retaining full stand-alone processing capabilities. The

●
LU 6.2 contains specifications that enable programs written in different languages under different operating systems to communicate with each other.

concept behind this protocol is that different computers running different programs (written in different languages under different operating systems) can interact easily with each other.

For years corporations have longed for the ability to download information from a mainframe directly into a personal computer running products such as Excel. Similarly, there is a real need to be able to upload customer files created under a Windows or OS/2 program (such as Microsoft Access or DB2/2) directly into a mainframe database. LU 6.2 provides this capability.

IBM developed SNA before personal computers were popular; its concept of distributed processing (which was incorporated under SNA) was a master-slave relationship. All communication under SNA goes through the main computer. Two end users who wish to send information to each other can do so only by going through the mainframe computer. Under LU 6.2, true peer-to-peer communications is possible. A personal computer as part of an SNA network is able to address a second personal computer directly, without going through the mainframe. Such a path is particularly valuable if the mainframe should fail.

LU 6.2 overcomes many of the limitations of SNA because it provides a true generic *application program interface (API)* between application programs and Systems Network Architecture. Because this interface includes hardware specifications, the network can be thought of as machine-independent—as long as all vendors adhere to these requirements. Rather than establishing a traditional master-slave relationship (the historical norm under SNA), LU 6.2 allows either node in a network session to initiate the session.

FIGURE 6.4.

The NAU elements found under SNA.

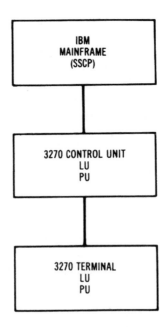

Micro-Mainframe Communications

The main areas of emphasis in this book are LANs, and how microcomputers on a network can communicate with each other (as well as with mainframes and minicomputers).

Despite the possibilities of LU 6.2, the dearth of software written for the interface means that for the foreseeable future, microcomputers will continue to communicate with the mainframe and minicomputer world by *terminal emulation* or through more popular protocols such as TCP/IP.

Local LAN Gateways

A single IBM PC in 3278 terminal emulation, connected directly to the cluster controller by coaxial cable, is using one of the controller's ports—this is a major limitation. Several PCs connected in this way would severely limit the mainframe's ability to serve all company users. Using coaxial cable, it is possible to connect an entire microcomputer LAN to an IBM cluster controller port via a gateway. As Figure 6.5 illustrates, any PC in such a network has access to 3270 terminal emulation. DCA and Wall Data are some of the many companies currently offering this coaxial-connect gateway. Novell's Netware for SAA is one of the most popular software gateways available, and makes it possible for any LAN or WAN to connect to the mainframe via the SAA gateway.

●
Although LU 6.2 has come to fruition in the IBM world, the main method for micro-mainframe and micro-mini communications continues to be the emulation of various terminal types.

●
A LAN gateway can be attached via coaxial cable to a 3274 cluster controller to provide a local micro-mainframe connection or to a 5394 controller to provide AS/400 Midrange access.

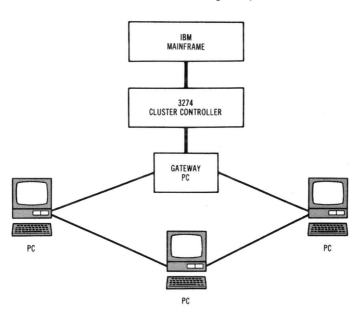

FIGURE 6.5.
An IBM PC with 3270 terminal emulation.

Remote Gateways

Remote gateways enable LAN users to communicate with a mainframe computer by using 3278 terminal emulation over a gateway PC. This gateway emulates a cluster controller and communicates with the mainframe computer via a modem, bridge, or router.

Useful as coaxial-connect gateways are, many companies have their LANs at one location, and their mainframe facilities elsewhere. In this situation, remote LAN gateways prove particularly valuable.

At the remote site, the designated gateway PC is equipped with a *gateway interface board* and special gateway software to effectively emulate a mainframe controller. As Figure 6.6 illustrates, each remote PC can emulate a mainframe terminal using the gateway PC's synchronous modem, bridge attachment or router to communicate over a wide area network with a mainframe computer. VISIO by Shapeware is a very good product to do this.

A variety of products can link LANs to the mainframe in this way, they include IBM Communications Manager and Novell's Netware SAA. You may recall from the discussion of the SNA world and the nature of SNA sessions that one user can find himself needing three or four editing sessions simultaneously. These mainframe sessions are very valuable; often the network administrator will establish some order of priority for using them.

FIGURE 6.6.

Remote 3270 emulation with a gateway PC.

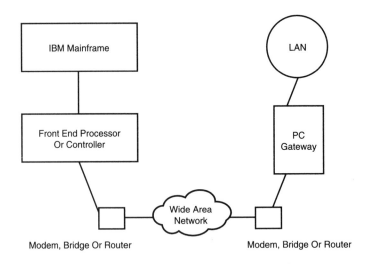

Micro-Mainframe File Transfers

Many of the micro-mainframe file transfer programs permit only the transfer of files. The microcomputer user can select key fields from a mainframe database and retrieve only this specific information.

You have seen that it is possible to link workstations in a LAN to a mainframe computer by using terminal emulation and a gateway. The major limitation of this emulation is that an intelligent PC is forced to assume the role of a dumb terminal. The terminal emulation software usually permits online inquiry using the mainframe programs and has the capability to save each screen of 3270 terminal information.

Unfortunately, this is not the major reason companies want to link their microcomputers with their mainframe computer. Users want to be able to download and upload selected information, not merely dump screenfuls of information.

Because microcomputers and mainframe computers are running different programs under different operating systems, file transfers in both directions create enormous problems. Even more serious, the very file structure of micro and mainframe application programs usually differ. IBM mainframe computers use an EBCDIC format, while microcomputers use an ASCII format.

Another a problem is the file-size limitations of a microcomputer; there is a fundamental difference in size between a micro and a mainframe. Mainframe files may not be downloadable simply because the microcomputer does not have enough disk space to handle them; the micro's software may not be able to handle the large number of records found within a mainframe file.

Many of the leaders in micro-mainframe communications offer *file transfer* programs with their 3270 terminal emulation products. These programs do not permit a user to manipulate the data within a mainframe's application program or select certain fields; they merely enable a microcomputer user to download or upload complete files.

Companies have developed intelligent links that tie together their own mainframe computer programs with major microcomputer software. Information Builders, for example, offers FOCUS for the IBM mainframe environment and PC/FOCUS for microcomputers. Using this program, it is possible to use the mainframe database for distributed processing. PCs tied to a LAN can be used as transaction workstations to enter data.

There are a few vendors who have begun to address the possibilities of LU 6.2 and its potential for facilitating data transfer from microcomputer to mainframe. Network Software Associates' AdaptSNA LU6.2/APPC is what the name implies—an implementation of LU 6.2 and PU 2.1. It enables a PC program to communicate directly with a partner program running on a mainframe or minicomputer. This implementation does away with the traditional SNA master-slave relationship, permitting peer-to-peer communication.

Wall Data's Rumba for Database Access (Rumba DBA) gives you transparent, direct access to IBM DRDA-compliant databases, which include DB2, SQL/DS, and OS/400, without LAN gateways and server components. RUMBA DBA provides easy access to corporate databases so you can build and execute queries quickly and easily while maintaining the security and integrity of corporate information. Products like Rumba DBA will begin to reduce the gap between mainframe and LAN databases. Enabling a company to best position its data, and yet provide its users with query and report creation facilities that they require.

Micro-Mini Communications

Just as it is possible to connect to a mainframe via a gateway and emulation packages, it is possible to connect to midrange or minicomputers in the same fashion. This process is similar to 3270 terminal emulation, except that the microcomputers need to be equipped with the following:

●

Through terminal emulation it is possible for microcomputers—individually, or as part of a LAN—to communicate with minicomputers such as IBM's AS/400 (as well as its older System 34, 36, and 38 computers).

- Suitable network cards to connect to the gateway supporting 5250 emulation.
- File transfer software to communicate with IBM minicomputers
- Corresponding software and hardware to communicate with DEC, Hewlett-Packard, and other major minicomputers

Several major vendors offer this combination of hardware and software. NetWare for example provides NetWare SAA that provides the gateway features to an IBM AS/400. Wall Data provides Rumba Office which provides connectivity to IBM Mainframe, IBM AS/400 and DEC computers in one integrated package. Rumba Office can also take advantage of a wide range of gateway hardware. Novell's Netware for LAT is their DEC connectivity solution.

Many of the same file transfer limitations found in micro-mainframe communications are also present in micro-mini communications. IBM addresses many of these problems with its PC Support and Client Access/400 products. Client Access/400 provides 5250 emulation under Windows and OS/2, Direct database access via ODBC, and File Transfer software.

Virtual Networking Systems

Banyan Systems has developed VINES software, which permits sharing of resources on a virtual network. PCs can actually share a mainframe or minicomputer hard disk.

On a *virtual network* all resources appear to be local so that the differences between microcomputers, minicomputers, and even mainframes are of limited importance to the end user. Banyan Systems, for example, has developed VINES software in conjunction with its family of network file servers. As Figure 6.7 illustrates, VINES permits the sharing of resources, applications, and information wherever they are located on a virtual network.

A microcomputer user can access files from a mainframe as easily as if this information were on his PC. The microcomputer can save information onto the *virtual disk* of the mainframe or minicomputer that is also attached to the Banyan file server. Because the software supports LU 6.2, it is extremely easy to communicate with other users, even if you do not know precisely where they are on the network. The software keeps track of users' addresses, and permits electronic mail transfer simply by indicating the receiver's name.

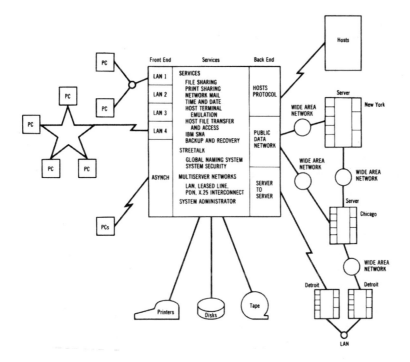

FIGURE 6.7.

Banyan's Virtual Networking System (courtesy of Banyan Systems, Inc.).

What Have You Learned?

1. Bridges connect LANs at the Data Link layer of the OSI model and filter or forward packets.

2. Routers connect networks at the Network layer of the OSI model and are protocol-specific.

3. IBM's mainframe and minicomputers utilize Systems Network Architecture (SNA).

4. Network-addressable units (NAUs) consist of logical units (LUs), physical units (PUs), and System Services Control Points (SSCPs).

5. LU 6.2 provides an application program interface (API) that will permit peer-to-peer communication.

6. With appropriate hardware and software, an IBM PC or compatible can emulate an IBM 3270 terminal and communicate with a mainframe.

7. An IBM PC or compatible can serve as a LAN gateway. The PC can be connected to the host in a variety of ways and provides terminal emulation for an entire LAN.

Quiz for Chapter 6

1. Which of these devices transmits packets most quickly?

   a. gateway

   b. bridge

   c. router

   d. IMOK

2. A device operating at the Network layer of the OSI model is the

   a. bridge.

   b. router.

   c. gateway.

   d. repeater.

3. Under SNA, the Path Control Network is concerned with

   a. traffic flow.

   b. transmission priorities.

   c. error recovery.

   d. all of the above.

4. An IBM PC or compatible can communicate with a mainframe computer if the PC is equipped with

   a. a dot-matrix printer.

   b. a 30MB hard disk.

   c. 3270 terminal emulation hardware and software.

   d. a Super VGA-compatible monitor.

5. Microcomputers that are part of a LAN might communicate with a mainframe located in the same building by using

   a. communications software.

   b. an IBM PC or compatible LAN gateway, connected via coaxial cable with a cluster controller.

   c. laser technology.

   d. fiber optics.

6. A gateway PC that is used only for this function is known as a

   a. gateway server.

   b. distributed server.

   c. dedicated gateway.

   d. remote job entry station.

7. A mainframe database file is likely to consist of

   a. EBCDIC characters.

   b. ASCII characters.

   c. ANSI characters.

   d. 8-bit words.

8. To communicate with an IBM System 34/36/38 or AS/400, the PC can emulate a

   a. Sun Sparcstation.

   b. UNIX server.

   c. 4829 color terminal.

   d. 5250 terminal.

Peer-to-Peer LANs

Peer-To-Peer Networks

About This Chapter

In this chapter, you take a look at the main peer-to-peer networks in the market-place. Peer-to-peer networks are networks that do not require a file server, and each client can talk to and share information with every other client.

About This Section

This section discusses Microsoft's Windows for Workgroups (WFW), a peer-to-peer network operating system that includes the Windows graphical user interface. You learn how basic functions such as printing and sharing a directory are handled with WFW. It provides you with some insight as to whether this network operating system is right for your computing environment.

Windows for Workgroups: User Requirements

Windows for Workgroups (WFW) only works in enhanced mode. PCs must be running at least an Intel-based 386SX microprocessor to run WFW V3.11.

While installation of WFW is not difficult, there are a couple of issues that might cause inexperienced network users some concern. Because users are likely to add some non-Microsoft software, there is a likelihood that there will be some software conflicts and inter-operability problems. Some users might be happier with a source of support in their immediate area.

●
WFW requires at
least an Intel 386SX-
based computer.

The network driver issue is another problem. Network drivers must be loaded in the PC's
CONFIG.SYS file and cannot be unloaded easily. This requirement makes reconfiguring
network adapters time-consuming and difficult.

WFW uses the NetBIOS Extended User Interface (NetBEUI) as its default transport protocol. One limitation is that this protocol cannot be routed. This means that if WFW is
used in conjunction with a NetWare LAN, for example, users can share all the resources
of this NetWare network, but they are only able to see other WFW users if they are on the
same segment. An external bridge can be used to route NetBEUI packets from one segment to another segment.

Windows for Workgroups supports Novell's Open Data Link Interface (ODI) drivers so
that WFW's peer services can run on NetWare's IPX protocol. Users also have the option
of supporting the Network Device Interface Specification (NDIS) that is found under
Windows NT.

●
32-bit Disk and File
Access can improve
WFW v3.11
performance.

32-Bit Disk and File Access

WFW v3.11 has built-in 32-Bit Disk and File Access. When enabled through the 386
Enhanced icon under the Control Panel, these options can significantly improve the reading
and writing of data from the computer's hard drive. Direct access to the computers hard
disk controller is provided by 32-Bit Disk access rather than through DOS. It must be
noted that 32-Bit Disk Access can be unreliable on some battery-powered portables.

Faster reading and writing to the disk cache is provided by 32-Bit File Access. Information read from the hard drive is kept in a disk cache in the computer's extended memory.
The next time an application or program tries to read that information from the hard disk,
the information is supplied directly from memory instead (which is obviously far faster
than the disk). Data to be written to disk may also be stored in the disk cache.

Connecting to Another Computer

With Windows for Workgroups, users press a Connect Network Drive button that opens
a window with a list of computers and share names. A user selects the computer and share
name and WFW assigns it the next drive letter, although this letter can be changed by the
user. By selecting an option it is possible to have specific computers automatically connected at the time that Windows for Workgroups is loaded.

Network Management
and Security Features

Although WFW does not offer strong network management features compared to client/
server network operating systems, it does compare favorably with network management

features offered by other peer-to-peer network operating systems. The NetWatcher accessory provides users with a display of the various connections to their local shared resources. The WinMeter utility provides a graphical display of how resources are being distributed between local applications and shared resources.

Although security is not a strong feature in WFW, an auditing button enables users to access a detailed log of events. Actual security consists only of password protection and not access control lists found in other programs such as LANtastic. Users can grant read access, all access, or none: all these levels of access depend on how the user decides to grant access to a resource or share.

Resource Sharing

WFW enables users to share data, directories, and printers. Let's examine each of these features.

Sharing Data

Actively linked data can be shared through network Dynamic Data Exchange (DDE). Under WFW, users can create live document links with DDE-compliant applications such as Excel. Several application files can be linked to documents being created on several network computers simultaneously.

As an example, Andy could be using CorelDRAW! to create a cartoon figure to be used as part of an employee safety campaign. Tina could be using AutoCAD to create a design of the corporate headquarters to pinpoint danger areas. Sally could be using WordPerfect to write up details of this new campaign. Sally's WordPerfect document includes Andy's drawing and Tina's design. If these individuals make changes in their work, these changes are automatically reflected in Sally's WordPerfect file.

WFW users also have the ability to cut and paste from each other's work. Items can be copied and pasted from a source document to a Clipboard. Because the Clipboard can only hold one item at a time, users can paste the contents of a Clipboard to their own ClipBook. This ClipBook not only holds several pieces of information, but it also can be shared with other users. A ClipBook page can be selected and then shared with other WFW network users by clicking a Share button.

A dialog box associated with the Share button appears so that the user can specify the level of access others will have to this page (Read-Only or full access). A password is required for each of these access levels.

Sharing Directories

Under WFW, directories can easily be shared. Users need only click on a tool bar to set security options. Figure 7.1 illustrates the Share Directory screen. Notice that the access level depends on the password used.

FIGURE 7.1.
*The Share Directory
screen under WFW.*

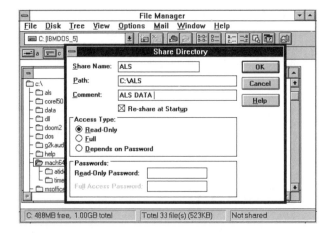

FIGURE 7.1.
*The Share Directory
screen under WFW.*

Sharing Printers

WFW users can use their own local printers as well as clicking a Connect Network Printer
button to view the shared printers on the network and specify the location of the printer
desired. By clicking on the Print Manager, it is possible to see the status of print jobs on
various network printers. Figure 7.2 illustrates the Print Manager screen.

FIGURE 7.2.
*The Print Manager
Screen.*

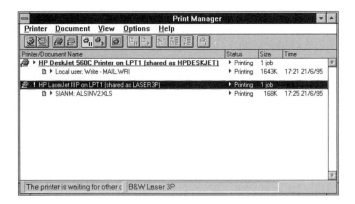

Under WFW, printers can be shared and unshared. Both printers and documents can be
paused. It is also possible with WFW to promote, demote, and delete documents from
the WFW print queue.

Communications Under WFW

WFW has a number of communications features, including real-time conversation, e-mail,
and scheduling. You will examine each of these features.

Chat

A Chat feature lets users exchange live e-mail in an almost realtime environment. As many as eight users can now take part in a conversation with a realtime conversation window. Microsoft has included a ringing phone icon and sound to alert users that someone wants to Chat. Figure 7.3 illustrates two users taking advantage of the Chat feature.

●

A Chat feature allows up to eight users to communicate with each other in realtime.

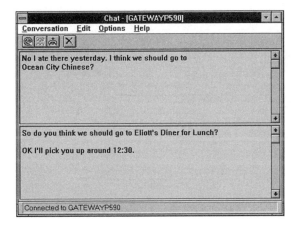

FIGURE 7.3.

Two WFW users take advantage of the Chat feature.

E-Mail Under WFW

WFW comes with built-in e-mail, which is a scaled down version of Microsoft Mail. When Mail is run as a minimized icon, it looks like a mail slot in a person's front door. A user receiving mail sees letters slip through the slot. An audible chime can also be set to alert the user that mail has arrived. Although it lacks some of the robustness of a full Microsoft Mail program, this version does allow users to compose, send, and forward messages. They also can read and reply to any letters they receive. Messages can be sorted by priority, sender, data, or subject, and can be stored in named folders.

One of the limitations of the e-mail version included with WFW is that only one workgroup post office (WGPO) is allowed for each workgroup. Also, one user must serve as the postmaster in order to create the post office (WGPO tree). The postmaster also must share the WGPO directory. Another limitation of Mail is that it does not include any gateways to other network e-mail systems. The features of Microsoft Mail have been covered in Chapter 4.

Schedule+

Microsoft includes a scheduler/calendar program called Schedule+ with WFW; it even has written a Visual Basic connection to Microsoft Project so that users can mail their "to do" lists for Schedule+ to other workgroup users. An Appointment book helps users manage their meetings and schedule up to six appointments and tentative appointments per time slot. Another user can be designated as an assistant and given the power to schedule his or her appointments. Figure 7.4 shows the initial Schedule+ startup screen.

FIGURE 7.4.

The Schedule+ initial start screen.

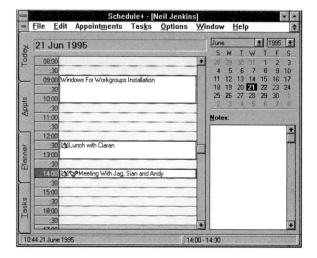

The Planner portion of the program enables users to display appointments several days at a time. The Calendar portion of the program notes with color any conflicts or openings. Figure 7.5 shows a meeting request screen. Notice that the recipient has the choice of accepting, declining, or tentatively accepting the request for a meeting. When a person accepts a request, the program automatically notifies the sender of this acceptance and then schedules the meeting in the recipient's Appointment Book.

FIGURE 7.5.

A meeting request screen.

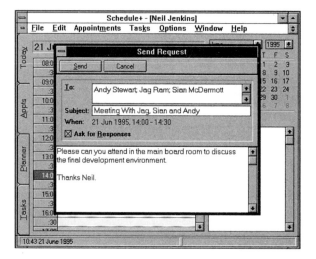

It's possible to edit appointments in a user's Appointment Book. By clicking on the Edit Appt option under the Edit menu, the user sees a display of appointments that have been made. The user can then set a reminder for any of these appointments. A small bell icon appears in the time slot of the appointment in the Appointment Book indicating that a reminder has been set. The program will remind the user of this appointment at the time designated for this reminder. The default is to notify the user 15 minutes before an appointment.

Microsoft makes Microsoft Mail and Schedule+ Extensions available to WFW users at an add-on cost of approximately $495. This product provides additional functionality for these two functions including the ability to create groups of post office users and gateways to communicate with external e-mail systems and other schedule programs.

Strengths and Weaknesses

Windows for Workgroups is remarkably easy to use. It is an extension of the extremely popular Windows operating system. Virtually all network activities including scheduling and electronic mail enable people to work in an intuitive way. The scheduling appointment book resembles a yellow pad with appointments written in. Simple prompts guide users through most activities. For a company needing to link a few computers to form a small network or their first network, WFW is ideal.

For companies having several computers to network or with an existing network operating system such as NetWare, WFW comes up short. Its security does not match that of competitors such as LANtastic. Its use of the NetBEUI transport protocol is also limiting, particularly if the company needs to route network packets to a remote network or to another LAN running a different network operating system.

What Have You Learned about WFW?

1. Windows for Workgroups (WFW) is a peer-to-peer network operating system that includes scheduling and e-mail programs.
2. Files created with different programs can be dynamically linked using dynamic data exchange.
3. The minimum PC microprocessor to use WFW is an Intel 80386SX.
4. Both the e-mail program (Mail) and the schedule program (Schedule+) provide minimum services, but Microsoft does offer an upgrade option to add functionality to these programs.
5. Because WFW uses the NetBEUI transport protocol, data cannot be routed.
6. 32-Bit Disk and File Access can seriously improve the performance of WFW.

Windows 95

Windows 95 is Microsoft's operating system successor to Windows 3.1 and Windows for Workgroups 3.11. Windows 95 is a 32-bit operating system with multitasking and multithreading. In this chapter, you read about the main differences in Windows 95 compared to Windows for Workgroups and how Windows 95 is set to make a significant impact on the networking world.

Windows 95 Built-in Networking

● *Windows 95 comes complete with 32-bit networking built-in.*

Windows 95 comes complete with 32-bit networking built-in to allow it to work directly with most of the major networks—including NetWare, Windows NT, and other Windows 95 peer-to-peer machines.

32-Bit Components

The networking components have been rewritten to take advantage of the 32-bit operating system. The redirector program, protocol drivers, network adapter drivers, and file and printer services now run in a true multitasking environment and do not take up any real mode memory.

Windows 95 also comes with 32-bit versions of an IPX/SPX-compatible protocol and TCP/IP. A variety of other protocols and 16-bit network clients are also supported.

Network Neighborhood

Once the network has been installed on Windows 95, each user has access to the Network Neighborhood. This option allows a user to look at, log on, and log off the network server that their machine can "see." This option is usually accessed from the Network Neighborhood icon on the Windows 95 desktop.

Network Management and Security

● *Windows 95 can take advantage of existing NetWare and NT server security.*

Windows 95 supports pass-through, server-based security for both NetWare and Windows NT networks, allowing each client computer to use the existing NOS security. This eases implementation of Windows 95 onto your existing LAN.

Windows 95 can be configured to request an existing logon and password before a user can use the operating system in a networked environment. Windows 95 can take advantage of the bindery information or user accounts on NetWare and Windows NT servers. By doing this, network managers can set security on a user-specific basis for all resources on the network including the optional file and printer sharing services in Windows 95.

Windows 95 provides additional security for remote dial-in networking, this includes encrypted passwords and callback options.

Network Management Tools

Windows 95 has an administration tool built in called System Policy Editor. This tool is used to set up rights and restrictions for specific users and computers as well as define general default settings. Network Administrators can use this tool to control access to the network, specify desktop configuration settings, and prevent users from modifying their desktop and applications. The editor can also limit users to running a defined list of applications.

In addition, Windows 95 provides support for SNMP agents to query and manage the registry on the client computer. As a result, network managers can use third-party or in-house developed software for network management.

The System Monitor provides graphical measurements of network traffic, file system performance, and other activities on remote computers.

The NetWatcher is similar to the same program in WFW 3.11. It allows the user to view and disconnect network connections and control file and printer sharing.

Dial-In Networking

Dial-In networking under Windows 95 allows the user to connect to network resources, such as files and e-mail as if they were locally attached. Windows 95 can use a point-to-point protocol (PPP) or server-based dial-in packages such as NetWare Connect and Windows NT RAS.

The Windows 95 Briefcase is a tool that allows remote users to track and update copies of files stored on two or more computers—usually at the office and on a portable. Files that need to be kept synchronized are placed in the briefcase, and Windows 95 prompts the user to synchronize the files. Briefcase then updates the file on the network to match the file on the portable.

Windows 95 Exchange

Windows 95 includes a completely new e-mail product called Exchange. The Exchange product is really several products in one. It acts as a single inbox and can send and receive Microsoft Mail, CompuServe Mail, Internet Mail, Electronic Fax, America Online Mail, and Microsoft Network Mail.

What Have You Learned about Windows 95?

1. Windows 95 is Microsoft's 32-bit replacement operating system for Windows 3.1 and Windows for Workgroups.

2. Windows 95 has faster 32-bit networking support for a variety of networking operating systems as well as its own peer-to-peer networking.

3. System Policy Editor, NetWatcher, and System Monitor are all peer-to-peer network management tools.

4. Microsoft Exchange acts as a single mailbox for a variety of mail services including CompuServe, Internet, Fax, and MS Mail.

Artisoft's LANtastic

In this section, you examine the market leader for peer-to-peer network operating systems, Artisoft's LANtastic. Rather than being a single product, LANtastic is actually a family of products designed for different platforms including DOS-based microcomputers and Apple Macintosh computers. You also look at the hardware that Artisoft offers for LANtastic LANs.

●
LANtastic uses a peer-to-peer configuration.

LANtastic

Artisoft's LANtastic is a network operating system that uses a peer-to-peer approach that enables each network workstation to share its resources (such as its hard disk's contents or printer) with other network workstations. For companies that do not need the security and additional features available with a centralized file server, the peer-to-peer approach is relatively inexpensive and efficient.

●
Security is robust on LANtastic. In addition to password protection, supervisors can limit users' network access to certain days and hours.

Security on LANtastic

LANtastic's Username with Password feature makes it possible to limit a user's access to certain hours and to certain days of the week. Users can be granted any or all of the following privileges.

- Read files
- Write files
- Modify files
- Create files
- Delete files
- Rename files

- Make directories
- Delete directories
- Look up directories
- Execute programs
- Change file attributes

Network managers can set up *Access Control List (ACL) groups.* ACL groups allow multiple users, such as users within a particular department, to have the same privileges regarding particular files on servers, or shared resources. Each user's individual account can be assigned specific additional access rights beyond those linked to the ACL group. ACL security can also be extended to individual files and groups of files located on shared resources.

●
Access Control Lists enable network managers to grant groups of users the same network rights.

LANtastic's Network Management Features

Artisoft's The Network Eye is a program that enables one user on a LANtastic network to sit at one network workstation and view the screens and keyboards of all other network workstations. A user can view up to 32 screens simultaneously. It is possible to copy, cut, and paste text or data from one PC to another PC.

One valuable use of this program, from a managerial perspective, is to give network users access to a modem or fax board installed on a networked workstation.

The Net Mgr utility program makes it possible to set up individual accounts. Users can be required to change their passwords, and their network access can be limited to certain times and days. A network manager can use this utility to define groups of users, so that network resources can be shared by all individuals within a group. Users can log on to the network and use this utility program's menu to see which servers and network resources are available; they can also access e-mail or view a printer queue.

Hardware for a LANtastic Network

On Ethernet networks, LANtastic supports thick and thin coaxial cabling as well as twisted-pair wire. The NodeRunner/SI Ethernet Adapter supports all three types of cabling. It contains a 32K RAM buffer (upgradeable to 64K), which can be used in either 8-bit or 16-bit slots. The buffer can sense the 16-bit slot and enhance its performance.

Adding an optional PROM chip (Programmable Read-Only Memory) from Artisoft makes it possible to boot up a diskless workstation from a network server. Network programs can be run on a diskless workstation, but because it has no disk drives, files cannot be downloaded. This approach provides greater security than does a standard PC.

The maximum network cable lengths per segment on a LANtastic Ethernet network are 607 feet (185 meters) with thin coaxial cable, 1,640 (500 meters) feet with thick coaxial cable, and 328 feet (100 meters) with 10BaseT twisted-pair cable.

Artisoft offers a 10BaseT hub/concentrator. Residing within a host PC, this device has five external 10BaseT ports that use modular RJ45 telephone-style jacks. Network management software makes it possible to view the status of all ports, and to enable or disable each port individually.

LANtastic for Windows

LANtastic's Windows interface enables users to take full advantage of its features, including dynamic data exchange.

Artisoft's LANtastic for Windows interface provides pull-down menus, icons, and online help in a Windows context. Users can open multiple windows to monitor printer queues, manage user accounts, and chat with multiple users—all at the same time.

With a Windows interface, LANtastic users can use pull-down menus to create and maintain shared resources like drives, printers, and other peripherals. These users can run the LANtastic for Windows utility in the background while running another Windows application. Because the LANtastic for Windows utility program supports the dynamic data exchange (DDE) standard, users can mail data from a spreadsheet or database window (via LANtastic's e-mail) without leaving the application.

LANtastic for OS/2

LANtastic for OS/2 is a 32-bit multitasking, multithreaded operating system.

Artisoft has a version of LANtastic designed to run on top of IBM's OS/2. It connects to LANtastic 5.0 and 6.0 DOS and Windows stations. The SMB protocol provides connectivity to Windows NT, LAN Server, and other SMB-based servers. It coexists with NetWare requester for OS/2 and LAN Server clients on the same machine, thus making it possible for each PC to be on multiple networks at once.

LANtastic for OS/2 looks and feels like OS/2's native interface. It supports OS/2 long file names and extended attributes with other OS/2 machines. LANtastic for OS/2 is a conversion of Artisoft's LANtastic 6.0 for DOS and Windows and it shares many of the features discussed later. Installation is very simple, and LANtastic for OS/2 supports NDIS-compliant network cards. However, LANtastic for OS/2 does not contain the Artisoft Exchange e-mail program, which is a major loss for a peer-to-peer networking system.

LANtastic for the Macintosh

Macintosh users can access a LANtastic LAN via a PC serving as a dedicated gateway between the LANtastic and Macintosh networks.

Artisoft offers a version of LANtastic for the Macintosh. Users can purchase hardware (LocalTalk adapter cards and cables) and software bundled together or software only. This version of LANtastic enables Macintosh computers to be linked to form a LAN that runs the LANtastic NOS and provides access to all its features as well as the ability to print to PostScript printers. The software only version provides drivers for EtherTalk, LocalTalk, and Token Ring adapter cards.

The LANtastic for Macintosh software establishes a PC to serve as a dedicated gateway between the Macintosh and LANtastic networks. PC servers on the LANtastic network are set up as logical drives on the gateway PC and appear to Macintosh network users as slightly modified computer icons. Thus, Macintosh users see PC files and directories as they would standard Macintosh files and directories and can select printers attached to the LANtastic network.

A dedicated gateway PC is used by PC users to access PostScript printers on the Macintosh network. These users can see Macintosh files saved onto the gateway PC's hard drive.

Both PC and Macintosh users can access other files that use the same file format such as Microsoft's Word and WordPerfect's WordPerfect software. File attributes and record-locking are supported in both directions. In addition, any PostScript-compatible printer—even non-AppleTalk interface printers such as the Hewlett-Packard's LaserJet series—can be shared simultaneously among all workstations, both Macintosh and PC.

LANtastic for TCP/IP

LANtastic for TCP/IP allows LANtastic clients to share documents and data files with other TCP/IP clients. It allows users to take advantage of other resources located elsewhere on a TCP/IP network.

LANtastic 6.0

Artisoft's latest version of LANtastic incorporates many features not found in earlier versions. In particular, it is much stronger in the areas of multi-platform connectivity, network administration, and security. This version supports 500 users per server versus the 300 users supported in earlier versions and is about 15 percent faster. The software is now much more modular, so you only load the features you need. A burst mode transfers data faster, while using less memory. This version also now has built-in file and record-locking.

●
LANtastic 6.0 can handle a maximum of 500 users.

Multi-platform Support

A major trend in large corporations is the drive toward enterprise-wide networking. This means that networks running different operating systems on different hardware platforms will have an increasing need to communicate with each other. LANtastic version 6.0 addresses this need. It provides bridging capabilities to UNIX's Network Filing System (NFS). This feature permits a LANtastic client that is also a UNIX client (running LANtastic for TCP/IP software or other UNIX client software) to serve as a bridge to the rest of the LANtastic network. Artisoft has also provided a bridge to NetWare LANs. A LANtastic client running as a NetWare client can also be set up as a NetWare bridge so that users on the LANtastic network can access the NetWare server's files. This task can be accomplished by installing an additional adapter to the LANtastic machine and appropriate NetWare workstation files.

Another common situation in an enterprise-wide environment is to have mixed topologies. NetBIOS in LANtastic 6.0 includes routable packets that permit users to connect different types of networks such as ARCnet, Ethernet, and serial port networks to form a single LANtastic LAN. An IPX routing option allows the use of Novell IPX-compliant routers.

The Linkbook

The Windows version of LANtastic has a feature known as the Linkbook. It functions like a regular Windows Clipboard except it can be used by other network users. In this storage area such items as text, graphics, and even sound files can be placed. The Linkbook can be set up with security so that network users can access items in it without being able to delete them or place new items in it.

Enhanced Network Administration

LANtastic 6.0 permits administrators to set up all user accounts on a single client that can share the user account information with other clients. A feature that is especially attractive to network managers permits them to control a network station remotely. This feature allows them to check every client's configuration, status, and performance. Screen and sound alerts tell when a network station's workload exceeds the thresholds a network manager sets.

Advanced Print Job Control

LANtastic 6.0 adds additional printing features. Delayed despooling means that users can specify the date and time they want a particular document printed. Remote despooling is a feature that permits a queue to be serviced by multiple remote printers. This feature is attractive to network managers who have a LAN that spans different buildings and even different sites.

"Talking" on the LAN

Windows users of LANtastic 6.0 who have Artisoft Sounding Boards installed can access the voice chat feature for realtime voice communication between two PCs and use LAN Radio for multiple channel "CB radio-like" communications across the network. Users can also create voice error messages using the Artisoft Sounding Board.

LANtastic's ACLs make it possible to restrict users' access to directories and files.

LANtastic's Access Control Lists

For each shared resource, an Access Control List (ACL) can be set up for each user or user group. Protection can be established for an entire shared drive, its subdirectories, or even a single file.

Because LANtastic is a peer-to-peer network operating system, users can limit access to a resource such as a printer to a particular user or a specific group of users. Unless an individual account has the "A" (Super ACL) privilege, a user would have only the rights specified from the types of access specified in Table 7. 1.

Table 7.1. Access control list rights.

Abbreviation	Function	Description
R	Read Access	Open files for reading.
W	Write Access	Write to files.
C	Create a File	Create files. Without Write Access enabled, users are not able to write to these files.
M	Make Directory	Create new subdirectories.
L	File Lookups (DIRs)	Display or search through directories.
D	Delete Files	Delete files.
K	Delete Directories	Delete subdirectories.
N	Rename Files	Rename files.
E	Execute Program	Execute programs.
A	Change file attributes	Change file attributes within a shared directory.
I	Indirect File	Create and use indirect files within this shared directory.
P	Physical Access	Use a special subdirectory to connect to DOS devices directly.

A drive can be set up so that other network users can read files and perform directory lookups but not make any changes in these files. Those users have the RLE access.

> **Note:** Providing access rights to other network users can cause serious security problems. LANtastic applies security rights on a disk resource downward through the entire directory. If, for example, a C-DRIVE is defined as pointing to C:\ and users have full rights to this access, they also have full rights to all levels within that C drive including all subdirectories. LANtastic also makes it possible to limit access to specific server files and directories.

Controlling Login Times

LANtastic makes it possible to control when a user is allowed to log on to a server. The user can be limited to certain hours and certain days. Time limits can be imposed in half-hour increments, so it is possible, for example, to restrict users to a time slot consisting of 1:30 PM to 3:30 PM on Thursdays.

Audit Trails Under LANtastic

Audit trails reveal if users have attempted to access an unauthorized device.

LANtastic offers an audit trail feature that makes it possible to view what types of network access were made or attempted by users. A network supervisor can filter the auditing process to audit only certain events such as a user attempting access to an unauthorized device such as a database server. Another advantage of audit trails is that a supervisor can establish charge-back procedures to charge network users for utilizing network resources such as printers or disk drives.

Figure 7.6 shows LANtastic's Audited Activities screen. Server Up refers to a server being started or shut down. Logins and Logouts refer to users logging on or off a server. Queuing refers to a user writing to a server's mail or print queues. LANtastic considers the Printing activity to be a print job completed for a user. The log entry contains the number of bytes sent to a printer. Finally, User Entry refers to a NET AUDIT command.

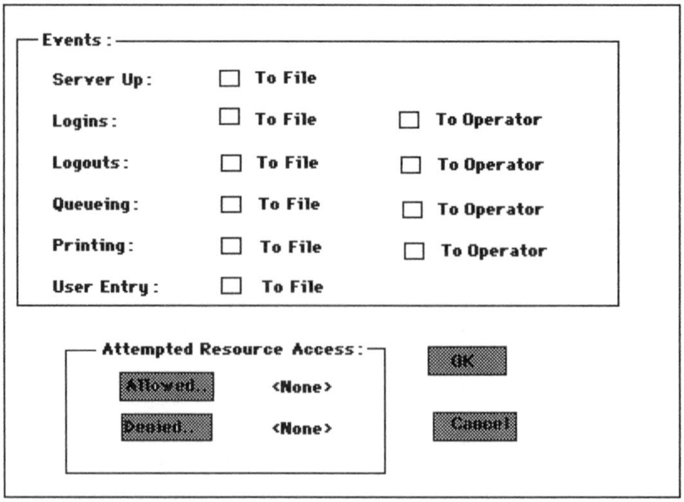

FIGURE 7.6.

LANtastic's Audited Activities Screen.

Printer Management

LANtastic takes files sent to a network printer and places them in a temporary storage location known as a print queue. These files are then printed in the order in which they were received. Users who have Super Queue (Q) privilege can control all jobs sent to a print queue. Other users can only control their own print jobs.

Table 7.2 illustrates a LANtastic print queue viewed by someone with Super Queue privileges. Print jobs can have any one of the following status conditions:

Print jobs can be held, updated, deleted, or rushed.

Table 7.2. The status of print jobs under LANtastic.

Status	Description
Despooling	The job is printing.
Waiting	The job is waiting in the print queue for its turn to print.
Held	A user can stop a print job while it is printing (despooling). Later this job can be deleted or restarted.
Updating	A user places an item in the queue.
Deleted	The print job has been deleted.
Rush	Someone with Q status has given this item higher priority.

LANtastic Mail System

Artisoft Exchange is an integrated store-and-forward system that includes sophisticated electronic mail. Users on a LANtastic LAN can exchange e-mail messages, files, and even voice messages if Artisoft Sounding Boards are present. Mail can be sent to any server selected. Artisoft Exchange is part of LANtastic 6.0's Windows interface.

It can also be used as a scheduler, fax machine, and pager. It has links to external mail systems such as MCI Mail and MHS-compatible systems.

User Communications with LANtastic

LANtastic users can "chat" with each other on the network.

LANtastic has a Chat feature that enables users to transmit text messages to each other. Figure 7.7 shows the Chat feature in action. A Chat session is initiated when a user selects the name of a computer with which to be connected and then clicks on the OK button.

The station called receives a pop-up message informing the person that a specific user wishes to conduct a Chat session. The network user at this station can complete this Chat connection by choosing "Call." Once the connection is established, the two users can type at the same time. One person's typing is displayed at the top of a screen while the other person's typing is displayed at the bottom of the same screen. A LANtastic menu makes it possible for users to save these messages and read them at a later time.

A terminate-and-stay-resident (TSR) program called LANPUP alerts users immediately when a message is received. If the Artisoft Sounding Board adapter is installed in network workstations, users can use the Voice Chat feature to converse with each other or even send a voice message that can be saved in digital format and replayed later, in just the same way a user might display electronic mail. Artisoft also offers a feature known as LAN Radio that enables users to communicate on a channel without having to use any of a company's phone resources. Up to 100 channels are available. Once a broadcast source such as a radio is attached to a network computer, LAN Radio can broadcast a variety of different types of information across a network. Users turn to a particular LAN Radio channel to receive this information.

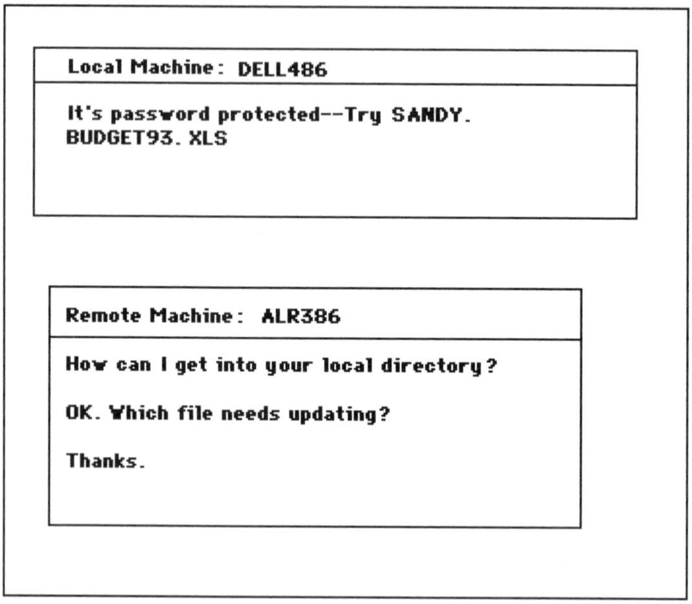

FIGURE 7.7

The Chat feature in action.

```
┌─────────────────────────────────────────────────┐
│  Local Machine:  DELL486                         │
├─────────────────────────────────────────────────┤
│  It's password protected--Try SANDY.             │
│  BUDGET93. XLS                                   │
│                                                  │
└─────────────────────────────────────────────────┘


┌─────────────────────────────────────────────────┐
│  Remote Machine:  ALR386                         │
├─────────────────────────────────────────────────┤
│  How can I get into your local directory?        │
│                                                  │
│  OK. Which file needs updating?                  │
│                                                  │
│  Thanks.                                         │
└─────────────────────────────────────────────────┘
```

LANtastic's Future

Artisoft has developed a new product called LANtastic PowerSuite. This product is an integrated, single-installation package that combines the LANtastic network operating system with leading products from other vendors. These include Lotus cc:Mail, Lotus Organizer, Cheyenne BitWare, and Cheyenne BitShare.

Offered in a variety of hardware and software combinations, the PowerSuite gives users everything they need to set up a network, start sharing files, printers, modems and other peripherals, schedule meetings and automatically notify attendees, and quickly send and receive faxes and e-mail messages.

LANtastic as an Enterprise Network?

Artisoft would like LANtastic to play a larger role in enterprise-wide networks. It is planning to add support for global directories, fault tolerance, and faster throughput for print and file services. Global directories up to now have only been found on very sophisticated client/server network operating systems such as Banyan's VINES and NetWare's 4.*x* versions. These directories keep track of network resources and enable a network user to access hardware and software resources across a network without having to know precisely where these resources are located.

What Have You Learned?

1. Network managers under LANtastic can limit users' network access to certain days and hours.

2. Access control lists enable network managers to grant similar rights to a group of users.

3. The Network Eye is a program used to view servers and displays of all other network workstations.

4. It is possible to use a local printer as well as network printers with LANtastic for NetWare.

5. LANtastic 6.0 can support up to 500 users.

6. All user accounts can be set up on a single server, which can share this account information with all other servers.

Macintosh Peer-to-Peer LANs

In this section, you examine Apple's Macintosh peer-to-peer local area network. You take a look at Apple's LocalTalk hardware and AppleShare software as well as its family of file servers.

Building a Macintosh Network

AppleTalk, Apple's family of network protocols, includes the network protocols necessary to transmit data over three different types of network topologies. Table 7.3 lists the topologies AppleTalk permits.

Table 7.3. Network topologies permitted under AppleTalk.

Type	Name	Transmission Speed
Proprietary	LocalTalk	230.4 kbps
Ethernet	EtherTalk	10 mbps
Token Ring	TokenTalk	4/16 mbps

● LocalTalk transmits data at 230.4Kbs over shielded twisted-pair wiring.

LocalTalk

LocalTalk is Apple's built-in network interface found in its Macintosh computers and LaserWriters. It handles the physical requirements of network transmission as well as media access. It can transmit data at 230.4 kbs, using a CSMA/CA method of media access control. The LocalTalk cabling system consists of shielded twisted-pair wiring configured, according to Apple, into a multidrop bus. A drop cable (a cable coming off the bus) connects a Macintosh to a connection box, which in turn is connected to the network.

● Macintosh computers can be part of an Ethernet network and transmit data at 10Mbps when EtherTalk cards are installed.

EtherTalk

EtherTalk is Apple's implementation of AppleTalk protocol to run on a LAN with an Ethernet network topology. EtherTalk adapter cards can be purchased and placed in Macintosh computers that then can be linked into an Ethernet LAN via coaxial cabling or twisted-pair wire. While EtherTalk cards are relatively expensive, they do provide 10 mbps network transmission speed.

● TokenTalk cards permit Macintosh computers to be part of a Token Ring network.

TokenTalk

TokenTalk is Apple's implementation of AppleTalk protocol for a Token Ring LAN. A TokenTalk card is placed in the Macintosh computers to be networked. These computers are linked via coaxial cabling or twisted-pair cabling to wiring concentrators which, in turn, are cabled together to form a non-contention LAN capable of either 4 mbps or 16 mbps transmission speeds depending on the type of TokenTalk adapter card installed.

LocalTalk is Apple's network hardware, and AppleTalk is Apple's family of network software protocols. These control everything from routing to file access. Before examining specific network products, you will spend some time looking at these important protocols.

AppleTalk Protocols and the OSI Model

Apple has long desired to become a major provider of Fortune 500 companies' local area networks based on its Macintosh, but only recently has it developed a strategy that seems to be working. By developing a set of protocols that are consistent with the OSI model (discussed in Chapter 2), Apple has provided major corporations with some assurance that its Macintosh-based networks will be able to communicate with any IBM PC-based LANs (because IBM has also moved toward OSI-model compatibility). If both computer giants provide OSI-compliant networks, then it is reasonable to assume these networks will be compatible, because they will use the same international standards.

Apple designed its AppleTalk network to be consistent with the OSI model. Apple's network architecture follows the layered approach developed by the OSI to facilitate communications among heterogeneous networks. It is worth taking some time to examine this architecture, because it is so critical to Apple's desire to make Macintosh-based LANs an integral part of corporate networks around the world.

The Physical Layer

Figure 7.8 illustrates the structure of the protocols found in an AppleTalk network within the context of the OSI model. At the Physical layer level, Apple provides an interface for its own LocalTalk hardware. The LocalTalk circuitry is included with every Macintosh, so that only a LocalTalk cable is needed to connect Macintosh computers. As mentioned earlier, the problem with LocalTalk for larger networks is its limited transmission speed (approximately 230 kbs). Protocol support for both EtherTalk and TokenTalk topologies are also supported.

> ●
> Apple's AppleTalk network architecture offers a set of layered protocols consistent with the OSI model.

> ●
> The Physical Layer is concerned with an interface to LocalTalk.

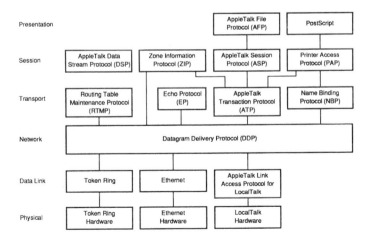

FIGURE 7.8.

The AppleTalk suite of protocols.

The Data Link Layer

The Data Link layer
is concerned with
formatting a packet
into frames.

At the Data Link layer, an AppleTalk network provides a link access protocol for Apple's own AppleTalk, as well as one for Ethernet and IBM's Token Ring hardware.

These link access protocols provide the Data Link layer with directions for formatting a packet into frames; the frames are given specifically defined fields, as well as a header and a trailer (which include important control information). These protocols also provide specific directions for handling data collisions. As indicated earlier, Apple provides a traditional CSMA/CA approach for both detecting and avoiding data collisions.

The Network Layer

The Network layer is
concerned with the
physical details
associated with
routing a packet
over the network.

The Network layer takes responsibility for the physical details of ensuring that a packet is routed correctly from one network to another. Apple includes a Datagram Delivery Protocol (DDP) that provides a means of addressing specific logical ports or sockets on different networks. This protocol is responsible for establishing the route a datagram takes from its source workstation address to its destination workstation address.

This Datagram Delivery Protocol is absolutely critical for Apple's interconnectivity with other networks, because it can access key information from routing tables to establish a network path for the datagram. It can also use a Name Binding Protocol (found in the Transport layer above it) to translate the network server's name into an acceptable internet address.

The Transport Layer

The Transport layer
is concerned with
the type of delivery
specified for a
packet.

An AppleTalk network's Transport layer consists of four distinct protocols, all designed to facilitate the arrangements necessary to route a datagram from one network to another. While the Network layer handles the nitty-gritty details of the routing, the Transport layer is responsible for deciding exactly what transport services are required (including acknowledgment of delivery, error checking, and so on).

The Routing Table Maintenance (RTM) protocol provides the key information necessary for bridges to connect similar networks, and for routers to connect different networks. This protocol provides detailed information on which bridges must be addressed (and how many "hops" it will take) to transmit a datagram from network 1 to network 4. The RTM protocol can provide not only the preferred route for transport, but also alternative routes if a particular bridge is disabled.

We have already mentioned a second Transport layer protocol—Name Binding Protocol (NBP)—in conjunction with the activities of the Network layer. The NBP is responsible for matching workstation/server names with Internet addresses. You might think of NBP as a service similar to one provided by many post offices. While post offices would like to receive full address information, often a letter addressed simply to "The Gas Company" will be routed (with the proper address added) to the city's lone gas company. The actual addressing is transparent to the network user.

AppleTalk Transaction Protocol (ATP) and Echo Protocol (EP)

The AppleTalk Transaction Protocol (ATP) provides a guaranteed class of service for transport of datagrams. It makes it possible to have an acknowledgment that a datagram was delivered error-free. This protocol is a critical component of OSI-compatible Transport layers, because a specific class of service may be required by certain network application programs.

The Echo Protocol (EP) is the final standard found in an AppleTalk network's Transport layer. It provides an *echo* function by enabling the destination workstation to echo the contents of a datagram to the source network workstation. This echoing technique enables the network to know that a particular workstation is responding and active; it also enables the network to measure the round-trip delays encountered.

The Session Layer

The Session layer on OSI-compatible networks is concerned with the establishment of a communications session. In an AppleTalk network, there are four protocols found in this layer: the Data Stream Protocol (DSP), the Zone Information Protocol (ZIP), the Session Protocol (SP), and the Printer Access Protocol (PAP).

> ●
> The Session Layer is concerned with the establishment of a communications session.

Data Stream Protocol (DSP)

The Data Stream Protocol (DSP) is concerned with the major task of the Session Layer: establishing a communications session between nodes. The DSP can establish full duplex communications, detect and eliminate duplicate datagrams, and request retransmission to ensure error-free service.

Zone Information Protocol (ZIP)

The Zone Information Protocol (ZIP) is involved in mapping networks into a series of zone names. These zone names become instrumental in helping the NBP determine which networks are found in which specific zones. This information is also critical for establishing a delivery path for both routers and bridges.

Session Protocol (SP)

The Session Protocol (SP) found at the Session layer in an AppleTalk network is concerned with the correct sequencing of datagrams when they arrive out of order. The Session Protocol is also concerned with packaging data into correctly sized datagrams, and with establishing break points during conversation sessions to ensure efficient communication.

Printer Access Protocol (PAP)

The Printer Access Protocol (PAP) found in an AppleTalk network is concerned primarily with stream-like service for devices such as printers (or streaming tape systems) when a network wishes to communicate with such a device.

The Presentation Layer

The Presentation layer is concerned with how data is actually represented.

The Presentation layer in an OSI-compatible network is concerned with how data is presented, and with the type of syntax that is used. In an AppleTalk network, two major protocols are located in the Presentation layer: the AppleTalk Filing Protocol (AFP) and the Postscript Protocol (PP). They coexist and provide different functions.

AppleTalk Filing Protocol (AFP)

The AppleTalk Filing Protocol (AFP) provides a critical interface for file server software, in particular, Apple's AppleShare and Novell's NetWare. Because other computers with Macintosh-like interfaces can now function as file servers on a Macintosh AppleTalk network, the AFP also provides the interface for them. The AFP is concerned primarily with file structure. It provides the foundation for a network's hierarchical structure of volumes, directories, and files—as well as appropriate login techniques. It also enables AppleTalk workstations to access a local (or even a remote) file server. A special Translator program within AFP translates native AppleTalk file system calls into whatever equivalent is required by the file server being accessed.

PostScript Protocol (PP)

The Presentation layer's PostScript Protocol (PP) provides the appropriate interface to ensure effective communications between network workstations and PostScript devices (such as Apple's own LaserWriter).

The first versions of AppleTalk software limited users to 32 workstations per zone (a workgroup unit assigned arbitrarily by a network administrator). There was also a 254-node limit per network. Under Phase 2 AppleTalk, however, it is possible to have up to 256 zones per network, with support for up to 16 million AppleTalk devices, and routing support for up to 1,024 interconnected AppleTalk networks. While these numbers are theoretical, this routing support for a large number of workstations does make interconnectivity easier for companies that have several small networks.

System 7.5 and Peer-to-Peer Networking

Apple not only offers the built-in hardware required for Macintosh networking via LocalTalk, but it also offers built-in peer-to-peer networking with its operating system known as System 7.5. System 7.5 is the latest version of the operating system designed for the Macintosh. It offers users the opportunity to designate a Macintosh as a client, a server, or both client and server simultaneously.

The peer-to-peer networking built into the Apple Macintosh computer makes it possible for one machine to share information with another machine. To perform this task, a user selects a server using the Chooser desk accessory as illustrated in Figure 7.9.

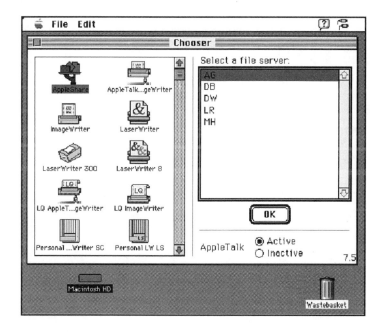

FIGURE 7.9.

Selecting a server with System 7.5.

Once a server has been selected, the user logs on either as a registered user or as a guest. Figure 7.10 shows a user logging on to a network as a registered user.

A user can share files. Once file sharing has been activated, the user indicates the specific folders and disks that are to be shared. Figure 7.11 shows how a user has made a folder and the files inside it available to a group. The following access privileges can be extended:

- See Folders. A user can see all folders in a current volume. Without this option checked, a user only sees documents contained in the root directory. Any folders in the current volume as well as documents contained in these folders are not visible.

- See Files. If this option is checked, a user can see all files including applications, documents, and system utilities in the current volume. Often this option is not checked by the registered owner so that people sending messages to that person cannot see the messages sent by others.

- Make Changes. If this option is not checked, a user can only copy files from the volume but not change the original. If this option is checked, users can save files to the current volume, create new folders, and so on.

FIGURE 7.10.

Logging on to a network.

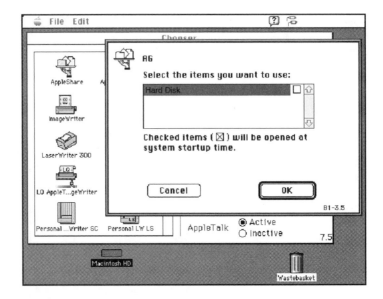

FIGURE 7.11.

Access to a Folder.

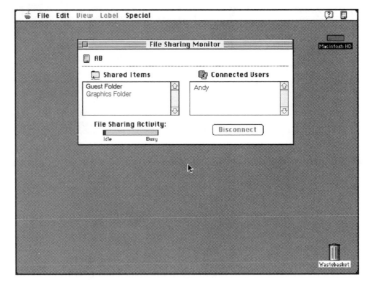

Security Issues with Apple's Peer-to-Peer Networks

One security issue associated with System 7.5's peer-to-peer networking capability is that some companies leave GUEST accounts enabled for new users. Often they discover at a later date that unauthorized people have been using these accounts. The ease that peer-to-peer networking offers on a Macintosh LAN must be balanced against the security risks.

Inter-Application Communication (IAC)

Apple's System 7.5 operating system contains a number of features that enhance peer-to-peer networking. One such feature is known as *inter-application communication* (IAC). With IAC a user can share data stored in RAM. Perhaps the best example of why IAC is so useful in a peer-to-peer environment is to consider the situation in which Tricia and Bill are working on a project and sharing the data found in Tricia's Excel spreadsheet. When Bill wants to look at data, he wants to be able to see any changes Tricia is currently making in her file and not the file she saved one hour earlier. IAC enables Bill to view changes that still reside in RAM.

By default, program linking is turned off. If Tricia wants to share her Excel data with Bill, she must first open her Sharing Setup control panel and click on the Start button in the Program Linking area at the bottom of the Sharing Setup window as seen in Figure 7.12.

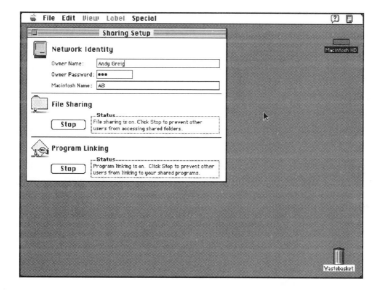

FIGURE 7.12.

The Sharing Setup control panel.

Because a user can selectively turn on or off access to particular programs, it is possible to permit colleagues to view changes in a Word document, for example, while restricting them from seeing changes made in a confidential Excel spreadsheet file.

Apple's Open Collaborative Environment (OCE)

Apple unveiled its *Open Collaboration Environment (OCE)* at the MacWorld Exposition in January 1992. OCE is a collection of application programming interfaces (APIs) that enable software developers to create programs that incorporate workgroup features in the Macintosh's System 7.5 software.

OCE is a collection of application programming interfaces that can be used to create workgroup programs.

●
AppleShare is
Apple's client/server
network operating
system. It provides
security at the folder
level.

AppleShare

While Macintosh computers on a LAN can communicate via the built-in peer-to-peer networking, larger LANs usually require a network operating system that is built around a centralized file server. Apple's AppleShare is an example of this approach. AppleShare is Apple's file server software for an AppleTalk network. Hard disks attached to the file server are known as *volumes*. Within each volume, files are stored in *folders* (which correspond to "directories" under MS-DOS). Interestingly enough, AppleShare provides security and access at the folder level, and not the file level. AppleShare's administrative software, Admin, is used for such supervisory chores as setting up network users and workgroups, and providing reports for network users. These reports can provide valuable information, such as the size and accessibility of individual folders on a volume.

Security includes logins, access to a folder as discussed previously, and even the ability to make files in a folder invisible to anyone but the person placing the files there.

AppleShare makes full use of the Macintosh graphic interface. PC users can connect to an AppleTalk network by installing a LocalTalk PC card. They then can access AppleShare files and printers. AppleShare PC software includes the MS-DOS Redirector, which converts all DOS file system requests to Server Message Blocks (SMBs). A special program then converts SMBs to AppleTalk Filing Protocol calls that can be understood on an AppleTalk network. The PC user still sees a conventional MS-DOS screen, because Apple's software follows all MS-DOS conventions.

AppleShare 4.1

AppleShare 4.1 is the latest release of AppleShare for the Macintosh Operating System. It is also the fastest AppleShare ever. While AppleShare 4.1 is not PowerPC native, it is tuned to run on PowerPC-based systems and will not install or run on 68K-based Macintosh computers.

AppleShare 4.1 runs, on average, 75% faster than AppleShare 4.0.2 on a similarly configured Power Macintosh or Workgroup Server.

What Have You Learned about Apple Macintosh?

1. LocalTalk describes the physical network hardware Apple offers for its network.
2. AppleTalk describes the family of networking suites offered by Apple.
3. AppleShare is Apple's centralized file-server software.
4. AppleShare's folders correspond to directories under DOS.
5. Apple's System 7.5 is a true multitasking operating system that enhances Apple network operation.

Quiz for Windows for Workgroups (WFW)

1. To run, WFW requires a PC with a minimum of an
   a. Intel 8086 microprocessor.
   b. Intel 8088 microprocessor.
   c. Intel 80286 microprocessor.
   d. Intel 80386 SX microprocessor.

2. For a transport protocol, WFW uses
   a. TCP/IP
   b. NetBEUI
   c. SPX
   d. CCP

3. PCs connected via WFW can communicate in real time using
   a. Talk
   b. Lisp
   c. a telephone
   d. Chat

4. WFW users can see a display of the various connections made to their local shared resources using
   a. WinMeter
   b. NetWatcher
   c. the Finder
   d. the Management Console

5. WFW users can see a graphical display of how resources are being distributed between local applications and shared resources using
   a. NetCheck
   b. WinMeter
   c. NetView
   d. NetConsole

6. Users under WFW can grant the following types of access to their directories:
   a. read, write, and secure.
   b. read, write, and delete.
   c. alter, delete, and save.
   d. read, all, and none.

7. With WFW, actively linked data can be shared through
   a. integrated link control.
   b. Microsoft linked data.
   c. dynamic data exchange.
   d. file link control.

8. Information can be shared with other network users via a
   a. share button.
   b. clipbook.
   c. infolink.
   d. Microsoft dynamic link.

9. The post office included with Mail under WFW is known as
   a. WWPO
   b. WGPO
   c. P.O.
   d. PBOX

Quiz for Windows 95

1. Windows 95 is a _____ Operating System.
    a. 16-Bit
    b. 8-Bit
    c. 32-bit
    d. 4-Bit

2. The Windows 95 Mail system is called
    a. Internet
    b. Mmail
    c. Mail-Moi
    d. Exchange

3. Which of these items are all Windows 95 Network Tools?
    a. System Policy Editor, NetWatcher, and System Monitor
    b. Doom, Doom2, and Heretic
    c. Wallpaper, Chat, and Exchange
    d. File Manager, Media Player, and Minesweeper

Quiz for LANtastic

1. Under Artisoft's LANtastic, users cannot be granted access to
    a. read files.
    b. make directories.
    c. modify files.
    d. execute directories.

2. Users within a group needing similar network access can be granted this access using
    a. access control lists.
    b. special group lists.
    c. access directories.
    d. birds of a feature directory.

3. The Network Eye enables the network manager to
    a. view who is outside his office.
    b. view network workstation screens.
    c. view network alarm conditions.
    d. view a cabling diagram of the network.

4. LANtastic 6.0 can support up to
    a. 100 users
    b. 200 users
    c. 500 users
    d. 1000 users

5. Delayed despooling is
    a. a cardiac condition curable through rest.
    b. an error condition during printing.
    c. caused by an over-filled print queue.
    d. specifying a later date and time for printing.

6. Multiple channel communication across a network takes place with

    a. LANTalk.

    b. LAN Radio.

    c. LAN Communications.

    d. TALK.

7. Users can be granted access to drives so they can read files, look at directories, but not make changes with the rights of

    a. RWC

    b. RML

    c. DRC

    d. RLE

8. Time limits can be imposed on a user in

    a. 5 minute intervals

    b. 10 minute intervals

    c. 30 minute intervals

    d. 60 minute intervals

9. A print job that is held later can be

    a. deleted

    b. restarted

    c. deleted or restarted

    d. rushed

Quiz for Apple Macintosh

1. Apple's network hardware is known as

    a. CheapTalk

    b. TinkerTalk

    c. AppleTalk

    d. LocalTalk

2. Apple's major network protocol is called

    a. SpeakEasy

    b. AppleTalk

    c. Apple Universal Protocol

    d. Macintosh OSI Protocol

3. AppleTalk networks transmit at speeds of

    a. 1 mbps

    b. 4 mbps

    c. 230.4 kbs

    d. 188 feet/second

4. AppleTalk provides link access protocol for all but one of the following:

    a. LocalTalk

    b. Ethernet

    c. Token Ring

    d. Xnet

5. AppleTalk networks are mapped into a series of

    a. zones

    b. area codes

    c. regional centers

    d. AppleAreas

6. Apple's LaserWriter requires the _____ protocol.

    a. Applesoft

    b. PostScript

    c. RS-232-C

    d. V.35

7. Security under AppleShare is at the
   _____ level.

   a. bit

   b. file

   c. folder

   d. document

8. Under Phase 2 of AppleTalk, it is
   possible to have up to _____
   zones per network.

   a. 32

   b. 64

   c. 128

   d. 256

9. Apple's operating system for the
   Macintosh that comes with built-
   in networking is

   a. System 5

   b. System 6

   c. System 7.5

   d. System 1

10. With Apple's built-in peer-to-peer
    network operating system, a
    workstation can act as

    a. server

    b. client

    c. receiver

    d. both client and server

11. Some people can gain unautho-
    rized access to a peer-to-peer
    AppleTalk LAN by logging in as

    a. Supervisor

    b. Guest

    c. Director

    d. King

12. Workgroup networking features
    will be created using

    a. ABC

    b. ODC

    c. ODE

    d. OCE

13. AppleShare 4.1 presently is
    designed to run on a

    a. 68020 microprocessor.

    b. 68030 microprocessor.

    c. PowerPC microprocessor.

    d. 68060 microprocessor.

14. Devices under Ethernet can be
    connected to devices under
    LocalTalk via

    a. bridges

    b. routers

    c. gateways

    d. repeaters

Client/Server LANs

Client/Server Computing

About This Chapter

Client/server computing as a term and buzzword has come to fruition recently. There are a variety of descriptions of what "client/server" actually means and what effect it has on a networked application or system.

In this chapter, you will develop a basic understanding of what client/server computing means and the effect it can have on your LAN. This chapter also serves as an introduction to the main network operating systems serving as client/server systems that are covered in the remainder of this book.

Client/Server Models

A definition of *client/server* aids you in understanding what this particular technology does.

In its simplest form, client/server identifies a system whereby a client issues a request to a second machine called the *server* asking that a piece of work be done.

The client is typically a personal computer attached to a LAN, and the server is usually a host machine such as a PC file server, UNIX file server, or midrange/mainframe.

● There are five basic client/server models.

The job requests can include a variety of tasks, including, for example:

- ● Return all records from the customer file database where name of Customer = Holly
- ● Store this file in a specific file server data directory
- ● Attach to CompuServe and retrieve these items
- ● Upload this data packet to the corporate mainframe

To enhance this definition you should also consider the additional requirements that a business normally has.

Terminal Emulation

● *Screen scraping allows a company to hide its mainframe and midrange screens and present them under a PC interface such as Windows or OS/2.*

As Figure 8.1 shows, the easiest model is to provide terminal emulation on the client alongside other applications. This approach is very easy to do using products such as WallData's Rumba or Attachmate but provides no real business benefit other than to begin a migration to client/server. Sometimes a company may use a more advanced form of terminal emulation whereby they hide the emulation screen and copy some of its contents, normally key fields, onto a Visual Basic or Borland Delphi screen. This copying is often referred to as *screen scraping*. The major benefit of screen scraping is that it allows a system to migrate from an old mainframe-based system to a new client/server system in small, incremental steps, the first step being to screen scrap.

FIGURE 8.1.

Terminal emulation and screen scraping.

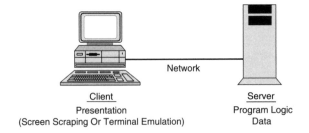

Network

Client
Presentation
(Screen Scraping Or Terminal Emulation)

Server
Program Logic
Data

Some Logic on the PC

It may be necessary to move some of the applications' program logic on the PC from the host computer. The second model, as shown in Figure 8.2, allows for some business/program logic to reside on the PC as well as the presentation. This is particularly useful when moving from a dumb terminal environment to a PC-LAN environment. The logic can be of any type, however, validation of fields, such as ensuring that states and zip codes are valid, are ideal types of logic.

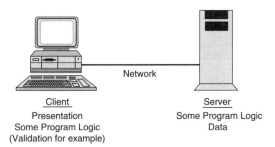

FIGURE 8.2.
*Business or program
logic on the PC.*

All Program Logic on the PC

A company can place all its program logic on a PC and have the databases stored on a server. This is the most frequent model in a client/server network. The size in terms of the volume of data often requires a file server or larger processor that has far more rigorous backup capabilities than a single PC. This client/server model is shown in Figure 8.3. The client/server networks discussed in this book readily support this model.

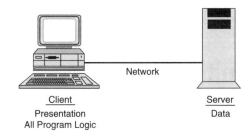

FIGURE 8.3.
*The entire application
resides on the PC.*

Some Data on the PC

The natural progression for a client/server system is to move some data to the local PC's hard disk. This is usually in the form of static data, data that doesn't change that often. An example of this may be a database of airline codes that only changes annually. Why should the PC have to access this data from the server when it is faster to get it from the local hard drive? It does not need to be shared, so it can quite happily sit on the local PC. Figure 8.4 shows this.

All Data on the Local PC

The final model is where all the data is stored and maintained on the local PC. The server is only used for network tasks such as file and printer sharing, communications, and possibly backup and recovery. Figure 8.5 shows this system. This system is not usually recommended as there are very few client/server systems that don't require multi-user access to databases. Nearly all network operating systems can support this model.

FIGURE 8.4.
Some data resides on the PC.

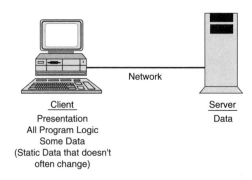

FIGURE 8.5.
All data resides on the PC.

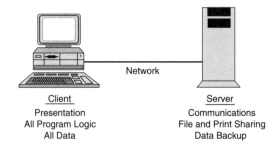

A Full Definition

As discussed, a client/server system can break down into any of the five models shown. They are not, however, mutually exclusive, and most good systems will use several of these styles to be effective and efficient. Over time, client/server systems may move models as the applications are replaced or enhanced.

In conclusion, a full definition of a client/server system is a system in which a client issues requests and receives work done by one or *more* servers.

The "more" servers statement is important because the client may need to access several distinctly separate network systems or hosts.

Why the Move to Client/Server?

The move to client/server has marked a major development in the evolution of the PC.

The move to client/server has marked a major development in the evolution of the PC. This was brought about by the recognition that companies had lavished vast sums of money on purchasing PCs in order to provide their users with desktop processing. Processing which, in theory, reduced the processing load on a central computer (usually a mainframe) and thus saved the company money. The mainstream use of PCs and LANs has typically been to provide the users with normal office working functions such as file sharing and printing. In order to capitalize on the expenditure on PCs, companies have needed to make more use of the PC than just office functions.

This need for better use of PCs in turn led to the idea of splitting up business applications so that some of the processing was done locally on the client and some remotely on the server. Taking this view further meant that companies could begin to move away from a centralized computer system (usually based around a mainframe) and could rely on a networked system of clients and servers to run their business. The ultimate goal became the removal of the corporate mainframe from the company and vast financial savings in turn. This process of moving away from a centralized computer system to a network is often referred to as *downsizing*. The vendors' promise of robust, fast, distributed client/server systems meant that many companies have begun to move along the client/server route for application development.

Client/server computing has become a major technology in the environment today. Yet it is still in its infancy. Currently, few tools are robust enough to provide the same level of performance and reliability as a centralized computer system. However, in turn, companies' business strategies are changing so rapidly that a centralized system cannot be developed or modified quickly enough to meet the business' needs. This is the main area where the implementation of a good client/server system can seriously improve a company's business systems. By having many servers providing distinct business functions, it is relatively easy to add new functions to the overall system. This is best illustrated by our example company.

Suppose The Widget Company has problems meeting the demand of a particular customer because the item the customer wants is out of stock and unavailable for several weeks. The Widget Company computer department has implemented electronically a gateway into a secondary supplier of these parts via a client/server system. When a salesperson requests this particular stock item, the application running on the salesperson's PC (the client) finds out that the item is out of stock from the main supplier and automatically seamlessly connects to the second supplier through the gateway. The salesperson doesn't need to know that Widget's supplies are coming from this second source because the customer receives his parts as usual and when the main supplier comes back online, the client program automatically detects this and once again uses this main supplier. Now consider that the Widget Company wants to offer the best price from either supplier. By slightly modifying the client program, both servers can be accessed at the same time and the lowest price retrieved and offered to the customer.

Why Client/Server is the Way to Go

Businesses are changing rapidly. The business marketplace is now more competitive than ever and will continue to be more and more so. Companies and organizations are faced with the challenge of keeping their business up to date, and in order to remain in the marketplace they must do business efficiently and cost effectively.

The computer systems that were developed in the 1980s tended to be based around a centralized computer system. LANs connected to this system, yet little or no real business processing was done on the LANs or the PCs. Because of this, any change to the business was made on the centralized system. If a new product was to be sold, or a new accounting system was to be implemented, they were usually placed on the main computer. As time went on and more and more systems were placed on the centralized computer, the costs of running this machine rose. But worse still, the time to change this system if a new business function was needed also increased. This has become so common that it is not unusual to hear of it taking in excess of three years to develop and implement systems when the product needs to be ready for the marketplace in six months. Clearly, companies cannot continue to take so long to get systems and product to market in today's fierce business environment.

Successful client/server systems break a company's major business areas into several distinct units and although integrated can be considered standalone. If development of these systems is done in the correct fashion, it is possible to deliver enhancements and new products to market faster than a centralized system. There are several reasons for this:

● The business area is smaller and can be changed more quickly.

● The changes do not usually impact as many users as a centralized system.

● Smaller systems can be prototyped quickly with a lot of user input, which leads to a faster development time.

● A network operating system can support many different types of servers, so implementing a new function on a specific server can be faster than trying to implement a new product on a mainframe or midrange.

Consider the Widget Company. As the number of parts the Widget Company supplies increases, the Board of Directors determines that they need to provide other companies' parts to their customers. They decide to build a new gateway server that connects to their other suppliers. They place this server on their LAN and develop a client-based interface to it. This system affects only the salespeople, so only those users are affected by the changes. The computer department brings in several salespeople to help them develop the client-based piece of the system so that they develop a system that works as the salespeople require. The sales orders are uploaded to the main Widget computer by the salespeople so the main computer does not need to be modified in any major way.

Building a Good First Client/Server System

Several considerations need to be made before a company begins to develop a client/server application. These considerations are often ignored, and as a result, the implementation of client/server systems can fail, often with expensive, disastrous results.

First and foremost, consider which sections of the business are going to be developed or redeveloped using the client/server models outlined above. Any development should benefit the business. It should make the company money by either increasing profitability or by reducing cost overhead such as automating data entry, doing automatic rather than manual validation, removing paperwork, and so on. You should not develop a client/server system without first determining the benefit it will provide. Otherwise, you may find that you have purchased equipment, training, and software and gotten no return on the investment. This occurs often in the client/server marketplace today.

Secondly, you should not develop any critical or core component on a client/server system until you have proved the client/server concept will work for your organization. It would be disastrous to develop a system that stored all your customer details only to find it kept crashing regularly, damaging data. Again, the return on investment will be very poor indeed.

Finally, choose an application that exists somewhere in the middle of the previous two. A client/server system that delivers business benefits without impacting the critical areas of the business will give you time to develop the staff using these systems, time to assess the impact on your LANs, and eventually the experience to provide bigger and better systems giving a bigger and better return on investment.

Client/Server LANs

The main client/server LANs with dedicated servers that can do work for clients include Windows NT Server, Novell NetWare 3.x and 4.x, Banyan VINES, and IBM LAN Server.

All of these network operating systems can act on, and process, requests from applications running on clients by processing the requests themselves.

Each of these systems can run additional software that can be run on the server doing work for each client on the network. These software products can include databases and communications. So it is quite possible for a LAN to be made up of separate servers. For example, one server may be a database server containing all the customer information. Another may be a communications server providing access to a mainframe and the Internet, and a final server may be running the network operating system, network management, and file and printing services.

> ● Windows NT Server, Novell NetWare 3.x and 4.x, Banyan VINES, and IBM LAN Server support client/server networking.

The Impact of Client/Server LANs

Due to the continual interaction between a client machine's application and the servers that it interacts with, network traffic invariably increases. You should not consider developing and implementing a client/server system without also considering (and possibly developing) enhancements to your network, or seriously learning about effects on any new network.

Typically, LANs operating in a networking mode (that is, really only sharing files and printers) can have far more users per LAN than a client/server LAN.

If the overall traffic of one client/server user has increased relative to a file- and print-sharing user, all clients have increased traffic to the server or servers. Therefore, there is more network traffic on a network with an unchanged bandwidth. If the bandwidth was under-utilized, then this is not usually a problem. If the bandwidth is close to full utilization, response-time problems occur. This can be resolved by either reducing the number of users per LAN, or increasing the bandwidth by moving to faster network topologies.

Client/Server and LAN Security

Client/server systems also have an impact on LAN security. The typical LAN user on a normal system invariably only connects to one file server. However, in a client/server system, the user may need to connect to many different servers on a frequent and infrequent basis.

This means that the user is often presented with a bewildering array of logons, passwords, and user IDs to all the different systems. If a user is required to access an AS400, Novell LAN, mainframe, and a UNIX server, they may have four different logons. There are two schools of thought on how client/server access should be handled. The first states an idealistic view that one logon and password should connect the user to all his required systems seamlessly. Each of the major network operating systems are trying to move toward this approach, including NetWare 4.1 with its NetWare Directory Services. This approach does have its problems. The main one is that there is a major security risk. Once a hacker or rogue user knows another user's password and user ID, they can access all the associated computer systems. If the passwords or IDs were unique, the intruders would only have access to one system.

The second method is to force users to have distinctly different passwords for each system. This gives the best security but does increase the amount of times a user has to log on to the different systems.

Planning for Client/Server

When you are planning for a client/server system it is important to consider a number of items.

1. The application development should include development, performance testing, and system testing across the network.

2. The network design should be completed and documented as part of the development process.

3. You should look at the current utilization of the networks and see if bandwidth and/or response-time problems may occur.

4. Reduce the number of users per LAN, or increase the bandwidth available to each client if there are bandwidth or response-time problems. If you do this, ensure that you have adequate lead time to implement these networks before the client/server system goes live. This reduces complications that may be network based when you are troubleshooting problems with the application.

A Short Note on Staff

If a client/server system is being developed by a company, it proves invaluable to have someone on the project team that understands LANs. All too often, client/server systems fail because very little consideration was given to network performance. This also helps to train network staff in the application development process, which in turn provides them with multiple skills, something that is particularly valuable in the client/server world.

As more and more applications take advantage of distributed networking, network staff will need to understand much more about the wider areas of computer systems such as programming, PC support, wide area networking, and system implementations.

What Have You Learned?

1. A client machine issues requests for work to be done to a server in a client/server system.

2. In a client/server system, a client can connect to multiple servers.

3. Client/server systems invariably increase network traffic.

Quiz for Chapter 8

1. In a client/server system, a client issues requests to "_____."

    a. Colin in Marketing

    b. an Apple Macintosh

    c. a Token Ring card

    d. a server

2. If performance degrades on a client/server system due to network performance, consider

    a. adding more cable.

    b. adding Pentium processors to the printers.

    c. reducing the number of users per network.

    d. implementing a network management system.

3. If performance degrades on a client/server system due to network performance, consider

    a. leaving the office early.

    b. implementing a faster network such as fast Ethernet.

    c. switching off the file server.

    d. asking users to work slower.

4. When building a client/server system, a development team should consider

    a. the impact on any new or current network.

    b. the format of the headers on their documentation.

    c. how often they hold a meeting.

    d. how often the development data code is backed up.

Novell's NetWare

About This Chapter

In this chapter we'll survey the LAN software that dominates today's market, Novell's NetWare. You examine its file-server software, sophisticated network security, and accounting options. In addition to viewing some of NetWare's powerful utility programs, you take a look at Novell's blueprint for the future, and its newest product, NetWare 4.1, designed for enterprise-wide networks. Depending on whose statistics you read, Novell has captured between 60 and 80 percent of the LAN Network Operating System marketplace. This chapter discusses the two main versions of Netware—3.12 and 4.1.

Novell's Philosophy

Novell's approach to serving the LAN user is unique in that it has chosen to concentrate its efforts on producing software that will run on other vendors' network hardware. NetWare runs on virtually any IBM or compatible, and supports all the major LAN vendor hardware discussed in this book—including the Apple Macintosh and ARCnet products. Novell's philosophy is to make itself a de facto industry standard by dominating the marketplace. Does a major corporation insist on purchasing IBM's Token Ring Network? Novell is happy to supply compatible NetWare to enhance the Token Ring's performance.

Topology

Novell's network operating system, NetWare, can run on a number of different topologies. Depending on the hardware you select, NetWare can run on a network configured as a star, a string of stars, a token ring, and even a bus. Running NetWare on 3Com's Ethernet bus hardware, for example, results in a bus topology. When running on ARCnet hardware, NetWare functions efficiently in a

NetWare supports a variety of network architectures, including star, bus, token ring, and a cluster of stars.

token bus environment. Northern Telecom and other PBX manufacturers offer their customers NetWare, utilizing the star topology of a PBX, while Proteon runs NetWare on hardware organized as a string of stars.

NetWare and the Concept of a File Server

NetWare is designed for true network file-server support. To understand this approach, it is helpful to study how a file server functions under Novell's software. Under the OSI model, Novell's file-server software resides in the Application layer, while the disk-operating software (DOS) resides in the Presentation layer. In effect, the file-server software forms a shell around the operating system such as DOS and is able to intercept commands from application programs before they can reach the operating systems command processor. The workstation user is not aware of this phenomenon. The user simply asks for a data file or a program, without worrying about where either is located.

To understand this interaction between the file server and the individual workstations, let's look at what happens when a workstation issues a request for a particular file. The network interface to the network file server (the *network shell*) resides in each workstation. It is responsible for intercepting network commands from an application program. The interface shell can run on DOS, Windows, OS/2, Macintosh, Windows NT, and Windows 95.

When an application program requests a specific file, the shell must first determine whether the request is for a local file (residing on the workstation's own disk drives) or a network request for information located on a file server. If the information is located on the workstation's own drives, the request is passed back to the command processor, where it is handled as a normal I/O operation. As a particular file is located and loaded into the workstation's CPU for processing, the user notices the red light on the disk drive go on.

What if the requested file is located on a file server? In this case, the request translator issues a "read" request to the file server—which locates the file and transmits it to the workstation in the form of a *reply packet*. The packet is received by a *reply translator*, which converts this information into a form the local workstation can handle. The command processor then provides the application program with this data.

The workstation is completely unaware of the internal mechanics of this operation. The network file server is so fast that local and network responses appear to be equally fast except in cases of unusually heavy network traffic.

●
Directory hashing is a method of mapping and indexing directories and their files to minimize the number of entries a file server must examine in order to locate a specific file.

Techniques for Speeding Up the File Server

NetWare uses a number of techniques to speed up the response time of its file servers. One technique is *directory hashing*, which can be likened to an efficient indexing system. The software maps all the directory files and keeps all this information in RAM. When a workstation requests a particular file, the file server need only examine a few directory entries to locate that file. Because this information is in RAM and not on disk, it is a very fast procedure.

Disk caching is a second technique Novell uses for rapid file-server response. It illustrates just how intelligent a Novell file server can be. In effect, the file server anticipates future workstation file requests and keeps an image of frequently requested portions of its drive in RAM. When a workstation makes a second request for additional material from this area of the server's hard disk drive, it is already located in RAM and does not require a second hard disk access. Because disk access is in milliseconds, while RAM access is in microseconds, a "smart" file server's use of disk caching can represent significant time savings for network users. Second and third requests for cached information can be processed one hundred times faster.

Another advantage of disk caching is that the file server can perform all disk writes as a *background* operation, which means it is capable of performing other procedures while sending this information to requesting workstations.

When a large file is accessed that is too big to cache into RAM, a *turbo-FAT index* is built on the FAT entries. Turbo-FATs are shared by multiple users accessing this file. This method improves search rates for records with the file, especially when several large files are accessed at the same time by multiple users (which is the norm for relational databases residing on the server).

Another technique used to speed up Novell's file-server response time is *elevator seeking*. Imagine a file clerk who is given a series of files to locate. The first three files are Johnson, Anderson, and Jackson. If the clerk actually pulled the files in this order, it would be inefficient, because two of the files are located in the same drawer. Elevator seeking is a technique that allows the file server to execute requests in the most effective manner relative to the current position of the disk heads. The result is a throughput increase (up to 50%) and a decrease in wear and tear on the disk drives.

Using the preceding techniques with normal multi-user file access removes the problems arising with disk fragmentation. Unlike a DOS or Windows-based system, NetWare's file system eliminates disk access speed as a main bottleneck. Unlike the and IBM LAN Server, Netware is its own operating system as well as a Network Operating System (The other two require NT and OS/2, respectively).

File Management Under NetWare

NetWare allows the supervisor to define directory access. In a moment, you take a look at how a department might establish its users. Presently, an even more fundamental issue is the nature of the files themselves.

Certain users may want to run single-user applications in a multi-user environment. The system administrator can designate a program or file as *shareable* (capable of being shared)

● Disk caching is a technique for keeping often-requested files in RAM for rapid response to workstation requests.

● Elevator seeking is a technique that enables the file server to determine the order in which to execute file requests, based on the current location of the disk heads.

or *non-shareable* (restricted to one user at a time). NetWare also contains a default file-locking function, which means these single-user programs could be accessed by different users, one at a time.

If a file is non-shareable, different users can view the file in Read Only mode, but they cannot write to it while it is being used in Read/Write mode by a specific user. Programs or files designated as shareable with record-locking capability operate in true multi-user fashion; several users can read and write to them simultaneously, as long as only one user is writing to a specific record at a time.

One feature of NetWare is that an application program can specify all the records it needs before telling the file server to lock these records. This technique ensures that two application programs which need overlapping records cannot create a deadlock in which both wait for unavailable records.

Setting Up Directories Under NetWare

NetWare uses a hierarchical file structure exactly like DOS. A diagram of this structure would resemble a mature tree, with main branches having smaller branches (which, in turn, have even smaller branches of their own). As an example, imagine that the Widget Company has just installed a NetWare network with several distributed file servers. Now it is time to set up some directories on the first file server.

Let's assume that Sales and Personnel will be using this file server. Beth and Barbara are the two sales administrators; Phil, Paul, and Peter handle personnel functions. As Figure 9.1 illustrates, Widget has named its first file server FS1. Under the SALES directory are these two subdirectories: BETH and BARBARA. Each sales administrator has created subdirectories under her own directory. Beth has created the subdirectories EASTERN.RGN, CUSTOMER.LST, and WESTERN.RGN. Notice that under WESTERN.RGN Beth has created two additional subdirectories: SALES.RPTS and PROSPECTS. Barbara has not yet created as many subdirectories, but she certainly has that option in the future.

The Personnel department has created directories for each of its administrators. Because Phil, Paul, and Peter all have distinct functions, each has created two subdirectories to handle his specialized reports.

Within the directories and subdirectories of both departments, the system administrator loads appropriate files. Under Beth's CUSTOMER.LST directory, for example, the following files are found: CURRCUST.E, CURRCUST.W, OLDCUST.E, and OLDCUST.W. To send a letter to former Widget customers living in the western region (to announce a new program designed to entice them to buy widgets again) Beth writes a form letter and performs a mail merge with the OLDCUST.W. and OLDCUST.E files.

FIGURE 9.1.

NetWare's File Structure.

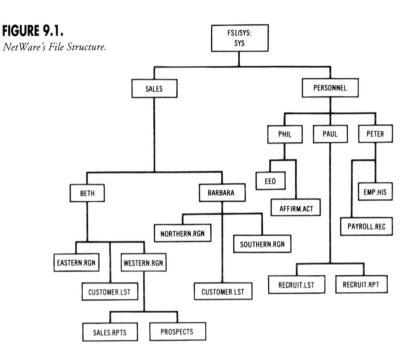

When designating subdirectories, Novell follows the convention that a slash (/) or a backslash (\) must be used to separate a directory from its subdirectory. The names of all succeeding subdirectories must also be separated in the same manner. To indicate the pathway for OLDCUST.W, for example, Beth may type

`FS1/SYS:SALES/BETH/CUSTOMER.LST/OLDCUST.W`

Because we have written a path for OLDCUST.W, the last directory named is the direc-tory we wished to specify. While this is the exact path, as you see in the next section, Beth would not have to type all of this to access the file with her application. The directory would be mapped and she would type `F:(filename)` to access it.

Mapping Network Drives: A NetWare Shortcut

NetWare requires that network directories be accessed via specific *network drives*. Net-work drives point to network directories and not to physical disk drives. Each workstation may assign 21 logical drive letters (F through Z). This assumes DOS uses its default A through E.

●

Network drives are logical, and not physical drives. By assigning directories to specific network drives, a user is able to move quickly from directory to directory, without having to remember the exact path.

Let's assume you want to assign the WESTERN.RGN directory to network drive F. You would type the following:

```
MAP F:=FS1/SYS:SALES/BETH/WESTERN.RGN
```

Typing the colon following the drive letter assigns this directory to the logical drive F. Now you can type **F:** from a DOS prompt to go directly to this directory. By assigning frequently used directories to different network drives, it becomes a simple matter to jump back and forth among network directories without having to remember paths or type in their long names correctly.

●
Search drives permit users to locate files, even though they might not know in which directory the files reside. They effectively add NetWare directories to the workstation's existing operating system path. It is even possible to locate files on other file servers using this technique.

Search Drives Save Time

One of the most common network error messages indicates that a file cannot be found. This usually means that the file doesn't exist in the directory in which you are working. Often you cannot remember exactly where it resides. To avoid this situation, use NetWare *search drives*. These enable the operating system to locate program files in directories other than your default directory. The software permits you to define up to 16 search drives (Search1:, Search2:, and so on). By placing universally used programs in publicly access directories and then mapping a search drive. The file server locates the requested programs even if they are not in the current directory from which the request is made. This approach has a major advantage: rather than having to copy the same program into several user's individual directories, you can map a single copy to a search directory, which allows everyone to access it from their current directories.

Search drives also can be mapped to directories on different file servers. The result is that a system administrator can make file access painless for novice users. All they need to do is specify a particular file or program that has been mapped to a search drive. Even if the file is located on a distant file server, it appears on the user's screen as if it resided on his or her local disk drive.

System Security

●
NetWare provides file-server security with its login procedure, trustee rights, directory rights, and file attributes.

Although vendors who market only network security systems may offer more elaborate systems, Novell's NetWare offers by far the most extensive security system available as part of a network package. NetWare provides file-server security in four different ways:

The login procedure

Trustee rights

Directory rights

File attributes

The Login Procedure

NetWare provides security at the login stage by requiring a valid *username* (user identity) and a valid password. The network administrator establishes a username standard by which all user IDs are created. One company may establish the employee badge number as the network ID, while another company may use the employee's first name and first initial the last name (for example, Fred Firestone's username, then, might be FREDF). Yet another company may set its standard to use the first initial of an employee's first name and the first seven letters of the last name (for example, Fred Firestone might be FFIRESTO).

The user also must know which file server he is using. Fred's login to file-server FS1, for example, might look like this (NetWare doesn't care if users use uppercase, lowercase, or a combination):

```
LOGIN FS1/FREDF
```

NetWare now waits for a password to be typed. The software doesn't announce the correctness or incorrectness of the login at this stage, but all three variables must be correct to clear this security level. In the event of an unacceptable login, NetWare does not indicate (for security reasons) whether the username, file server, or password is incorrectly typed. Let's observe Fred's login procedure.

```
LOGIN <ENTER>
Enter your login name:
FS1/FREDF <ENTER>
Enter your password:
```

For security reasons, Fred's password does not appear on the screen when he types it. One important point to make here is that the password is associated with the user, and not with the machine. With his username and password, a user can work on any available workstation.

NetWare requires a valid username, file-server name, and password at login.

Trustee Rights

The network administrator (Novell's term is network supervisor) is responsible for the network's security as well as its operation. The supervisor makes each user a trustee, and provides each with specific rights in certain directories. These rights usually extend through all subordinate directories, unless the supervisor specifically limits a user's access. The rights may be extended to the user either as an individual or as part of a user group. The range of possible trustee rights is listed here (these vary from version to version):

Each user has up to eight usage rights assigned by the network supervisor.

Read	Read from files
Write	Write to files
Create	Create (and simultaneously open) new files

Erase	Delete existing files
Access control	Grant access and modify rights filter in directories and subdirectories)
File Scan	Scan directories
Modify	Modify file attributes
Supervisor	(all rights, nonrevokable, in directories, subdirectories, and files below where it is granted)

Users can be given any combination of these rights in a directory. A user with Read, File Scan, and Write rights (for example) can open any file in that directory, read its contents, and write to the file. Without File Scan rights, however, the user would have to know the name of the file in order to access it; he or she would be unable to search for it with the DOS DIR command. Notice, also, that without the Erase right, a user would be powerless to delete any existing files.

Netware trustee security has many different levels and potential combinations. A user needs Erase rights, for instance, to delete an entire subdirectory. The network supervisor is usually the user that establishes the file system security. Users have the ability to grant access to other users in their own home directories (Access Control).

When a directory is created, a complete Inherited Rights Mask is added to the directory. This mask allows user rights that were granted to a directory higher in the structure to "flow" down into the new directory. The network supervisor can take away rights from the Inherited Rights Mask if she wants to "block" user rights from flowing down into subdirectories at lower levels in the structure. The network supervisor can also override the Inherited Rights Mask by granting rights to a user in a directory thus "going below" the Inherited Rights Mask. For example, the Accounting Group, of which Sue is a member, has rights to read, see (file scan), write, create, and erase in the ACCTG directory. The network supervisor wants to block the group rights from "flowing" down into the PAYROLL directory under ACCTG, so she changes the Inherited Rights Mask to block the read, write, create, erase, and file scan rights. Then she goes down to the PAYROLL directory and assigns the same five rights to the payroll administrator, Sue. The Accounting Group has rights to use the accounting applications and data files, but cannot use the payroll application or see the data files—only Sue can.

● Through security equivalencies, a supervisor can set the trustee rights of a particular user as equivalent to the rights of a particular user group or groups, or a number of different individuals.

The network supervisor assigns each user to a *user group*, and then may assign trustee rights directly to the entire group. These rights may also be assigned to user groups indirectly, through *equivalencies*. A user or user group may have up to 32 security equivalencies.

For example, a supervisor may establish that one user group may have all the rights already found within another user group; the two groups become equivalents. The supervisor may set up a group called "Everyone" and make all user groups' rights equivalent with this group. Obviously, this is more efficient than setting rights for each user. All members of the word processing pool, for example, are part of the same user group and share the same trustee rights. A NetWare supervisor, setting an assistant's rights as temporarily equivalent to his or her own, would enable the assistant to function as supervisor.

A user's *effective rights* comprise those as an individual user, plus those as part of a user group, plus all the trustee rights of any other users or user groups for which this user has a security equivalence.

File Attributes Security

NetWare security permits a user to determine whether an individual file may be modified. Let's assume that Christine, the NetWare supervisor, has been having trouble with other network users changing the contents of a particular file (CSTCONFG). Her rights include Modify privileges for this file's directory. Using the FLAG command, she restricts the file's use to Read Only. Christine is in her default directory (where the file resides), so to effect the change she types

```
FLAG CSTCONFG S RO <ENTER>
```

Now the CSTCONFG file can be shared by other users who can read—but not change— the contents. Christine could have changed all the files in her default directory to the same shareable Read Only status by typing

```
FLAG *.* S RO <ENTER>
```

There are four combinations of attributes that a user can select for a file (or group of files) with the FLAG command:

> Shareable, Read Only
>
> Shareable, Read/Write
>
> Non-Shareable, Read Only
>
> Non-Shareable, Read/Write

By typing **FLAG** and pressing Enter within a directory, you can see a list of the flags on files within that directory.

File attributes take precedence over trustee rights, because NetWare uses a logical AND function to determine rights. Let's assume that Bart has Read/Write rights to a particular directory. The CUST file in that directory has been flagged as Shareable, Read Only. NetWare examines Bart's user rights and the file's attributes, using an AND function that accepts only those terms that appear in both lists. Because the Read function appears in both lists, Bart can only read the CUST file.

●
A user re-establishing a file can set the attributes for that file using the FLAG command. File attributes prevail over individual trustee rights.

● SYSCON enables
users to view
information about
the file servers they
are logged into,
their login proce-
dure, the user
groups that include
them, and their
trustee rights and
network security
equivalencies. With
proper network
security, users can
change these
variables through
the utility.

Network Utilities

The four levels of network security are all handled by NetWare's powerful series of utility programs. Now we examine the two utility programs used in conjunction with network security: SYSCON and FILER.

The SYSCON Utility

The SYSCON utility is used for system configuration. It handles many of the security functions we have been discussing (such as establishing passwords, user groups, access to file servers, trustee rights, and equivalencies).

Because some of its functions can be performed by nonsupervisors, SYSCON is loaded into the SYS:PUBLIC directory. SYSCON is a menu-driven program. From DOS, typing SYSCON and pressing Enter gives the Available Topics menu shown in Figure 9.2.

FIGURE 9.2.

*SYSCON's Available
Topics menu.*

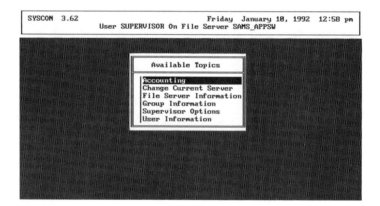

Notice that even though you might not be a network supervisor, you can still view information regarding your own status on the network. For example, you can view a list of user names (Figure 9.3). The Available Topics for users (as we saw in Figure 9.2) include Change Current Server, File Server Information, Group Information, Supervisor Options, and User Information.

Figure 9.4 displays the groups to which a particular user belongs. An editorial department, for example, might want to make all staff members part of the WRITERS group, and give them Read and File Scan to the word processing application or data directives. Any member of this group would be able to look up a project file for basic information, but only certain members of the department would have individual trustee assignments enabling them to change a file.

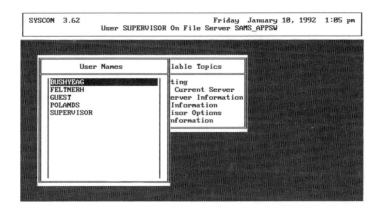

FIGURE 9.3.

Viewing users on a file server.

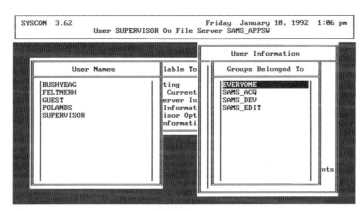

FIGURE 9.4.

Identifying a user's group.

Novell's NetWare allows users to examine their own security equivalencies and trustee assignments. In Figure 9.5, the supervisor has chosen to examine his security equivalencies—and discovered he has security equivalencies with Polands, as well as with the groups EVERYONE, SAMS_ACQ, SAMS_DEV, and SAMS_EDIT.

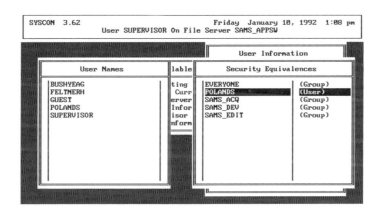

FIGURE 9.5.

Displaying security equivalencies.

As you saw earlier, this system makes it easy to add new users and to duplicate trustee rights without having to list each of several dozen files that a user should be able to retrieve. A new Personnel Department clerk, who will cover Christine's assignments during her summer vacation, can be given security equivalence to Christine—automatically giving the clerk all the group rights, as well as the individual rights Christine now enjoys. When Christine returns from vacation, the clerk can be given a security equivalence to another department clerk.

●
SYSCON can be used to specify the days and times a user can log into the network.

Enhancing Security with SYSCON's Accounting Restrictions

SYSCON contains a number of account restriction functions that enable a supervisor to control the degree of users' network access. Let's look at a couple of examples of how NetWare permits supervisors to perform these tasks. As Figure 9.6 reveals, a supervisor can designate the hours an employee can use the network. In this example, Carol has been restricted to logging into the network between 7:00 a.m. and 7:00 p.m. on weekdays.

FIGURE 9.6.

Carol may log in between 7:00 a.m. and 7:00 p.m. Monday through Friday.

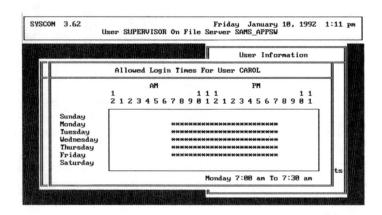

The supervisor can limit incorrect password attempts and lock an account that has exceeded the limit, as shown in Figure 9.7. Other account restrictions enable a supervisor to establish an account expiration date for a temporary employee. Supervisors can also require users to change passwords at certain intervals and use passwords of certain lengths. Finally, accounting options permit a supervisor to charge users for their disk storage and processing time. Users can even be charged higher rates during peak computing time to discourage unnecessary file transfers and report printing.

●
Login scripts are used to set up a network user's environment by automatically mapping network data and application search drives and displaying key information at login.

NetWare's Login Scripts

At any given time, a user can use the NetWare utilities menu to examine his or her *login script* and make any necessary changes. The login script is a shortcut, a way to tell NetWare how to go through a pre-assigned set of steps to customize the network's environment, and to display certain information when you log in to the network.

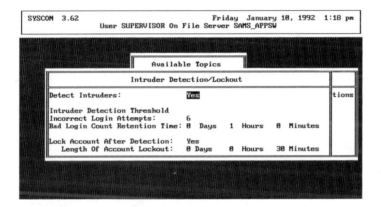

FIGURE 9.7.

Intruder Detection locks an account after a specified number of incorrect login attempts.

Although it is possible for each user to design an individual login script, one of the major advantages of this procedure is that the network supervisor can set up a login script for a new user that shields the novice from the intricacies of a network environment.

Although NetWare permits the mapping of different search network drives, this information is erased each time the user logs off the system. One of the major uses of a login script is to provide NetWare with this information automatically when the login script is executed. A login script for Peter might include the following:

```
map F:=sys:user/Peter
map G:=sys:sales/cust.lst
map S1:=sys:public
map S2:=sys:apps/wp51
map S3:=sys:apps/sprdsht
```

With this login script, Peter is able to access files in different directories, without knowing the full pathname. As a new user, Peter need not even know what a pathname is, as long as his network supervisor has set up this login script for him.

NetWare provides that a number of different variables can be placed in a login script—including the time, day of the week, month, and year. The login script can also identify the specific file server the user is addressing. Scripts use a command language that is clearly explained in Novell's documentation. The commands include an IF...THEN combination that permits you to individualize scripts for each day of the week. Christine, for example, might want to remind herself of a staff meeting that is always held Mondays at 10:00 a.m. She could have the following login script:

```
IF DAY OF WEEK="Monday" THEN
WRITE "Another week. Don't forget the staff meeting at 10 a.m."
```

When Christine logs in on Monday morning, her computer screen displays the following:

```
Another week. Don't forget the staff meeting at 10 a.m.
```

You can individualize each day's script, not only with the date and time and standing appointments, but also with the actual set of procedures normally performed that day. A payroll clerk may only go through the actual check-printing routine on the 1st and 15th of the month. The script could specify that if the date were the 1st or the 15th, the network should log the clerk into a different file server where the check-printing program resides, load the program, and make sure the appropriate printer is on-line. The clerk would need only to use the correct login name and password to begin the check-writing procedure.

●

The INCLUDE command enables you to link a number of text files written in login script format and place them in a login script.

Another useful login script command is INCLUDE. This command enables you to establish a series of text files that can serve as subscripts for your login. It is possible to have as many as 10 levels of INCLUDE commands, accessing different subscripts.

There are a number of very practical uses for these subscripts. Let's say several people are working on a project with a tight deadline. Although some of these individuals are scattered throughout a large four-story building and others are at remote locations, it is essential that they all know the progress of the project on a daily basis. A project manager could establish a file for announcements under the PROJECT directory. Each night before leaving work (or even late at night from home, with the proper remote equipment), the project manager could use the word processing program to write a text file that addressed all members of the team. Each member's login script then would have an INCLUDE command to access this file. As a team member, Christine might include the following in her login script:

```
IF DAY OF WEEK="Monday" THEN BEGIN
WRITE "Another week. Don't forget the staff meeting at 10 a.m."
INCLUDE SYS:PROJECT/ANNCMENT
END
```

●

NetWare's interpretative shell permits workstations with different operating systems to share information.

NetWare—particularly its login script procedure—addresses a critical problem for many major companies: the proliferation of different types of computers and operating systems. On a NetWare file server, different operating systems can share files because of the interpretive shell. MS-DOS 6.22 files can co-exist with PC DOS 7.0 and OS/2 files.

A company can establish an identifier command within users' login scripts to ensure that a user with PC DOS 7.0 software, for example, loads the proper 7.0 versions of his programs, and not 3.3 programs. Novell suggests the following login script to map search directories for differing machines and operating systems:

```
MAP S2:=SYS:PUBLIC\%MACHINE\%OS\%OS VERSION
```

The FILER Utility

The FILER menu utility program controls volume, directory, file, and subdirectory information. Earlier we discussed a situation in which Christine wanted to ensure that other users did not change a file within a directory she had established. To accomplish this, Christine could change the directory's inherited rights mask or change the file's attributes. As the network supervisor, Christine has *absolute control* of the network.

Let's assume that Christine wished to make the change at the directory level. Using the FILER utility, she could examine the inherited rights mask for that current directory. The inherited rights mask consists of the following:

Supervisor

Read

Write

Create

Erase

Modify

File Scan

Access Control

Christine places the selection bar (displayed on the screen) on the right she wishes to delete, and then presses the Delete key. NetWare asks if she wishes to revoke this particular right (Yes or No). When she presses her Select key, the right is revoked and removed from the inherited rights mask.

The FILER utility also permits adding, viewing, or deleting trustee rights for a particular directory, as well as viewing and deleting file attributes. A security feature available under FILER is the ability to specify a *directory exclusion pattern*.

A network supervisor, for example, could establish a network-wide directory exclusion pattern for all directories whose names begin with PROJ. This would mean that the directories for the Jove, Jupiter, and Saturn projects (PROJJOV, PROJJUP, and PROJSAT) would not be displayed with a directory listing.

It is also possible to specify a file exclusion pattern within directories. Let's say that within the directories of each of the secret projects is a budget file (PROJBUD) only the project manager needs to see or use. A file exclusion pattern for the .BUD pattern ensures that even those users with sufficient security to enter the project directories won't be able to see the budget files listed when they request a listing of all the files in that particular directory.

●
FILER permits users to display and change for security reasons key information about directories and files that they control.

Printing Utilities

NetWare offers the PRINTDEF utility to define print devices, modes of printing, and types of forms. The CAPTURE/ENDCAP utility is designed to redirect a workstation's LPT ports, while the PRINTCON utility is used to set up print job configurations.

PRINTDEF

PRINTDEF is a printer definition utility program that enables the network supervisor to define the types of network print devices (printers, plotters, and so on), the modes of network printing (draft quality or final printout), and even types of forms (8.5" X 11", wide, etc.). By typing **PRINTDEF** and pressing Enter, you see the PrintDef Options screen. Selecting Print Devices at this point reveals a list of print devices that have been defined.

A network supervisor can define the control codes associated with the network's various printers once, and then use other NetWare printing utilities to create customized printing jobs. Using PRINTDEF, a supervisor can define several print modes required for a specific print job. A desktop publishing program's print definition might include emphasized printing and proportional spacing (for example), while budget analysts might want a print job defined for printing very wide spreadsheets in compressed mode.

CAPTURE/ENDCAP

The CAPTURE/ENDCAP utility is designed to allow you to redirect a workstation's LPT ports to network printer devices, queues, and files. CAPTURE is capable of redirecting up to three LPT ports. These ports are logical so that a PC need not have three physical ports. In fact, CAPTURE does not work with serial ports COM1 and COM2.

CAPTURE is particularly valuable for a network supervisor who wants to redirect printing away from workstation hardware and out to the network. You can redirect the print data to the network's print queue 2 as follows:

```
CAPTURE LOCAL=1 QUEUE=PRINTQ_2
```

Note that these CAPTURE commands are temporary and are effective only until another CAPTURE command is executed, an ENDCAP command is used, or you log out of the file server.

PRINTCON

The PRINTCON utility can be used to set up print job configurations using the options available under the CAPTURE and PCONSOLE utilities. As a supervisor you may define standard configurations for specific users and their specific documents (because this data is stored in the mail directory on the server normally logged on to by each user). Figure 9.8 illustrates a typical print job for a routine text file using a laser printer.

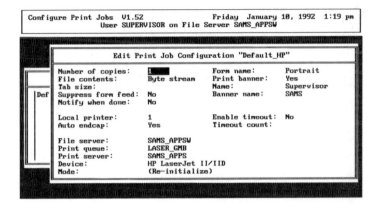

FIGURE 9.8.

A typical print job configuration.

Once these configurations are defined, a user simply selects one, without having to specify print options. You can specify Carol's LOTUS standard printer configuration (as well as her WORDPERF configuration) once, and she will never have to grapple with answering printer definition questions.

NPRINT

Once a job configuration has been set up under PRINTCON, it can be used with the NPRINT command. Because PRINTCON contains a detailed description of your form, printer, number of copies, and so on, all you need to specify with the NPRINT command is which file you want printed.

NPRINT file job =BUDMONTH <ENTER>

● NPRINT is a fast way to print a document on a network using print configurations already established.

The specific parameters you defined in the BUDMONTH configuration are used for printing the document. As another example, assume you wanted to print three copies of the WESTERN file without a banner. You would issue the following command:

NPRINT SYS:MARKETNG\SALES\REGIONS\WESTERN C=3 NB <ENTER>

PCONSOLE

The PCONSOLE utility controls network printing. This program enables you to access and print files on other file servers, examine jobs waiting for printing in a print queue, change the way a job is printed, physically change the contents of a print queue, and view information about both print servers and print queues. In Figure 9.9, the supervisor is both a user and a designated print queue operator (designated by her network supervisor) who may view a particular print job as it waits in a print queue.

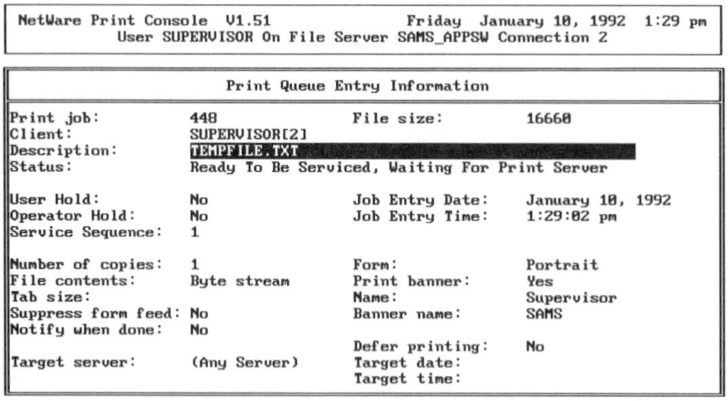

FIGURE 9.9.

NetWare displays print queue information.

```
┌──────────────────────────────────────────────────────────────────────────┐
│ NetWare Print Console  V1.51           Friday  January 10, 1992  1:29 pm   │
│           User SUPERVISOR On File Server SAMS_APPSW Connection 2            │
└──────────────────────────────────────────────────────────────────────────┘

┌──────────────────────────────────────────────────────────────────────────┐
│                       Print Queue Entry Information                        │
│ Print job:          448              File size:        16660               │
│ Client:             SUPERVISOR[2]                                          │
│ Description:        TEMPFILE.TXT                                           │
│ Status:             Ready To Be Serviced, Waiting For Print Server         │
│                                                                            │
│ User Hold:          No                Job Entry Date:   January 10, 1992   │
│ Operator Hold:      No                Job Entry Time:   1:29:02 pm         │
│ Service Sequence:   1                                                      │
│                                                                            │
│ Number of copies:   1                 Form:            Portrait            │
│ File contents:      Byte stream       Print banner:    Yes                 │
│ Tab size:                             Name:            Supervisor          │
│ Suppress form feed: No                Banner name:     SAMS                │
│ Notify when done:   No                                                     │
│                                       Defer printing:  No                  │
│ Target server:      (Any Server)      Target date:                        │
│                                       Target time:                        │
└──────────────────────────────────────────────────────────────────────────┘
```

NetWare Bridges, Routers and Gateways to Other Networks

NetWare not only allows intrasystem operation but supports routers and gateways that link networks to other networks.

Bridge Software

NetWare makes it possible for networks to communicate with other networks, as well as with mainframe computers. A router connects networks using different hardware. One network, for example, might use ARCnet's interface cards and cabling, while another network uses IBM's Token Ring interface cards and cabling. NetWare provides router software, which permits these two networks to share information.

The software can reside on a dedicated workstation (ROUTER.EXE) but is now built into the Netware operating system and thus is another process for the file server to handle. In order to handle routing internally, there must be at least two available expansion slots, one for each network interface card for each respective network. The router remains invisible to users whether it is running on a dedicated PC workstation or as a process within the Netware file server.

Novell's Multiprotocol Routing Software

Novell offers multiprotocol routing software that runs on NetWare LANs. This software routes several different protocols including UNIX's TCP/IP and Apple's AppleTalk so that users on these different networks can communicate with NetWare LAN users.

SNA Gateway for Micro-Mainframe Communications

Novell's NetWare for SAA in conjunction with its NetWare 3270 LAN workstation for SAA enables multiple gateways on the same network, sending mainframe print jobs to LAN printers, viewing the current status of the gateway, and pooling LU sessions.

Because the IBM mainframe world uses synchronous communications, Novell recommends its Synchronous/V.35 Adapter board (which contains an RS-232-to-V.35 interface). This adapter, when used with an Intel 80386-based workstation serving as a gateway, makes transmission speeds of up to 64 kbs possible.

NetWare Connect

Novell also offers NetWare Connect. This is a software product that allows users to dial into a server or LAN. It can also be used to dial out by LAN users using LAN based communications packages.

System Fault Tolerant NetWare

Any company that relies completely on computers for information processing is fearful of a system failure. Novell has developed System Fault Tolerant NetWare to overcome this potential disaster. There are three different levels of system fault tolerance, depending on the degree of protection required.

What makes Novell's approach so unusual is that while it has provided the software tools for hardware duplication (to prevent downtime), the user may purchase off-the-shelf hardware in order to realize significant cost savings.

Level I NetWare protects against partial destruction of the file server by providing redundant directory structures. For each network volume, the file server maintains extra copies of file allocation tables and directory entries on different disk cylinders. If a directory sector fails, the file server shifts immediately to the redundant directory. The user, not inconvenienced, is unaware of this automatic procedure (depicted in Figure 9.10).

When a Level I system is powered up, it performs a complete self-consistency check on each redundant directory and file allocation table. It performs a read-after-write verification after each network disk write to ensure that data written to the file server is rereadable.

Level I software's *hot fix* feature checks a sector before trying to write data to it. If a disk area is bad, the disk drive controller writes its data to a special hot fix area. The hot fix feature then adds the bad blocks to the bad block table, so there is no possibility of losing data by writing it to these bad blocks in the future.

●
Novell offers gateway software and hardware for its NetWare LANs enabling network users to communicate with IBM mainframes.

●
NetWare's system fault-tolerant features reduce the chances that a file server's data will be lost.

FIGURE 9.10.

*The hot fix feature of
System Fault Tolerant
NetWare.*

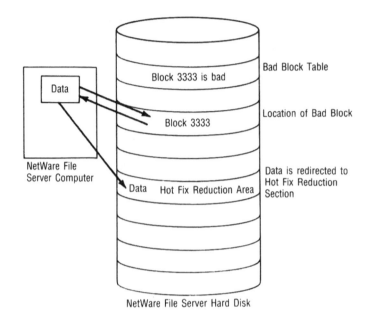

Level II software includes the protection offered by Level I, plus a number of additional features. At this level, Novell offers two options to protect the LAN against the total failure of the file server. The first option is *mirrored drives*, which means supporting two duplicate hard disk drives with a single hard disk controller (as illustrated in Figure 9.11). Every time the file server performs a disk write function, it mirrors this image on its duplicate hard disk. It also verifies both hard disk drives to ensure complete accuracy. If there is a hard disk failure, the system switches to the mirrored drive and continues operations with no inconvenience to users.

The second option under Level II is for *duplexed drives*: virtually all the hardware is duplicated, including the disk controller and interface, (as illustrated in Figure 9.12). If a disk controller or disk drive fails, the system switches automatically to the duplexed alternative and records this in a log. The performance of a duplexed system is far superior to that of a single system because of split seeks. If a certain file is requested, the system checks to see which disk system can respond more quickly. If two requests occur simultaneously, each drive handles one of the disk reads. In effect, this technique greatly enhances the file server's performance.

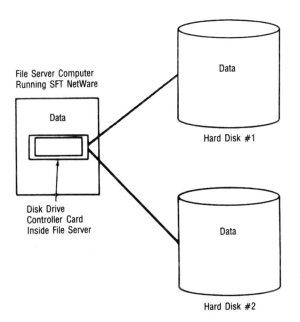

FIGURE 9.11.

Disk mirroring with System Fault Tolerant NetWare.

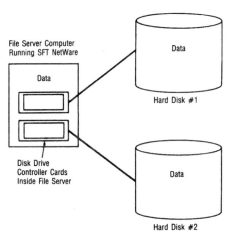

FIGURE 9.12.

Disk duplexing with System Fault Tolerant NetWare.

Level II also includes a Novell feature known as the *transaction tracking system (TTS)*, which is designed to ensure the data integrity of multi-user databases. The system views each change in a database as a transaction that is either complete or incomplete. If a user is in the middle of a database transaction when the system fails, the TTS rolls the database back to the point just before the transaction began. This action is known as *automatic rollback*. A second procedure performed by the TTS is roll-forward recovery: the system keeps a complete log of all transactions to ensure that everything can be recovered in the event of a complete system failure.

Level III software incorporates all features from Level II and adds a duplicate file server connected by a high-speed bus. If a file server fails, the second file server immediately assumes control over network operations. This is by far the best, most resilient system to have; however, it is also the most costly.

Novell, NetWare, and the Future

Novell believes that future enterprise networks will require seamless connectivity among different computing platforms.

In this section, you examine Novell's future plans for NetWare. You look at Novell's vision of a universal architecture that will be able to accommodate a number of different protocols concurrently. You also examine Novell's three major client/server network operating systems: NetWare 3.12, NetWare 4.*x*, and Unixware.

Novell believes the computer industry is now well into a second stage of LAN connectivity, in which LANs are connected to mainframe and midrange computers by gateways or by direct interfaces. Over the past several years, Novell has planned an architecture to be consistent with a future characterized by increased connectivity, seamless flow of information between large and small computers, and multivendor compatibility. Novell's plan, known as Universal Networking Architecture (UNA), is to move toward a network architecture that will encompass any platform.

The major emphasis today in many large corporations is still on the mainframe or host computer. The LAN user is concerned with accessing mainframe applications, and not with direct peer-to-peer communications between a microcomputer program and a mainframe program. Such concepts as peer-to-peer communication, ease of use, and transparency for end users will characterize the next (or third) stage of LAN connectivity.

Novell sees this third stage as a time in which, for example, an individual database record can be updated with information from various programs running on different-sized computers using different protocols and operating systems. All these differences will be resolved by NetWare in a manner that is transparent to the end user.

One evidence that Novell is very serious about its UNA is its inclusion of MHS in every package of NetWare. Licensed from Action Technology, MHS provides CCITT X.400 electronic mail standards. These standards are the key to making electronic mail programs that run on different computers able to provide a universal "envelope." The destination LAN's own electronic mail program can open and decode this "envelope."

NetWare versions 2.2 (now discontinued) and later reflect Novell's philosophy in yet another way. IBM has been modifying its System Network Architecture to incorporate peer-to-peer communications. The idea is to let programs communicate directly with other programs, without having to go through a mainframe computer. NetWare v2.2 permits Advanced Program-to-Program Communications (APPC) through the use of Netware Loadable Modules (NLMs).

NetWare and the Use of Heterogeneous File Servers

Novell has been developing file-server software that enables a variety of different types of computers to serve as file servers under NetWare. A DEC VAX computer, for example, can do so with NetWare VMS. The VAX's file-server capabilities are transparent to the end user, who still sees DOS files in their familiar format. NetWare for the Macintosh now permits an IBM DOS-based machine to serve as a file server for an AppleTalk network. NetWare translates the native AppleTalk commands from Macintosh workstations into its own Network Core Protocol, processes the commands, and then translates its own commands back into the AppleTalk protocol the Apple workstations understand. This entire process is transparent to Apple users and PC users alike.

In December 1988, Novell announced its NetWare server strategy would include support for Network File Systems (NFS) and IBM's Server Message Block (SMB) protocols. Novell also indicated it would support LAN Manager clients with the NetBEUI/DLC protocol. Novell's long-range NetWare server strategy, however, is to provide a broad platform capable of supporting several different kinds of file servers; including those running under UNIX, VMS, and OS/2.

Later in this chapter you examine the current NetWare 4.1 version, and what Novell promises in future versions. Support of OS/2 includes support for Microsoft's Named Pipes and IBM's APPC. Figure 9.13 represents what Novell calls its "Novell Vision" of a heterogeneous file-server environment.

FIGURE 9.13.

The Novell vision.

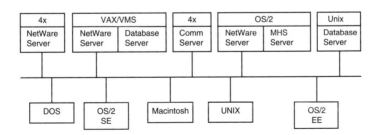

Novell differentiates between *native-mode* and *host-mode* file servers. Native-mode file servers are designed for a specific hardware platform (a dedicated NetWare Intel 80486-based file server, for example) and so are inherently more efficient. Host-mode servers, on the other hand, run on top of an operating system such as UNIX or OS/2 (which also supports such services as file and print functions).

There is a considerable movement in the computer industry toward server-based database applications that use such host-based server platforms as OS/2, Windows NT, and UNIX. Novell has indicated it will support both its own native-mode server and those host-mode servers which support database applications.

NetWare for UNIX

● A portable version of NetWare written in C can be ported easily to mini-computers and UNIX machines.

Novell has licensed version 3.12 of NetWare to a number of vendors including Data General, IBM, and HP. These vendors ported NetWare to run on their own UNIX environments. This product was known as Portable Netware and is now known as Netware for UNIX. All the standard DOS and NetWare commands can be used with it.

Novell is planning a version of Portable Netware that is processor independent, Processor Independent NetWare (PIN) as it will be known will operate on a variety of different processor-based machines. This way NetWare can harness the strengths of the individual chip types such as Intel, RISC, mainframe and so on.

Novell is working with several traditional minicomputer vendors including Hewlett-Packard, Digital Equipment Corporation (DEC), and Sun Microsystems to develop native NetWare versions that will run on reduced instruction set computing (RISC) chip-based systems—powerful machines based on the HP-PA chip, DEC's Alpha chip, and Sun's SPARC chip. The advantage for users of running native NetWare (in contrast to portable NetWare) on a RISC-based computer is that the network operating system's performance will be optimized for that particular computer.

NetWare's Movement Toward Protocol Transparency

A virtually universal NetWare platform would provide support for multiple protocols—and Novell has been moving toward this vision. It would enable a user to have transparent access to a number of computing resources. These might include multiple server/client protocols and various subnet protocols.

Novell views the future as a time when the microcomputer will be at the center of computing, and not a mere appendage to mainframe computers. To make this dream come true, however, the artificial barriers separating computing resources must be eliminated.

The various protocol differences create incompatibilities for UNIX-based minicomputers, DEC computers running VMS, SNA-based IBM mainframe computers, and other computing resources (such as Sun workstations running NFS protocol). Novell envisions a time when its software will help break down the barriers that make communication difficult among these different platforms.

Novell's Open Data Link Interface

Open Data Link Interface (ODI) software offers an interface between LAN adapter cards and different protocols. The Open Data Link Interface serves as a Novell response to Microsoft's Network Device Interface Specification (NDIS). ODI can handle as many as 32 transport protocols—and 16 different adapters— simultaneously. A single network is able to support multiple protocols and different types of adapter cards.

Instead of leaving the network manager to grapple with the multi-protocol issue, ODI makes the entire matter transparent to users. In effect, ODI acts as a standard network interface, so that vendors need only develop network software with one generic driver. ODI provides the necessary translations required, as well as the appropriate network drivers.

Open Data Link Interface is composed of a Link Support layer (LSL) which contains two programming interfaces: *Multiple Link Interface (MLI)* for LAN-adapter device drivers, and *Multiple Protocol Interface (MPI)* for LAN protocols. The Link Support layer coordinates packet sending and receiving by sorting the packets it receives into the correct protocol stack—which could consist of as many as 32 queues for such disparate protocols as IPX/SPX, TCP/IP, OSI, and AppleTalk.

Among the many vendors who welcomed Novell's ODI announcement in early 1989 were Apple, Compaq, and Western Digital Corporation. Sytek Corporation also indicated support for ODI by incorporating it into its Multiple Protocol Architecture and LocalNet Integrated Network Connectivity products. Sytek will develop drivers for baseband and broadband network adapter cards that use Novell's Multiple Link Interface. Novell indicated it would provide ODI-compliant drivers for its own LAN adapters, as well as for those offered by IBM and 3Com Corporation. Open Data Link Interface is consistent with Novell's philosophy of offering a universal platform for different network operating systems.

NetWare 3.12

In May 1989, Novell announced the products it described as its "server platform for the '90s"—NetWare 386 v3.0 and v3.1. This network operating system (now called NetWare 3.12) was not a replacement for NetWare 2.2; it is a separate product. NetWare 3.12 supports up to 250 nodes per server, up to 4G of RAM, 32 physical drives per volume, and 2,048 physical drives per server. It allows 100,000 concurrent open files and 25,000 concurrent transactions. It also can handle more than 2 million directory entries per volume, with a maximum file size of 4G, and a maximum volume size of 32 TB. A feature providing Level III system fault tolerance permits redundant file servers and third-party applications.

● Open Data Link Interface (ODI) software provides an interface between up to 16 different LAN adapter cards and up to 32 different protocol stacks.

● NetWare 3.12 supports up to 250 nodes per server, up to 64 volumes, 100,000 concurrent open files, and 32 Terabytes of disk space.

Novell's NetWare 3.12 approach is modular. Users can add functions to their server platform by using server-based applications called NetWare Loadable Modules (NLMs). Printing functions, LAN drivers, and various NetWare utilities are among the features available as NLMs. Databases, electronic mail, and office automation servers can be written as NLMs; that way they can be loaded or unloaded while the server is running. Figure 9.14 illustrates this feature of NetWare 3.12 architecture.

FIGURE 9.14.

NetWare 3.1x architecture (courtesy of Novell, Inc.).

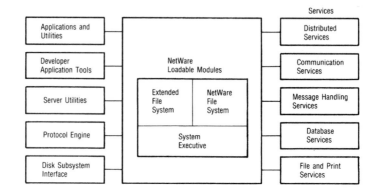

● NetWare 3.12 supports IPX/SPX, TCP/IP, OSI, and SNA protocols.

NetWare 3.12 supports multiple transport protocols concurrently—including IPX/SPX, Transport Control Protocol/Internet Protocol (TCP/IP), Open Systems Interconnect (OSI), and Systems Network Architecture (SNA)—as illustrated in Figure 9.15.

FIGURE 9.15.

NetWare 3.1x supports multiple protocols.

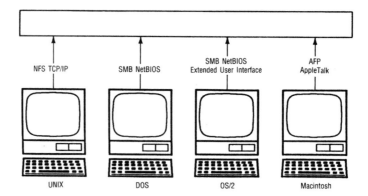

NetWare 3.12 also supports Microsoft's Named Pipes and Server Message Block, IBM's NETBIOS Extended User Interface, Advanced Program-to-Program Communications, Apple's AppleTalk and Apple Filing Protocol (AFP), and Sun Microsystems' Network Filing System (NFS).

NetWare 3.12 adds a number of significant network management features. These include better network statistical reporting, better print services (including print servers), and password encryption. NetWare 3.12 provides network status—even monitors and alerts—as well as access to management functions from remote consoles.

This version of NetWare also offers extended (installable) file system support for CD-ROMs and WORM drives. NetWare 3.12 can configure its server memory automatically, which reduces installation time substantially. Its Extended File Salvage facility enables NetWare 3.12 to retain all user-deleted files until the server runs out of disk space, unless the user has flagged those files for purging. When there is no longer any disk space available, the files are purged in order of deletion.

NetWare 3.12 incorporates other evidence of artificial intelligence. It is capable of fine-tuning its own operation by observing the number of users accessing an application, and when this number drops, it can adjust the amount of memory needed at each stage of optimum caching.

NetWare 3.12 is also "80486-aware." This means that if an Intel 80486 processor or Pentium is installed in the server, the operating system is aware of it and uses the extra 80486 instructions available to it to perform with greater efficiency. The 80386 version has approximately three times the performance of Novell's previous 80286-based products.

Network supervisors considering NetWare 3.12 will find communications a vital area of concern. NetWare 3.12 supports Ethernet, Token-Ring, LocalTalk, ARCnet, and Synchronous Data Link Control, as well as T-1 and asynchronous media.

Novell's Network Management System (NMS) can manage nodes on a NetWare 3.12 LAN. Its network reporting system is based on the categories and packet formats of the OSI Common Management Information Protocol. This format enables NetWare networks to report information to other CMIP-based systems, as well as to NetView (IBM's mainframe network management system). IBM and Novell currently are working together so that NetView understands over 100 of NetWare's alerts.

Novell offers a NetWare Programmers' Workbench, which provides developers with everything necessary to write distributed applications in the NetWare 3.12 environment. These essentials include two C programming language compilers, supplied to Novell by Watcom Systems.

The NetWare 3.12 Network Loadable Module for the Macintosh

NetWare 3.12 utilizes network loadable modules (NLMs) to add network functions. NetWare for the Macintosh NLM enables Macintosh users to take full advantage of NetWare services, and allows them to access information on an Intel-based file server. Enhanced printing support enables Macintosh users to manage their own print jobs within a queue. Macintosh, DOS, and OS/2 users can send print jobs to an Apple LaserWriter and compatible printers. The printers themselves can be connected to the serial or parallel port of a NetWare 3.12 file server, a NetWare Print Server, or a DOS workstation serving as a remote printer.

The Macintosh NetWare NLM includes an AppleTalk router that can determine its own network and zone configuration by analyzing data it receives from AppleTalk. This feature frees network managers from having to provide configuration information. AppleTalk data packets can be routed across ARCnet, Ethernet, LocalTalk, and Token Ring cabling.

Bridging the Gap Between the Macintosh and IBM PC

Macintosh workstations under NetWare can see and access files and printers on both Macintosh and PC file servers.

Because NetWare is a distinct and hardware-independent network operating system, it provides an effective bridge between the IBM and Apple worlds. A Macintosh workstation utilizing NetWare v2.15 (and above) is able to see and access both the Macintosh and the PC files displayed on its NetWare file server. DOS files are stored in standard HFS format. In addition, no conversion is needed for files produced by application programs available for both machines (such as Microsoft Word, PageMaker, and WordPerfect).

One major advantage of Novell's approach is that a Macintosh network can utilize Intel 80286-, 80386-, 80486-, and Pentium-based computers as file servers. These units provide high performance at lower prices than comparable Macintosh units. Also, because NetWare is capable of handling up to 32 terabytes of disk storage on a single file server, large-capacity hard disks are still less expensive for IBM machines than their Macintosh counterparts.

Equally important, NetWare supports Macintosh print spooling because it is compatible with the AppleTalk Printer Access Protocol. IBM PC workstations under DOS or OS/2 can access ImageWriters and LaserWriters that are part of an AppleTalk network. These printers can be configured on IBM software (as C Itoh Prowriters and Diablo 630 printers, respectively). The network also has PostScript printer drivers built into its AppleTalk protocol suite.

Because NetWare is able to distinguish its own IPX packet format from Apple's format for its own file server, AppleShare file servers can also be accessed on a NetWare network. Similarly, Macintosh computers using EtherPort network interface cards and running NetWare can access IBM PC workstations that use standard Ethernet network interface cards and also run NetWare.

Because the two operating systems have different rules for naming files, NetWare for the Macintosh contains a utility program that converts Apple file names to DOS file names. DOS limits file names to eight characters without spaces between the letters; Apple files can contain up to 31 characters. DOS interprets a period in a file name as the separator between file name and extension, and lists the first three letters after a period as the extension. The Apple file name My Proposal is translated into the DOS file name MY; the Apple Mr.and Mrs. Smith file becomes MR.AND in DOS.

One problem with this automatic conversion process is that because the program truncates Apple names, it is possible that two files could appear to have the same DOS name. The solution is to convert the two Apple file names in such a way that the last character in the second file name in the DOS display appears as a number. This way, the Macintosh files MY.FILE 1 and MY.FILE would appear on a DOS workstation's screen as MY.FIL and M1.FIL. DOS files are displayed in Apple folders with the word DOS appearing in the document icon, and all letters appearing in uppercase. Figure 9.16 shows what a Macintosh user would see.

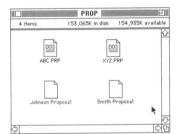

FIGURE 9.16.

DOS and Apple files displayed.

Depicting NetWare Volumes on the Macintosh

NetWare displays a list of available volumes in a volume dialog box. You may select as many volumes as you wish. One very nice feature of this login process is that you can specify that your name and password be saved along with the list of volumes you have selected. From that point on, each subsequent time you log in to the network, you'll be logged into these volumes automatically.

NetWare volumes on the Macintosh are depicted using the Macintosh icons (pictures). A SYS volume, for example, could be selected and clicked to reveal several file folders (including LOGIN, MAIL, PUBLIC, and SYSTEM).

A volume can contain several different types of folders: gray, dropbox, plain, black-tab gray, and black-tab plain.

- A gray folder is unavailable for use. This means you cannot open it, copy files into it, or make any modifications.

- The arrow above dropbox folders symbolizes that you can drop files into these folders, but you cannot see what's inside.

- Plain folders permit you to open them and see the files it contains. Your rights, a subject we discuss shortly, determine what else you can do with these files.

- Finally, black-tab folders enable you to modify the folder's security. You can change your own rights in the folder, which may result in a change of the folder's color from gray to plain. (You cannot read the files in black-tab gray folders.)

Several of these folder types are shown in Figure 9.17. To create a new folder, you simply select the New Folders command from the File menu. When an unlabeled new file folder appears on your screen, you can type a name for it. NetWare converts a Macintosh file folder name (by eliminating spaces and truncating it) into a form DOS accepts.

FIGURE 9.17.

Different types of available folders.

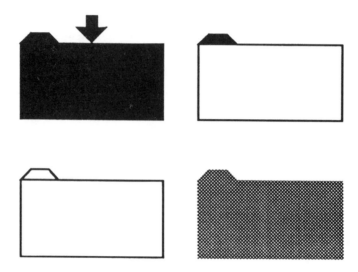

Files can be named and saved directly into a specific folder existing on a specific volume, as shown in Figure 9.18. Files can be flagged to give them any of the following special attributes: Read-Only, Shareable, Hidden, Archive needed, System, and Transactional.

FIGURE 9.18.

Files can be saved directly into a specific folder.

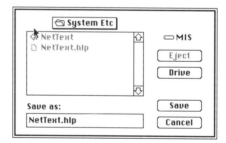

The NetWare Control Center

The heart of NetWare for the Macintosh user is the NetWare Control Center. Here network information concerning users, groups, servers, volumes, folders, and files may be viewed and modified.

The Network Control Center appears as an icon in a folder on the Macintosh desktop. When you double-click on this icon, it begins to search for NetWare file servers. If you are not logged on to some of these file servers, you may do so by double-clicking on the file server icons as they appear.

The NetWare Control Center menus include the following: Server, Volumes, Folders/ Files, User, and Groups. A sample screen appears in Figure 9.19.

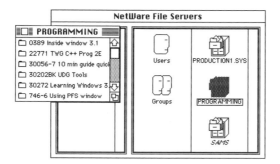

FIGURE 9.19.

The NetWare Control Center.

Note that the Server window is divided into left and right panels. The left panel contains icons for each file server on the network, while the right panel contains icons that enable you to access appropriate information on users, groups, and volumes linked to that file server. You may access information on only one file server at a time.

Printing Under NetWare for the Macintosh

On a mixed NetWare network containing both IBM and Apple computers and printers, PCs can use both the Apple printers and their own non-Apple network printers. The Macintosh workstations, on the other hand, can print only to the Apple printers. One major limitation of AppleShare software is that it does not use a print spooler; instead, it sends files directly to its printers.

Novell developed its Netware for Macintosh Connectivity product so that Macintosh workstations can spool to an AppleTalk queue server that emulates an Apple printer. This queue server then forwards the files to a NetWare print queue for spooling and eventual printing.

The Chooser menu permits Macintosh users to see NetWare queues and the Apple printers attached to the network. Novell suggests that the supervisor create a separate print queue for each AppleTalk printer on the network.

NetWare 4.x

NetWare 4.x is Novell's network operating system designed for enterprise computing. It can accommodate up to 1000 users on a single server. Netware 4.x is based on the 32-bit architecture of the Intel 386-Pentium processor range. Version 4.x is similar to the 3.12 operating system, yet significant improvements have been made. The major feature of 4.x

---

●

On a NetWare LAN with both PCs and Macintosh Computers, PCs can print on both Apple and non-Apple printers.

●

NetWare 4.x is designed to handle Enterprise level LANs. Up to 1,000 machines can concurrently connect to a single server.

is Netware Directory Services (NDS). NDS is an enterprise-wide service linking file servers and network resources, such as printers, into a hierarchical, object-oriented directory. NDS is based on the CCITT's X.500 directory linking standard. It is a globally distributed database that provides a single point of login and is built to allow easy partitioning and replication to all servers.

Designed for large networks, NetWare 4.*x* enables a network manager to manage dozens of file servers from a single console. It also offers enhanced remote communications. The software uses Novell's *Packet Burst and Large Interpret Packet* protocol designed to permit larger packets to be transmitted and cuts back on the number of acknowledgments needed to be sent to ensure that transmissions are received accurately.

Another major feature found in NetWare 4.*x* is a set of specifications Novell jointly developed with Kodak. Among the services provided are the ability to receive, transmit, and store images over the network.

Security has been greatly increased under NetWare 4.*x*. A network manager can restrict use of various network resources to authorized users. These rights define file privileges such as read, write, and delete. The network manager can also define the actions a user or program are allowed to perform. NetWare 4.*x* also adds powerful auditing functions. The network manager can audit collections of network containers—collections of network objects—and server hard-disk volumes and the events that occur with these objects. He can assign separate auditors by using different auditor passwords.

Still another significant security feature implemented in NetWare 4.*x* is packet authentication. The network operating system now attaches a unique, randomly generated signature to each packet generated by a workstation or server. This approach prevents intruders from capturing packets and forging a user's session identification to gain access privileges.

NetWare 4.*x* can take advantage of the Intel Pentium processor. It does this by using the Pentium's *multithreading* capabilities that allow two 32-bit instructions to process at the same time. Dependent on the file server's load, this feature can improve performance by 35 percent.

Novell has stated that it will no longer develop or enhance NetWare 3.12 and is stating that companies should transition to NetWare 4.*x*. For more detailed reading on Novell's NetWare 3.12 and 4.1, I recommend that you read *NetWare Unleashed* by Rick Sant'Angelo, Sams Publishing.

Unixware

● Unixware is a network operating system that can handle UNIX System V release 4 files and NetWare files.

Novell's intention to be the strategic partner of major corporations with enterprise-wide LANs has led it to add a UNIX-based product to its networking portfolio. Unixware is a network operating system that adds native NetWare's SPX/IPX protocol to UNIX's System V release 4 (SVR4.2). It includes support for X-Window as well as the ability to mount NetWare volumes.

A graphics-oriented desktop manager interface is found on both the personal Unixware and unlimited-user server version, the Application Server. The GUI can be configured to look like the industry standard Motif OpenLook or HP Openview interfaces. Unixware is ideal for companies that are already running NetWare over LANs as well as UNIX. It makes it possible to view and access both NetWare and UNIX files from the graphical user interface.

What Have You Learned?

1. System fault tolerance enables NetWare to provide redundancy of key hardware and software elements to prevent network failure.

2. Three techniques NetWare uses to speed up its file-server response time are directory hashing, disk caching, and elevator seeking.

3. By mapping network drives and utilizing the principle of search drives, a user can retrieve a file without knowing where it is located.

4. NetWare's many levels of network security include the login procedure, trustee rights, directory rights, and file attributes.

5. New network users can immediately enjoy all the rights of another network user if they have the same network equivalencies.

6. NetWare users can learn information about their login scripts by using the SYSCON utility.

7. Using the FILER utility, network users can establish directory and file exclusion patterns.

8. Novell's NetWare router software and hardware permit two networks to be linked.

9. Novell's SAA gateway software permits users on a NetWare LAN to access an IBM mainframe.

10. NetWare can search for potential bad disk sectors—and then avoid them—using the hot fix feature of system fault tolerant software.

11. The integrity of a database is maintained, even in the event of network failure, by the Transaction Tracking System (TTS).

Quiz for Chapter 9

1. ARCnet uses a series of active and passive hubs tied together with
- a. fiber optics.
- b. twisted-pair wire.
- c. coaxial cable.
- d. lasers.

2. NetWare file servers keep often-requested files in RAM for rapid response to requests. This is known as
- a. directory hashing.
- b. disk caching.
- c. elevator seeking.
- d. rapid response retrieval.

3. NetWare minimizes wear and tear on disk drives by retrieving files closest to the present location of the heads, instead of simply processing retrieval requests in the order in which they are received. This technique is known as
- a. directory hashing.
- b. disk caching.
- c. rapid file retrieval.
- d. elevator seeking.

4. NetWare workstations need not contain floppy disk drives as long as they have
- a. a remote system boot PROM.
- b. NetWare v2.2 and above.
- c. EGA graphics.
- d. at least 256K of RAM.

5. Workstations using different versions of DOS can coexist on a NetWare network because

- a. each workstation does not use the file server.
- b. NetWare provides an interpretive shell.
- c. the differences in DOS versions are not significant.
- d. different machines need different versions of DOS.

6. The PCONSOLE menu utility is designed to handle
- a. printing requests.
- b. photocopying requests.
- c. filing requests.
- d. micro-mainframe communications.

7. Novell's System Fault Tolerant NetWare automatically places bad sectors in a "bad block" table by using
- a. a hot fix feature.
- b. elevator seeking.
- c. mirrored disk drives.
- d. the Transaction Tracking System.

8. The automatic rollback feature of the Transaction Tracking System ensures the integrity of a database by
- a. duplicating each data entry.
- b. rolling back to before the data entry if the entry was disrupted before it was complete.
- c. keeping a log of all data entries.
- d. completing an entry if it is disrupted.

9. The concept of mirrored drives means that

    a. all drives are the mirror opposites of each other.

    b. a second drive keeps an exact copy of the file server's information.

    c. all hardware and software are duplicated, including disk controllers and interfaces.

    d. if one disk drive becomes cracked, the other drive also is cracked.

10. Duplexed drives increase the speed of a file server by about

    a. 3 times

    b. 4 times

    c. 2 times

    d. 6 times

11. Novell's UNIX-based application server is

    a. Unixware

    b. NetWare PEER

    c. NetWare Shrink

    d. NetWare SNA Gateway

12. Portable NetWare is written in

    a. COBOL

    b. FORTRAN

    c. C

    d. 4GL

13. NetWare enables the file server to locate a file quickly, without searching through every directory, by use of

    a. disk caching.

    b. directory hashing.

    c. elevator seeking.

    d. remote system boot PROMS.

14. Network disk drives are really

    a. hard disk drives.

    b. floppy disk drives.

    c. network file servers.

    d. logical disk drives.

15. Different networks can be linked using

    a. a remote PC.

    b. a router PC.

    c. a disk server.

    d. spooled disk files.

16. NetWare LANs can communicate with IBM mainframe computers by using

    a. a bridge PC.

    b. an SAA gateway server.

    c. an asynchronous communications server.

    d. both b and c.

17. Users can shorten the set up of their network workstation environment by

    a. using the NetWare manuals.

    b. using electronic mail.

    c. using elevator seeking.

    d. using login scripts.

Microsoft's Windows NT Server

About This Chapter

Microsoft supplies a File Server Network Operating System called Windows NT Server. The NT Server software runs on top of Microsoft's 32-Bit Operating system Windows NT. In this chapter, you will discover some of the advantages of this Network operating system.

Client/Server Computing

Client/server computing consists of a front-end client application program accessing a back-end server. While these applications can take many forms—including e-mail, spreadsheets, project management, and so on—the first major client/server products have focused on database management programs.

When running a client/server database management program on a Windows NT Server network, a client workstation requests certain records from another workstation serving as the database server. This database server, rather than sending the client workstation all its database records (as well as the entire program), sends the specific records requested. The client workstation then uses its front-end software to display these records.

The advantages of client/server systems running under NT Server include a significant reduction in network traffic. Fewer records need be transmitted, and the program itself need not be transmitted to the client workstation.

A database server running a database program provides the key records requested by a client workstation running front-end client/server software.

Windows NT is a
32-bit network
operating system
that includes such
features as
multitasking,
multithreaded
processes, and pre-
emptive interrupts.

Windows NT Overview

Microsoft's Windows NT is a very powerful true 32-bit network operating system that is available in client and server versions. Among NT's key features are pre-emptive multitasking, multithreaded processes, portability, and support for symmetrical multiprocessing. Pre-emptive multitasking permits simultaneous foreground and background multitasking. NT, rather than specific programs, determines when one program should be interrupted and another program executed. Multi-threaded processes refers to the threads under NT that function as execution agents. Multiple threads of execution within a single process means that threads allow a process to execute different parts of a program on different processors simultaneously.

Windows NT uses the NT File System (NTFS). This file system supports file names up to 256 characters. It also permits transaction tracking. This means that if the system crashes, NT rolls data back to its previous state just before the system crashes.

Windows NT data links include support for the IEEE 802.2 specifications (Token Ring and Ethernet), the Synchronous Data Link Control (SDLC) protocol, the X.25/QLLC protocols, and the Distributed Function Terminal (DFT) specification.

Windows NT's
architecture is
modular. It consists
of several sub-
systems, a kernel,
and a hardware
abstraction layer
(HAL) that is the only
part of the program
that is hardware-
specific.

Windows NT's Architecture

As Figure 10.1 illustrates, Microsoft designed Windows NT to be modular and portable. It is composed of a kernel as well as several different system subsystems. Subsystems are available for applications running OS/2 and POSIX-compliant programs. A Virtual DOS machine (VDM) runs MS-DOS and 16-bit Windows applications.

The kernel is responsible for NT's basic operations. It allocates and synchronizes multiple processors as well as handling interrupts and error exceptions. An NT Executive manages the interface between the kernel and various subsystems. An I/O Manager handles device-independent input/output requests. The Hardware Abstraction Layer (HAL) is system-specific. It translates the NT Executive's commands into a form that can be understood by the hardware found in the physical platform running NT. By isolating hardware-specific NT commands into the HAL, Microsoft has created an architecture that makes it easy for it to port this network operating system easily to other platforms. For enhanced portability, virtually all of NT, with the exception of the HAL, is written in the C programming language.

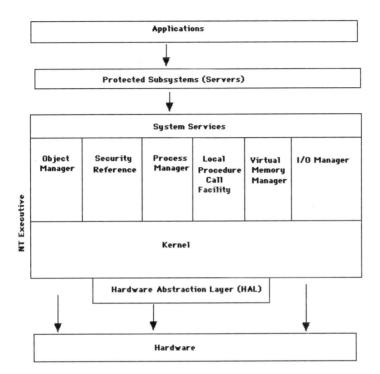

FIGURE 10.1.
Windows NT's Architecture.

Performance Features of Windows NT

Windows NT is a true 32-bit network operating system. Applications can execute multiple commands simultaneously. It also supports systems with multiple processors and provides the ability to perform *symmetric processing.* This means that several processors can divide the work equally. Using symmetric processing, a company needing exceptional performance can purchase a superserver with several microprocessors, and NT will be able to take advantage of all this processing power. Symmetric multi-processing allows system and applications requirements to be evenly distributed across all available processors, thus making everything perform much faster.

NT includes peer-to-peer networking software so that NT users can share files and applications with other users running NT or Windows for Workgroups. Another major performance advantage of NT is its method of accessing memory. It uses a flat memory model that, unlike a paged memory approach, enables applications to access up to 2G of RAM. Now application programmers can write larger applications.

The performance possible under NT comes at a price. The program requires at least an Intel-based 486 DX machine with at least 12M of RAM and 100M of secondary storage. Microsoft also has agreements with several companies including Digital Equipment Corporation and MIPS Computer Systems to provide NT on a number of hardware platforms. These latest generations of microprocessors currently include Intel and RISC systems such as the MIPS R4000 and Digital Alpha AXP.

Security Under NT

Windows NT requires users to enter a password each time they start the operating system, whether or not they're connected to a server. Another security feature of NT is the *User Manager*. This program ensures that passwords adhere to corporate policy. The User Manager permits each NT machine to be configured for the number of users, with all users given their own privilege level. It is also possible to create groups and give everyone in a group the same privileges.

Another key security feature is the *Event Viewer*. This program enables network managers to view a log of all network errors and violations, including the time, date, and type of violation as well as where the event occurred and the name of the user involved. Each time NT is started, a password is required. Users must reboot their machines to make sure the password dialog box pops up.

NT is certifiable at U.S. government C2-level for secure environments. Microsoft has indicated that it will offer enhancements in the future that will raise NT's security level and make it even more appealing to government agencies.

Running NT with Other Network Operating Systems

Windows NT Server provides built-in file-sharing and print-sharing capabilities for workgroup computing and an open network system interface that includes built-in support for IPX/SPX, TCP/IP, NetBEUI, and other transports. NT Server is compatible with existing networks such as VINES, NetWare, UNIX, LAN Manager 2.*x*, and Windows for Workgroups.

Windows NT features application program interfaces (APIs) permitting network operating systems (NOS) vendors to write client software for their products to run with this product. Windows NT supports Simple Network Management Protocol (SNMP) so server activities can be managed by any SNMP network management program.

NT supports Macintosh clients, treating them as equal citizens on the network. It supports AppleTalk File Protocol v 2.1 and has full AFP security built-in. PC-created files appear with the correct Macintosh icons and resource information—Macintosh users can double-click on these files to start the right application. Macintosh users can access NT Server the same as any AppleShare server.

NT's printing subsystem can handle all Macintosh PostScript print jobs on NT-based printers and send PC-originated print jobs to AppleTalk-connected printers.

Connecting NT to the Rest of the World

Windows NT comes with a service known as *Remote Access Server*—a feature that enables DOS, Windows, and NT clients to dial into an NT network and log in and work as if they were LAN connected, only slower. Up to 256 connections can be handled, and Remote Access Server uses NT's basic security scheme, including Data Encryption Standard (DES) encrypted passwords and optional call-back. For remote communications, Windows NT also supports the X.25 protocol and Integrated Services Digital Network (ISDN). Security can be set up so that a dial in user has access to the entire LAN or just the server they dial in to.

SNA Server

The *SNA Server* for NT service provides connectivity to IBM mainframes via 3270, Advanced program-to-program communications (APPC), NetView, and to the IBM AS/400. SNA Server uses a client/server architecture to distribute the communications processing, and each PC uses standard LAN protocols to connect to the SNA Server.

Systems Management Server

The *Systems Management Server* allows you to centrally manage hardware and software on your LAN. You can manage PCs as assets and distribute new software and patches to them from this server. The Management Server also allows you to conduct network protocol analysis and to troubleshoot individual PCs. As a result, the Management Server is a very valuable tool in an NT Server enterprise network.

E-mail and Scheduling with Windows NT

Microsoft's NT includes a copy of Workgroup Connection along with copies of *Mail* and *Schedule Plus* workgroup products. Figure 10.2 illustrates a Scheduler screen. This program includes an appointment calendar, planner, note pad, and task list. It can schedule appointments via the network to which it is attached.

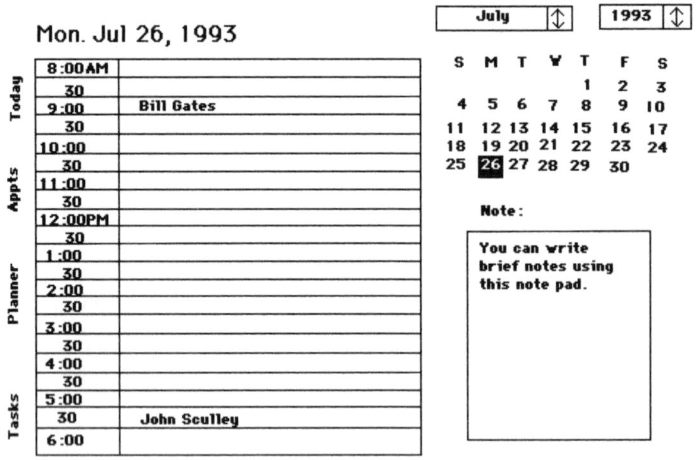

FIGURE 10.2.

NT's Scheduler.

Mon. Jul 26, 1993

Today	8:00AM		
	30		
	9:00	Bill Gates	
	30		
	10:00		
Appts	30		
	11:00		
	30		
	12:00PM		
	30		
Planner	1:00		
	30		
	2:00		
	30		
	3:00		
	30		
	4:00		
	30		
Tasks	5:00		
	30	John Sculley	
	6:00		

July ⬍   1993 ⬍

S	M	T	W	T	F	S
				1	2	3
4	5	6	7	8	9	10
11	12	13	14	15	16	17
18	19	20	21	22	23	24
25	**26**	27	28	29	30	

Note:

You can write
brief notes using
this note pad.

What Have You Learned?

1. Windows NT Server is Microsoft's NT-based network operating system.

2. Windows NT Server uses the NTFS high-performance file management system.

3. Windows NT features multitasking, multithreaded processes, and pre-emptive interrupts.

4. Windows NT supports symmetric multiprocessing.

5. Windows NT provides support for both remote computing and connections to mainframes and minicomputers.

Quiz for Chapter 10

1. The ability of NT to control when interrupts take place is known as

    a. multithreaded processes.

    b. multitasking.

    c. symmetric processing.

    d. pre-emptive interrupts.

2. The ability to evenly divide up a processor's work among several additional processors is known as

    a. symmetric processing.

    b. asymmetric processing.

    c. unisymmetric processing.

    d. polysymmetric processing.

3. Windows NT supports a file system known as

    a. HPFS

    b. PTFS

    c. NTFS

    d. NTSF

4. The portion of NT that is hardware-specific is

    a. the kernel.

    b. the kernel executive.

    c. the I/O Manager.

    d. HAL.

5. Most of NT is written in

    a. Cobol

    b. Fortran

    c. C

    d. BASIC

6. Passwords under NT are managed by the

    a. Password Manager

    b. User Manager

    c. Viewer Manager

    d. Security Manager

7. Network logs are viewed using the

    a. Event Viewer

    b. Log Viewer

    c. Security Viewer

    d. User Manager

8. NT supports Macintosh clients via a protocol known as

    a. the Finder.

    b. the Macintosh operating system.

    c. System 7.

    d. AppleTalk File Protocol.

9. Encryption under NT is provided using the

    a. Encryption User Standard.

    b. Data Encryption Standard.

    c. Government Encryption Standard.

    d. Encryption Government Standard.

10. NT connectivity with IBM mainframes is via

    a. the HOST Connection Program.

    b. the SNA Server service.

    c. Remote Server.

    d. AS/400 Server.

IBM's LAN Server

About This Chapter

IBM's LAN Server started as a derivative of Microsoft's LAN Manager but has differentiated itself significantly from that product. Perhaps the major improvement found in LAN Server is the enhanced communications links to IBM midrange and mainframe computers. This chapter examines some of this network operating system's major features and explores reasons why some readers might find this program desirable for their local area networks.

LAN Server

LAN Server is a network operating system that runs under OS/2. This file server software provides what IBM terms "requester/server relationships" (and what the rest of the industry refers to as client/server relationships).

Regardless of the term used, the software, when running under a truly multitasking operating system, permits distributed databases on a LAN to become a reality. Users need only request a particular record, and the actual processing takes place elsewhere on the network. IBM offers several products that enhance the feature set of both OS/2 and LAN Server. The Communications Manager product provides Advanced Peer-to-Peer Communications for OS/2. The DB2/2 Database Manager product provides distributed database technology that can span from PC file servers right up to corporate mainframes.

LAN Server offers enhanced database access functions because of the availability of the optional Distributed Database Connections Services/2 (DDCS/2), a component of IBM's Systems Applications Architecture. This feature permits connections between host databases and the databases on remote network client stations.

● LAN Server is a
network operating
system that runs
under OS/2.

● A domain is a group
of workstations and
one or more servers
on a network under
LAN Server.

The concept of a *domain* is very important on a LAN Server network. A group of workstations and one or more servers comprise a domain. A user who is given a user ID for the domain can log on to the domain from a requester workstation and access the domain resources. The network administrator designates one network server within each domain as the domain controller; it manages that domain and coordinates communication between servers and requesters. LAN Server requires that a minimum of one domain be created, and that a server act as a domain controller. A further server can be designated the backup domain controller.

One very valuable feature of LAN Server (known as location independence) enables the network administrator to treat a group of network servers as a single server. In such a case, users can access files on any server without being required to know on which server that information resides.

A *requester* is a network workstation that allows users to access shared resources as well as the processing power of a server. A requester has either OS/2 LAN Requester or DOS LAN Requester installed. A DOS application running in DOS compatibility mode at an OS/2 LAN Requester workstation can access printer and disk resources on an OS/2 LAN Server.

Figure 11.1 illustrates a typical user's LAN Server screen. Unlike other network operating systems, this program utilizes OS/2's power to track network activity and issue alerts. Its graphics-oriented user interface is consistent with IBM's Systems Application Architecture (SAA), the company's long-range plan for providing a uniform interface across its product line. Another SAA goal is to provide transparent movement of information across IBM's range of computers. LAN Server is preferable to other network operating systems for customers who have a heavy investment in IBM mainframe equipment. It offers enhanced micro-mainframe communications with its Communications Manager, and enhanced access to mainframe databases with its DB2/2 and DDCS/2 range.

FIGURE 11.1.

*A typical user's LAN
Server screen.*

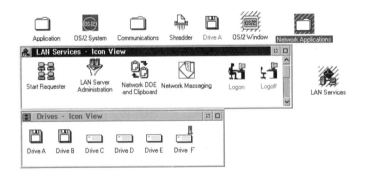

● Fault tolerance is
available with LAN
Server's Advanced
Package.

Customers can purchase an Entry Package or an Advanced Package. The Entry Package is designed for use on a PC that is non-dedicated. The PC can therefore be used as both a file server running LAN Server and a network workstation. If the additional features of

the Advanced package are not required, LAN Server-Entry provides a lower cost alternative. The Advanced Package includes such system-fault-tolerant features as disk mirroring
and disk duplexing. Both versions support the Network Device Interface Specification.
This means that a number of network interface cards (not just IBM hardware) can be used
with this software. The Advanced package adds the following server features:

- 386 high performance file system (386 HPFS) superior to the HPFS supplied
  with OS/2
- Fault tolerance for fixed disk drives through disk mirroring and disk duplexing
- Local security for the 386 HPFS
- Optimized code to take advantage of the Pentium Chipset from Intel to further
  improve performance

Regardless of the package purchased, LAN Server 4.0 coexists with TCP/IP for OS/2. When
TCP/IP is installed with NETBIOS, a LAN Server network gains access to a wide area
network, and LAN requesters can use TCP/IP for communication between different LANs.
The LAN requesters included in the LAN Server pack are only for use on the installed
server. You must purchase one license per installed network workstation that is to attach
to the LAN Server.

LAN Server and OS/2

While Microsoft's LAN Manager and IBM's LAN Server started out as very comparable
products, the two companies have chosen to go their separate ways. When LAN Server is
run in conjunction with IBM's OS/2 version 2.0 or higher, differences with LAN
Manager become apparent. LAN Server can take advantage of the fact that OS/2 is a true
32-bit operating system. Users can run DOS, Microsoft Windows, and OS/2 as network
clients. IBM does not offer LAN Server support for Macintosh computers yet.

LAN Server can generate alerts about printers, nearly full disks, and power problems. These
alerts can be interpreted by LAN Server's own network management program as well as
by the NetView program running on a host computer.

LAN Server's Graphical Interface

LAN Server 4.0 features a brand new graphical user interface (GUI). The administrative
tools within LAN Server now use the object technology that is part of IBM's OS/2 Workplace Shell. This significantly eases setup, management, configuration, and administration of the network by using drag-and-drop screen objects. Figure 11.2 shows the LAN
Server Environment.

●
LAN Server 4.0 uses
the graphical
environment of the
OS/2 Workplace
Shell to ease
network administra-
tion.

FIGURE 11.2.

*The LAN Server
environment.*

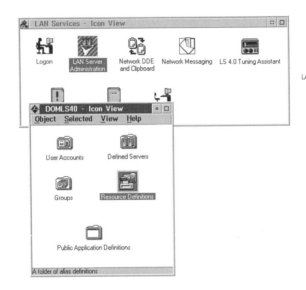

All network resources are now represented by OS/2 icons. You can add a user by picking up the new user icon and dropping it on a specific group. Access to drives, CD-ROMs, directories, and printers can be done in the same way.

Administrators can manage multiple domains through the interface regardless of where the domain servers are actually located.

Security Under LAN Server

User Profile Management (UPM) enables network administrators to require validation for a user ID and password at logon time. LAN Server's access control system provides additional security by providing a set of permissions that allow a network administrator to grant users various levels of access to shared resources. The following permissions can be granted:

- Read files and run EXE files
- Write to files
- Create subdirectories and files
- Delete subdirectories and files
- Change file attributes
- Create, change, and delete access control profiles

Network administrators can also grant various operator privileges for such areas as Accounts Operator, Print Operator, Comm Operator, and Server Operator. A user with Accounts Operator privileges can manage users and groups within a domain. This user has the privileges to add, modify, or delete users and groups. Figure 11.3 illustrates the information a network administrator provides when creating a new user.

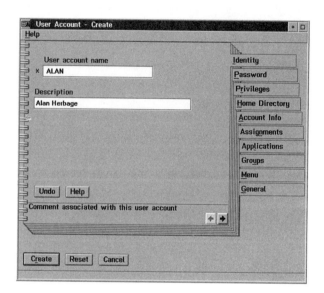

FIGURE 11.3.

Adding a new user.

Users with Print Operator privileges can manage print queues and print jobs. They can create, modify, or delete printers or queue servers within a domain. They also can share print queues and manage remote jobs on shared queues. These management tasks can be performed by using Print Manager or from the command line.

Users with Comm Operator privileges can manage serial devices. This means that they can share serial devices and manage shared serial devices.

Users with Server Operator privileges can manage aliases and other shared resources. They can view network status within a domain. They also can create, modify, or delete aliases or other shared resources. An *alias* is a nickname for a resource. These nicknames are created because they are much easier to remember and use than the more official *netname* for a resource. Figure 11.4 illustrates directory alias creation.

FIGURE 11.4.

Adding a directory alias.

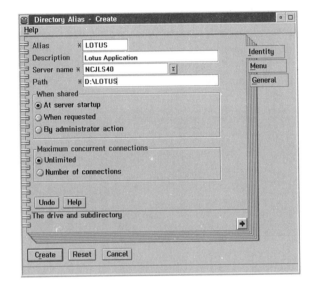

IBM LAN Server/400

IBM has recently released a similarly named product called LAN Server/400. What is interesting about this product is that it is a file server running on an adapter card that fits into IBM's Midrange AS400 Computer. This means that a company can consolidate its main computer (AS400) with its file servers. The card is referred to as the File Server I/O Processor or FSIOP for short. Currently the card acts as a LAN Server 3.0 file server. Support for Novell Netware is intended. The benefit of using this approach includes the potential availability of the disk drives on the AS400 (up to 128G per FSIOP).

What Have You Learned?

1. LAN Server is IBM's OS/2-based network operating system that groups file servers by domains.

2. LAN Server can be enhanced by adding Database Manager and Communications Manager.

3. Resources can be accessed by using their aliases.

4. IBM LAN Server/400 is effectively a file server operating inside an IBM AS400.

5. LAN Server is an excellent network operating system choice for a company where the network emphasis will be on LAN to mainframe communications.

Quiz for Chapter 11

1. LAN Server is a network operating system that runs under
   a. Windows NT
   b. PC-DOS
   c. OS/2
   d. UNIX

2. Requester/Server is IBM's term for
   a. peer-to-peer relationships
   b. client/server relationships
   c. master/slave relationships
   d. one-to-many relationships

3. Under LAN Server, a group of workstations and one or more servers comprise a
   a. domain
   b. subnet
   c. sub-domain
   d. area

4. A file server running LAN Server can be linked to an IBM mainframe using
   a. Micro-mainframe Link
   b. HostLink Manager
   c. Database Manager
   d. Communications Manager

5. A network administrator can treat a group of network servers as a single server because of LAN Server's
   a. global directory
   b. group directory
   c. location independence
   d. SQL compatibility

6. LAN Server's graphics-oriented user interface is consistent with
   a. SNA
   b. SAA
   c. FAA
   d. Token Ring Network

7. The Advanced Server package provides users with
   a. fault tolerance
   b. ODIC
   c. 486 High Performance File System
   d. UNIX compatibility

8. A Requester under LAN Server can be known by its
   a. nickname
   b. alias
   c. global name
   d. path

9. An alias is another word for a resource's
   a. nickname
   b. global name
   c. netname
   d. path

10. A network administrator can permit a user to add, modify, or delete users and groups by making this person
   a. a print operator
   b. a comm operator
   c. an accounts operator
   d. a fax operator

Banyan VINES

About This Chapter

In this chapter, you examine Banyan Systems' VINES network operating system. Designed for large enterprise-wide networks, VINES offers a preview of the next stage of network connectivity. Its transparent bridges and global directory (StreetTalk) make it a leader in internetwork connectivity.

An Overview of VINES

Banyan Systems' VIrtual NEtworking System (VINES, previously an acronym and now a trademark) is a network operating system based on a heavily modified version of UNIX. VINES places a premium on internetwork connectivity, security, and transparent operations. The company offers a number of add-on products, including electronic mail and network management software, which we discuss later in this chapter.

VINES supports a wide variety of hardware platforms including IBM's Token Ring, SMC ARCnet, Interlan Ethernet, 3Com's EtherLink and EtherLink Plus, and Proteon's ProNET-10. It requires a dedicated file server.

●
Banyan's software technology is a group of integrated services delivered consistently across multiple networks throughout an enterprise network.

All VINES services, including naming, file, printer, and mail, execute as UNIX processes. These services can be stopped and started from the server without disrupting other services. While computer industry experts have long extolled the multitasking and multi-user capabilities of UNIX, they have pointed out that its wide acceptance by the general public would be hindered by its lack of a user-friendly interface. Although the VINES user interface is menu-driven (as illustrated in Figure 12.1), and VINES is UNIX-based, a user must exit this network environment before being able to use UNIX.

FIGURE 12.1.
The VINES Menu.

```
VINES:  VIRTUAL NETWORKING SYSTEM




          1 - Mail
          2 - Catalog of StreetTalk Names
          3 - Printer Functions
          4 - File Sharing
          5 - Password Update
          6 - Communications with Other Computers



    Use arrow keys to highlight a choice and press ENTER.
    Press F1 for HELP.     Press ESC to exit this screen.
```

VINES version 6.0 provides support for clients running DOS, Windows, Windows 95, OS/2, Macintosh, and a variety of UNIX clients. A VINES 6.0 server can communicate with clients supporting the following protocols: VINES/IP, IPX, IP, AppleTalk, and NetBIOS.

●
The key to VINES' internetwork connectivity is its distributed database, StreetTalk, which provides a global directory for network communications.

StreetTalk

StreetTalk is VINES' distributed database, which serves as its resource-naming service. Resources can represent users, services (such as printers, file volumes, or gateways), and even lists. The StreetTalk name structure is threefold, with each part separated by the @ symbol.

object@group@organization

As an example, Frank Jones, an account executive in PolyTex General's Western regional office, might have a StreetTalk name such as the following:

FRANK JONES@SALES@WESTERN

Frank would be added to the VINES system via a screen similar to Figure 12.2.

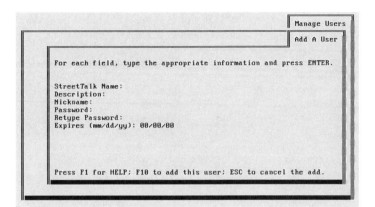

FIGURE 12.2.

Adding a user to Banyan VINES.

With StreetTalk and VINES, a user does not need to know pathways, or the location of users (or other resources). If Frank needs to send a message to Bill Taylor working in the Southwestern regional office, he needs only to know Bill Taylor's name. StreetTalk takes care of the mechanics of finding Taylor's node address and routing the material to him accurately.

To make matters even easier, StreetTalk permits the designation of aliases, or nicknames, for users. Figure 12.3 illustrates the screen a network manager uses for adding a user's nickname.

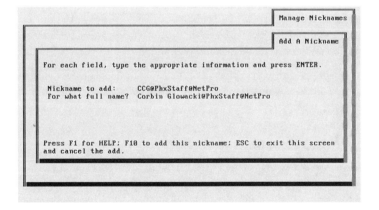

FIGURE 12.3.

Adding a user's nickname under VINES.

If Frank only knew Taylor by the nickname "BT," he could consult the StreetTalk catalog (using a screen similar to the one pictured in Figure 12.4) and find the name corresponding to BT.

Similarly, if Frank had proper access, he could request a file without knowing the directory or even the physical location of the file server that contains it. Frank could request BUDPROJ89, and let StreetTalk find and retrieve it, because each file server on a VINES network maintains a StreetTalk directory of all resources known to the network.

FIGURE 12.4.

A StreetTalk catalog.

```
What would you like to look at?


        Users              Nicknames
        File Volumes       Groups
        Printers           Organizations
        Lists              Servers
        EXIT this screen (ESC)  HELP (F1)



    Use arrow keys to highlight a choice and press Enter.

    ------------------------------------------------------------


    You are Frank K. Olsen@Sls@Polytex
```

Because of StreetTalk's global naming capability, the process is the same whether Frank needs to access an IBM mainframe in Arizona or an Ethernet network running VINES in New Jersey. The network operating system handles network addressing and communications with the mainframe (which runs SNA) or the Ethernet network (which uses an addressing scheme different from that used by Frank's Token Ring network). All this work is transparent to Frank, the end user. In each case, he simply selects (from a VINES menu) the name of the resource with which he wants to communicate.

Behind the scenes, the various VINES file servers communicate and exchange StreetTalk information, using what are called *outbound blasts*. These communications occur whenever a new server joins the network, when the administrator adds or deletes group or service information, and every 12 hours from the time the last server came online.

StreetTalk is a global directory service designed to handle multilingual organizations. Support is provided for six different languages and character sets: English, French, German, Spanish, Japanese, and Hangul.

StreetTalk Management

Banyan added several new management features with its StreetTalk III version. Network managers can re-name users and move groups across a network. This approach is vastly superior to the former method of deleting users and lists and then re-entering them with new names and profiles.

A StreetTalk Directory Assistance (STDA) feature functions as a replicated, advanced, easy-to-use, fast StreetTalk name lookup service comparable to an automated white and yellow pages directory. Users can search lists, printers, file services, and other services or nicknames by name, description, attributes, or patterns. Figure 12.5 shows an example of the STDA when using Mail to look up a recipient.

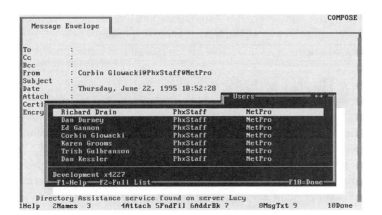

FIGURE 12.5.

Using StreetTalk Directory Assistance within Mail.

Banyan Systems has taken several VINES system level services including StreetTalk and incorporated them in its Enterprise Network Services for NetWare (ENS). This product enables Novell NetWare LANs to enjoy the single-login directory services enjoyed by VINES users. Because many companies have several LANs running different network operating systems, ENS offers network managers with LANs running both VINES and NetWare to manage these LANs using VINES superior system services.

Security Under VINES

VINES provides several different layers of security. A network administrator can require a password for login to the network. He or she can also specify the hours and days permitted for a particular user to log in to the network. VINES' version 3.0 and later contains security software known as VANGuard. The VANGuard menu is shown in Figure 12.6.

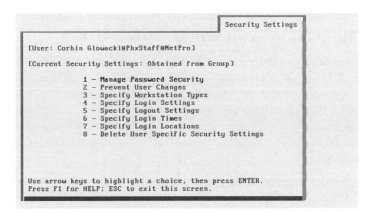

FIGURE 12.6.

VANGuard provides security for VINES.

VANGuard lets the administrator limit the number of simultaneous logins, set specific locations from which users must log in, and require users to change their logins at specified intervals. In addition, users' access can be restricted to a specific file server.

Under VINES, each user, service, and communications link has an access rights list (ARL), which specifies the users who are authorized to use it. The network administrator can establish the access rights to a file volume, but individual files cannot be restricted.

Printing Under VINES

Under VINES, printers linked to network PCs can be shared in the same way as printers attached directly to file servers. This eliminates the printer-to-server distance limitation and makes printer location a much more flexible operation. The network administrator determines which printers are available for which users by assigning a virtual connection for each print queue listed in a user profile. The SETPRINT program permits a user to look at jobs in any print queue, use a different print queue, or change printer settings. The Show Print Queue menu in Figure 12.7 illustrates how a user could hold or cancel a print job in a queue.

FIGURE 12.7.

The VINES Show Print Queue Menu.

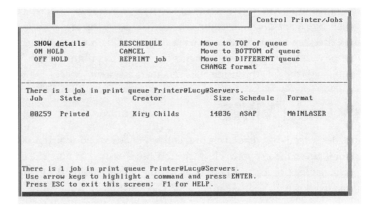

Communicating with Other VINES Users

For intranetwork communications, VINES includes two standard network packages, SEND and CHAT, and offers an optional electronic mail program. SEND is a command that enables a user to send a one-line message appearing at the bottom of another user's screen. To use this command, a user would type **SEND** and press Enter. Prompts request the message (enclosed in quotation marks), as well as the name of the recipient. By indicating ALL, a user can send a one-line message to all other users with LANs connected to the sender's server.

The CHAT program creates a window enabling a user to chat with up to four others at one time. The program opens conversation windows for each user. If you are chatting in a private conversation with another user, and a second user expresses a desire to chat, you can either add that user to the discussion or place the first user on hold. Since CHAT works on all VINES networks, five users at different locations can have a sustained "conversation" on a particular project very much like a conference call.

While VINES does come with an electronic mail package, Banyan's mail program known as Intelligent Messaging (IM) is available as an add-on. One major advantage of this program over others is that it uses the StreetTalk naming convention so that names and nicknames are consistent. It also features a store-and-forward approach that enables it to utilize high-speed links between servers. The VINES Mail program menu displayed in Figure 12.8 shows that it provides most basic mail services, including the ability to organize documents into appropriate folders and a text editor for composing.

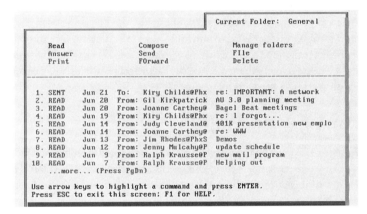

FIGURE 12.8.

The VINES Mail Menu.

Banyan offers a MacVINES Mail Gateway software option that provides communication between Macintosh and IBM microcomputers. VINES Network Mail, in conjunction with CE Software's QuickMail, provides the necessary DOS and Macintosh file conversions. VINES Network Mail includes the Listener and Bridge. The Listener runs as a service under VINES, and talks to the Bridge using AppleTalk protocols. Figure 12.9 illustrates how Macintosh computers and PCs can exchange mail on a VINES Ethernet backbone network.

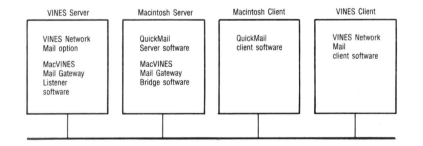

FIGURE 12.9.

Macintosh and IBM-Compatible PCs exchange mail on a VINES network.

VINES and OS/2

VINES (version 4.10 and later) supports OS/2 application programming interfaces (APIs), including APIs to named pipes and mail slots. Because named pipes support both DOS and Windows, workstations running DOS and Windows are able to access OS/2-based application servers (such as SQL Server). The addition of mail slots enables a DOS or OS/2 workstation to send information to any application on the network that communicates with others with mail slots.

In order for DOS and OS/2 workstations to share files on VINES version 3.x or higher, the OS/2 workstation must use DOS-compatible filenames. This means limiting filenames to an eight-character name and a three-character extension. Users with High Performance File System files must rename these files (before saving them to a VINES file server) to be consistent with the DOS file-naming scheme.

VINES and the Macintosh

The VINES option for the Macintosh supports an unlimited number of Macintosh clients across a Banyan network. A Macintosh workstation anywhere on a VINES network can access resources residing anywhere else on the network. The VINES Macintosh software is AppleTalk File Protocol (AFP)-compatible.

Macintosh users access VINES network services as though they were on an AppleShare server. They select VINES servers through the Chooser and access files on the server by double-clicking the mouse on the server icon. If VINES Mail for the Macintosh is added, Macintosh users can send e-mail across the network without the need for a separate Macintosh mailbox.

Macintosh users can send files to PostScript-compatible printers anywhere on a VINES network, even those connected directly to PCs. VINES for the Macintosh also includes built-in wide-area packet routing. (A *wide area network*, or *WAN*, links workstations located at sites covering a large geographic area.) This means that if a Macintosh user wants to send a packet to another user on a network running the TCP/IP protocol, the user's AppleTalk packets are encapsulated in Internet Protocol (IP) packets and sent over the links connecting the various VINES servers on the WAN.

VINES Gateways to Other Networks

The major strength of VINES is its ability to provide transparent access to network resources, regardless of where they are, or what protocol they happen to be using. Banyan's TCP/IP routing software enables a PC user to access TCP/IP resources whether they reside on a local network or a wide area network without worrying about these physical details.

As an example, VINES mail can be sent to SMTP mail users using the SMTP Mail Gateway option. VINES mail addresses are automatically converted into the standard SMTP format (user@host@domain) or UUCP-style address (host!host!host!user). The VINES' TCP/IP program encapsulates TCP/IP packets within VINES packets for travel across a VINES network. A server equipped with the TCP/IP routing option strips the VINES headers and sends the packets to an attached TCP/IP host or gateway.

Emulating an IBM 3274/6 cluster controller, the VINES 3270/SNA option supports up to 96 concurrent sessions per server with up to 32 sessions supported by a single communications link. The software permits up to four concurrent host sessions and one DOS session per PC. In addition to providing 3278/79 terminal emulation, the software permits host print jobs to be performed on local PC printers, file transfer, and APIs so that users can build DOS-based applications to communicate with SNA host applications.

Banyan also offers a VINES SNA Communications Server. This software includes 3270 terminal emulation features, NetView support, and up to 254 concurrent sessions. This server offers access to IBM Advanced Program-to-Program Communications (APPC) at both the desktop and server. This allows client/server applications to interact at the desktop, server, and host.

VINES and Symmetric Processing

A number of "super" file servers have been developed that use multiple processors. Multiple processors use either symmetric multiprocessor processing (SMP) or asymmetric multiprocessor processing (AMP). Under SMP, work is divided among processors on the basis of volume of work with each processor receiving an equal share. Under AMP, work is divided on the basis of job type. VINES (4.0 and later) offers support for SMP on servers such as Compaq's dual-processor SystemPro and AT&T's four-processor StarServer E.

●
VINES supports symmetric multiprocessing.

The VINES Applications Toolkit

The Banyan VINES Applications Toolkit is an advanced UNIX System V development environment for VINES, providing C language APIs for X.25, TCP/IP, and serial interfaces to support network communications. Several other features are noteworthy.

- The Toolkit provides access to VINES Socket Communications protocols, enabling developers to write media-transparent applications.

- A UNIX/DOS Bridge File Service enables DOS-based programs to share and interchange source code with the UNIX environment.

- A Network Compiler implements Remote Procedure Calls, which generate the code required for application-to-application communications.

VINES Network Management

Banyan offers network management software that provides LAN and LAN-interface statistics, as well as detailed information about servers, disk activity, and overall network performance. Designed as a network diagnostic tool, this software provides network administrators with information on file server cache size, percentage of cache hits, the number of times the file system was unavailable, and such "vital signs" of overall network performance as total messages sent and received, number of messages dropped, and the average amount of swapping. In addition, network administrators can view activities across multiple servers simultaneously.

Banyan offers the VINES Assistant for enhanced network management functions. This software enables a network manager to modify global network configurations, automate maintenance tasks, and monitor server capacity.

The VINES Assistant can perform historical performance analysis. Network managers can graphically view and analyze historical performance metrics as well as closely monitor server resources and performance.

VINES now supports IBM's NetView, enabling an IBM host running NetView to monitor a VINES network. VINES also supports the Simple Network Management Protocol (SNMP), which provides the "hooks" necessary to link with SNMP-based network management systems.

The VINES T-1 Server-to-Server Option

In addition to LAN support for leased-line, dial-up, X.25, SNA, TCP/IP, and ISDN server-to-server connections, Banyan also offers a T-1 Server-to-Server option. Users can take advantage of the full T-1 1.54 mbps bandwidth or alternatively use fractional T-1 in any increment desired. The major purpose of this option is to provide substantial bandwidth for large data applications shared between remote sites. Multiple data and voice transmissions can be merged on a single T-1 line. One major advantage of this option is that real-time T-1 statistics, network alarms, and alerts can be viewed on a VINES network management screen.

The VINES ISDN Server-to-Server Option

If ISDN is available, a company can connect its remote sites running VINES by using an ISDN link and Banyan's ISDN Server-to-Server option. This software runs on VINES software and an ISDN card, which resides in a server expansion slot. Users can access call management information via menus.

The Future for VINES

Banyan has a number of plans for VINES to run on additional platforms. The company plans to add UNIX and Windows NT client support, enhance VINES' e-mail capabilities, and provide new system-level services. It has already developed a Santa Cruz Operation UNIX version of VINES and has indicated development of software that will enable VINES users to exchange files with NetWare users. One system level service that could make VINES more interesting to managers of enterprise-wide networks is the ability to support large image and sound files.

In order for VINES to remain attractive to companies with enterprise-wide networks, the product's ability to facilitate communications with other communications platforms will be improved according to Banyan Systems. The company intends to enhance its Intelligent Messaging system to act as a server platform for messaging-enabled applications such as work-flow management. Intelligent Messaging will support Vendor Independent Messaging (VIM), Novell's Message Handling System (MHS), Microsoft Corporation's Mail application programming interface, and Apple's Open Collaborative Environment (OCE).

Banyan Systems also will add support of the CCITT X.400 and Simple Mail Transfer Protocol (SMTP) e-mail standards directly into its Intelligent Messaging system.

What Have You Learned?

1. VINES is a UNIX-based LAN operating system that runs on a wide range of hardware platforms.
2. StreetTalk is VINES' distributed database, which serves as its resource-naming service.
3. Enterprise Network Services (ENS) provides VINES' distributed database to NetWare users.
4. VINES provides effective gateways to TCP/IP networks and IBM networks.

Quiz for Chapter 12

1. VINES is based on
   a. AppleShare
   b. UNIX
   c. NetWare
   d. LAN Manager
2. The distributed database serving as VINES' resource-naming service is called
   a. Oracle
   b. SQL Server
   c. TownTalk
   d. StreetTalk
3. A VINES user can communicate with four other users simultaneously by using
   a. Mail
   b. Bulletin
   c. CHAT
   d. SEND
4. VANGuard provides VINES with
   a. security
   b. speech
   c. remote communications
   d. e-mail

5. Banyan does not provide VINES support for

   a. OS/2

   b. UNIX

   c. the Macintosh operating system

   d. MVS

6. The VINES Assistant provides

   a. security

   b. enhanced network management

   c. remote communications

   d. coffee, tea, and soft drinks

7. VINES can only run with a

   a. remote server

   b. local server

   c. shared server

   d. dedicated server

8. File servers under VINES communicate with each other and exchange StreetTalk information with each other using

   a. outcalls

   b. inservice calls

   c. outbound blasts

   d. FS calls

9. The StreetTalk structure consists of three parts, each separated by the symbol

   a. @

   b. !

   c. %

   d. #

10. VINES is available in all the following languages except

   a. French

   b. Italian

   c. Spanish

   d. Japanese

11. StreetTalk services are available for NetWare users with

   a. EDS

   b. SDS

   c. SNS

   d. ENS

IV

Putting It All Together

UNDERSTANDING

The Future of Networking

About This Chapter

How will networking change during the next few years? In this chapter, you examine a number of trends that are likely to dominate the networking industry. The need for more bandwidth is leading the industry toward transmission technologies such as Fast Ethernet and asynchronous transfer mode (ATM). Applications such as multimedia will require extensive bandwidth.

As networks become larger, more users will be dialing in from remote locations. Furthermore, an increasing number of users will have mobile computers and will use wireless network links. As companies link LANs throughout the country and world to form wide area networks, the integrated services digital network (ISDN) might finally find a receptive audience. All the outlined systems in this chapter are costly to install for the average network, but as prices reduce and new technology improves them, they will become the normal working infrastructure. Read on as you take a peek at a very exciting future for networking.

The Movement Toward Higher Bandwidth

Network applications continue to become more complex and include more use of video images. Furthermore, as companies migrate mainframe applications down to the network, these applications tend to be much larger. The result of these trends is a growing customer demand for greater network bandwidth with which to carry data associated with these applications.

When Ethernet was designed, its 10 mbps bandwidth and contention media access approach seemed more than adequate. Unfortunately, the *bursty traffic* that Ethernet has been designed to handle (short bursts of information exchange such as an inquiry and brief response) has been replaced by traffic that often is uniformly heavy on large LANs. While Token Ring topology was created as a non-contention network approach to handle heavy traffic, its maximum of 16 mbps bandwidth is already proving inadequate for some companies with larger, heavily used LANs.

Fiber Distributed Data Interface (FDDI)

Some companies have opted to prepare for the future by installing LANs with fiber distributed data interface (FDDI) that are able to provide 100 mbps bandwidth. This topology is discussed in Chapter 2.

FDDI has been accepted as a standard since 1990, yet high cost has meant that companies have not implemented it widely, preferring to use it only on their LAN backbones. The high cost of FDDI adapters has caused many companies to look at a twisted-pair wire alternative to FDDI: Copper Distributed Data Interface (CDDI).

There are a broad range of FDDI products currently available from a variety of vendors including Cisco, 3Com, Hewlett-Packard (HP) and DEC.

Copper Distributed Data Interface (CDDI)

Copper Distributed Data Interface (CDDI) is a network topology that is based on the FDDI standard and enables FDDI packets to be transmitted over twisted-pair wire. With a price per port under $995 and 100 mbps bandwidth, CDDI has attracted some interest. Unfortunately, though, many large companies have chosen to wait for a high bandwidth topology offering an even better price/performance ratio: fast Ethernet.

●
Fast Ethernet offers the promise of 100 mbps transmission using the traditional Ethernet frame format. Users will need new network interface cards and hubs but can retain existing cabling and software.

Fast Ethernet or 100Base-T

What makes fast Ethernet so appealing to many large companies is that users retain existing Ethernet software compatibility and, in many cases, are able to keep existing cabling. Only the network adapter cards and hubs must be modified. The idea of being able to increase network bandwidth from 10 mbps to 100 mbps with network adapter cards that likely are going to be priced under $400 is intriguing to network managers faced with increasing network traffic congestion. Fast Ethernet cards are now readily available, and this technology can be implemented. Because of the ease of transition from existing Ethernet to Fast Ethernet, this is an approach a lot of companies will take.

100VG-AnyLAN

The 100VG-AnyLAN networking technology is supported by AT&T, IBM, and HP. 100VG-AnyLAN is a logical system upgrade to both Ethernet and Token Ring. It is based on a star topology at both the physical and logical levels. It places intelligence in the central hub to provide network management. 100VG-AnyLAN products are already available from Hewlett-Packard.

Asynchronous Transfer Mode (ATM)

Asynchronous transfer mode (ATM) is already having an impact on local area networks. This cell-based transmission technology will have an even greater impact on both LANs and WANs in the near future. ATM, with its specifications developed by both the CCITT and by an ANSI committee, uses a cell-switching technology to achieve transmission speeds from 1.544 mbps to 1.2 gbps. A virtual circuit is established between network users, very much the same approach used by a telephone system. As much bandwidth as necessary can be allocated for these circuits through which ATM's cells are transmitted. Cells consist of 48 bytes of user information and a five-byte header.

> Asynchronous transfer mode (ATM) is a cell-based technology that can be used to gain transmission speeds of up to 1.2 gbps.

A major advantage of ATM is that because all cells are the same 53-byte size, network delays can be predicted so that this type of transmission can be used to carry real-time information such as voice and video. Because this is a switch-based technology, it is scaleable. Greater traffic can be handled by adding additional switches.

> ATM uses 53-byte cells. Because of the fixed cell size, network delays can be calculated and real-time video transmitted.

Another major advantage of ATM is that it is independent of upper-layer network protocols. A variety of protocols including FDDI can be used at the physical layer.

Figure 13.1 illustrates how routers could provide the connectivity from existing LANs to an ATM-based LAN. It is also possible to connect ATM directly to the desktop. In this example, the ATM switch is also connected directly to a high speed workstation.

What really appeals to many network managers, though, is the prospect of using ATM with a minimum transmission speed of 155 mbps as a common ground for a single, global infrastructure, as well as a high-speed backbone for enterprise networks. The advantage of using ATM on a LAN as well as on a WAN is that the interface between the two is seamless. A group of vendors known as the ATM Forum is working on a complete set of ATM specifications that will cover all key elements including the LAN/WAN interface.

Because ATM is still not well understood, let's take a few moments to examine ATM's cell structure. Figure 13.2 illustrates this structure. Some flow control information is followed by a Virtual Path Identifier (VPI) and Virtual Circuit Identifier (VCI). This information is used by ATM switches to route their cells efficiently. On a WAN, for example, there could be several different networks and/or ATM switches that could be part of the route that cells take to reach their destination.

FIGURE 13.1.
ATM-based LANs.

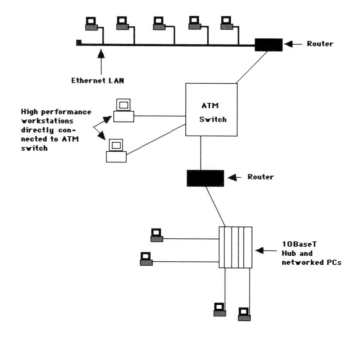

FIGURE 13.2.
ATM's cell structure.

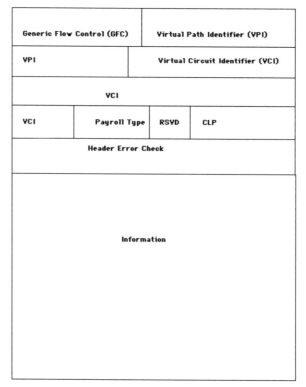

Multimedia and the Future LAN

True Multimedia on LANs is still in its infancy, but already industry experts are predicting that it will become a significant network application by the end of 1996. The hardware required for this technology is almost in place. Intel's Pentium chip and some of the new RISC chips offer the processing power to create and transmit video images over a LAN.

Multimedia on a LAN will probably use multimedia servers, servers optimized for this function. This means that these servers will have the most powerful processing chips available, fast-access high-capacity, storage devices including CD-ROMs and optical jukeboxes, and video compression chips. It is likely that fast Ethernet and ATM switches will be used to ensure that video information is transmitted rapidly enough so that it can be viewed by users in real time.

One way to glimpse what multimedia will look like on future LANs is to examine the LAN industry leader's vision of how this application will function under NetWare. Among the major uses of multimedia on the LAN envisioned by Novell are education, corporate training, kiosks with which to view information, video messaging, videoconferencing, and even cable TV-based information services.

To optimize transmission of multimedia information over a NetWare 4.1 LAN, Novell has announced enhancements to its network operating system including 64K block sizes, burst mode, and special NetWare multimedia directory services. Burst mode refers to Novell's method of sending several packets followed by an acknowledgment rather than requiring an acknowledgment every time a NetWare packet is transmitted over a network.

One very significant portion of Novell's multimedia strategy is the support for several different network client platforms including the Macintosh System 7.5 and Windows 3.1. Novell has developed network-loadable modules (NLMs) called NetWare Video that run on the server and optimize the disk and network I/O subsystems for use as a video server.

Until there is widespread acceptance of bandwidth over 100 mbps, the use of multimedia in everyday applications will not be a reality for most companies.

An interesting question to ask is, "When desktop video conferencing becomes widespread reality, what will happen to the telephone?". As soon as it is possible to call your family or friends via your home PC and see and discuss and interact with them no matter where they are, it would seem reasonable to suggest that the telephone will begin to seriously change functions. Similarly, when a PC can present video with the same audio and picture quality as the best Laserdisc players, video recorders, and movie theaters, what happens to the television? It will probably become a PC monitor with built-in dedicated PC for video. Downloading the latest blockbuster from the video store rather than going out in the rain will become a reality—and the store won't run out of copies!

The Growth of Remote Networks

A significant number of corporations have installed large local area networks at their head-quarters. Gradually, more and more branch offices are being equipped with smaller LANs. One of the major trends in networking is the growth of remote LANs. In order for a re-mote LAN to communicate efficiently with a LAN installed at the corporate headquar-ters, it needs a remote bridge or router and some kind of dial-up modem line or leased line, depending on the amount of traffic on the network.

The corporate LAN must be equipped with the appropriate dial-in communications soft-ware, and the remote LAN must also run communications software for users on the re-mote LAN to be able to have all the network benefits of local users on the corporate LAN.

Combinet has become one of the leaders in creating efficient dial-up LAN bridges between two LANs. This company offers a remote bridge that is able to use switched 56 (56 kbps dial-up service) when it is available. The bridge also can use the telephone companies' integrated services digital network (ISDN) when this 64 kbps transmission technology is available. Figure 13.3 shows a remote LAN bridge linking Ethernet LANs running at two different sites.

FIGURE 13.3

A remote bridge links Ethernet LANs running at two different sites.

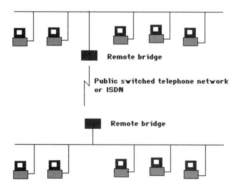

The two most common network protocols currently found on networks are NetWare's IPX and TCP/IP. Several network operating systems including IBM's LAN Server and Microsoft's LAN Manager utilize the NetBEUI transport protocol. Unlike IPX and TCP/IP, however, NetBEUI cannot be routed over interconnected LANs and wide area net-works.

A PC user communicating with a remote LAN using NetBEUI protocol must operate via a direct link that, in effect, is a bridged extension of the LAN. What this means is that a remote user with NetBEUI protocol cannot dial into a local LAN node and then be routed to a remote destination LAN via the network.

Wireless LANs and Mobile Computers

Today, wireless LAN technology is at a serious competitive disadvantage when competing against conventional LAN cable technology. The low price of cabled LANs, particularly Ethernet, has restricted wireless LANs to specific market niches. Companies with isolated reception, or warehouse buildings, for example, install wireless LANs in these areas and then bridge them to existing cabled LANs. Other current users of wireless technology include field auditors who move from location to location, and salespeople who need to become local users of their corporation LAN whenever they visit headquarters.

As the visual displays of mobile computers continue to improve, and the battery life increases, the convenience of these machines will encourage users to request them for their desktop computing. A standard interface for these computers, the PCMCIA (Personal Computer Memory Card International Association) specifications, has made it possible for vendors to introduce network interface cards using the PCMCIA credit card footprint.

Network operating system vendors including Novell and Microsoft currently are working on extensions to their directory services to make it easier for a mobile computer to become a network node via a wireless LAN connection. For example, drivers have been developed that enable two notebook computers with PCMCIA cards and Windows for Workgroups installed to communicate via wireless connections. Figure 13.4 illustrates how this process works. Proxim, a wireless LAN adapter vendor, already offers a PCMCIA card that includes its wireless LAN spread spectrum radio transmission technology.

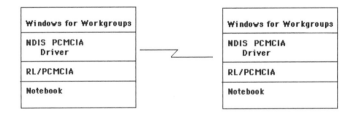

FIGURE 13.4.

Two notebooks with Windows for Workgroups communicate using wireless technology.

One possible result of the explosive growth of mobile computers is that these units eventually will include wireless LAN connectivity built-in, as well as having peer-to-peer LAN software installed in their firmware. This means that when these machines are turned on, they will immediately be ready to link to any other computers in the area that are similarly equipped. Artisoft, as an example, already has designed Ethernet chips that include the LANtastic network operating system.

ISDN and the Future Office

Study Group XVII of the CCITT worked four years (1980-1984) to develop a set of standards for future voice and data integration. Taking a broad view of future global telecommunications, the committee planned an architecture that would provide integrated access to circuit-switched and packet-switched networks, as well as end-to-end digital transport of data.

The resulting model—the Integrated Services Digital Network (ISDN)—represents a network of the future. It includes truly integrated voice, data, and even video, traveling smoothly (over the same pathways) from one type of network to another.

The ISDN concept of a universal interface means that each terminal will understand every other terminal. It will be possible to send information such as interactive videotex and facsimiles at the relatively high speed of 64K. ISDN standards define a digital interface divided into two types of channels: B channels for customer information (voice, data, and video) and D channels for sending signals and control information. These D channels utilize a packet-mode layered protocol based on the CCITT's X.25 standard.

The CCITT committee defined two major interfaces that use these B and D channels. The Basic Rate Interface (BRI) is used to serve devices with relatively small capacity such as terminals. A second interface, Primary Rate Interface (PRI), is used for large-capacity devices such as PBXs. Both interfaces utilize one D channel and several B channels, transmitting at 64K.

Because it can be used for a variety of data types, voice, video data, and so on, ISDN can be applied to a variety of applications. As Figure 13.5 shows, ISDN can be applied to many different computer applications scenarios.

FIGURE 13.5

The potential usage of ISDN.

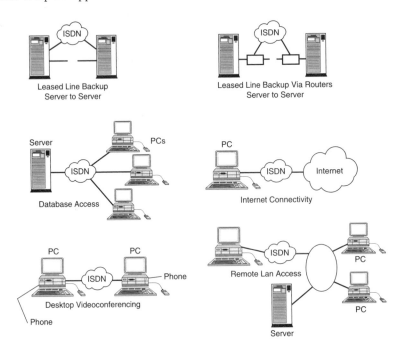

The Growth of Enterprise Networks

A trend that will continue for the next few years is the linking of one company's several different networks to form enterprise-wide networks. Many companies have realized that their computing environments consisted of several different isolated network islands. A mainframe might use PROFS for its electronic mail while handling the company's manufacturing computing. A Digital Equipment Corporation VAX minicomputer might be part of a DECnet network that handles the same company's accounting activities as well as its research and development computing tasks. Finally, the newest addition, a local area network, might link together that company's PCs and Macintosh computers to share productivity software such as word processing, spreadsheet, and database programs, while also sharing expensive laser printers. Finally, the engineering department might have several Sun workstations linked via Ethernet to share computer-aided engineering (CAE) and computer-aided design (CAD) files.

The network manager in the 1990s has been charged with creating a single enterprise-wide network of all these diverse computing elements. Every employee using such a network would have access to the resources available on any one of these previously isolated computing networks, assuming that this individual has the appropriate security. The access must be seamless, timely, and reliable.

As part of this enterprise-wide network, users can expect to see a more uniform graphical user interface regardless of hardware platform. Furthermore, the end user will eventually not need to even know what computing platform contains specific software. By clicking on an icon representing a specific business task, the user will call up an application regardless of where it is physically located. Similarly, many large databases will be dispersed on different servers that could be located in different cities. Once again, all the complex computing required to make these functions work will be invisible to end users. Mainframe programs can now appear on a user's PC screen looking identical to PC-based programs. No longer do network users need to be forced to learn how to use a keyboard that is functioning under mainframe or minicomputer terminal emulation mode.

Network Management Software

Today, there are several software programs available to manage networks, but there are several problems that remain. On enterprise networks, it is likely that a mainframe might be managed by a comprehensive network management program such as NetView. Hewlett-Packard minicomputers are likely to be managed by the company's OpenView program. In addition, there are dozens of programs currently available that utilize the Simple Network Management Protocol (SNMP) to receive information from network devices and report on their status.

While SNMP-based network management programs are very common in networks where UNIX is used, many managers have hesitated using this protocol to manage their PC LANs

●
Enterprise Network Management across multiple locations and multiple platforms is still in its infancy, yet it will develop quickly as companies pursue required structure management of their systems.

because it would add additional overhead to run a second protocol (TCP/IP) over a LAN that more than likely is already running NetWare's IPX protocol or LAN Manager's NetBEUI protocol.

Many current LAN management programs manage only a small portion of a network. Some programs manage PCs attached to a hub, for example, while other programs might only manage file server activity. It is sometimes necessary for network managers to run several different LAN management programs to provide comprehensive coverage. On an enterprise network, information from the LAN devices must still be integrated with information regarding the status of devices on minicomputers and mainframes.

Today, companies typically use a variety of products to manage their enterprise network. Yet increasingly there are a number of comprehensive network management programs that can track all types of LAN devices as well as integrate information from mainframe and minicomputers. Because networks are becoming increasingly more complex and larger, network management software continues to grow in popularity.

Here Comes UNIX!

For several years, some industry observers have been predicting that UNIX will gain popularity on PC-based LANs. UNIX does offer several advantages over current network operating systems. It offers symmetrical multiprocessing, meaning that several processors can divide up the processing load of a server. Microsoft's Windows NT offers this feature as does VINES, while NetWare still does not provide this feature. UNIX also offers built-in communications, a powerful script language, and program portability from one UNIX hardware platform to a second hardware platform. Perhaps equally important, UNIX was designed specifically for large networks and for providing security on such networks.

In 1993 Novell began shipping Unixware, a client/server operating system designed for seamless integration with NetWare. This NOS is able to run on Intel's 80386, 80486, and Pentium chips. Based on UNIX System V release 4.2, Unixware was designed to run UNIX applications on a NetWare LAN as well as share UNIX files with NetWare LAN users.

Historically, UNIX has failed to dominate the LAN NOS market because it required very fast processors and extensive memory resources, both of which were very expensive until recently. Also, UNIX is complex enough to require a very well-trained support person as well as users who have been trained it its basic commands. As Unixware illustrates, though, UNIX will grow in popularity on PC-based LANs because it now can overcome its heretofore most serious limitation, its reputation for being a very user-unfriendly environment. Unixware demonstrates that PC-based UNIX implementations will have a user-friendly, graphics-oriented interface very similar to Windows. More and more throughout the late 90s, LANs will also include UNIX servers as part of their structure, providing server resources to a variety of client workstations.

RISC-based Desktop Servers

While Intel-based machines have dominated PC-based LANs, a flurry of recent activity indicates that more reduced instruction computer (RISC) chips will be found on desktop LAN servers. These chips offer tremendous power at economical prices.

A recent trend is the development of native NetWare implementations on RISC chips. Hewlett-Packard's PA-RISC chip implementation of native NetWare offers very powerful, responsive performance because the chip's powerful processor does not have to use any of its resources to translate NetWare commands; these commands in native NetWare can be interpreted and processed very rapidly. The network industry will see an increasing number of RISC-based servers through the late 90s.

What Have You Learned?

1. Fast Ethernet is a network topology offering 100 mbps transmission speed while retaining its frame format compatibility with standard Ethernet.

2. Asynchronous transfer mode (ATM) is a 53-byte cell-based technology that can provide transmission speeds up to 1.2 gbps.

3. ATM offers the possibility of seamless interface between LANs and WANs using this technology.

4. Multimedia will become a major application on LANs, probably with the growth of ATM and fast Ethernet.

5. Remote access to LANs will continue to grow in popularity; faster links will become common.

6. Integrated services digital network (ISDN) will grow in importance as companies begin to use it to link branch offices to corporate headquarters.

7. UNIX will gain more popularity as a network operating system on desktop PC-based LAN servers.

Quiz for Chapter 13

1. Fast Ethernet has a maximum transmission speed of
   a. 10 mbps
   b. 25 mbps
   c. 50 mbps
   d. 100 mbps

2. Asynchronous transfer mode (ATM) transmits
   a. Ethernet-style packets.
   b. X.25 switched packets.
   c. 53 byte cells.
   d. very large frames for greater efficiency.

3. ATM can achieve a maximum speed of

    a. 100 mbps

    b. 500 mbps

    c. 1 gbps

    d. 1.2 gbps

4. Multimedia on LANs requires all of the following except

    a. compression chips.

    b. CD-ROMs.

    c. Windows.

    d. very fast microprocessors.

5. Burst mode refers to

    a. frames with too many bytes.

    b. packets routed over too many LANs.

    c. ATM cells.

    d. more efficient NetWare transmission.

6. Switched 56 refers to

    a. 56 users who switched from MCI to AT&T.

    b. leased data lines.

    c. dial up service at 56 kbps.

    d. lines that switch from leased to dial-up.

7. The NetBEUI protocol is

    a. not able to be routed.

    b. found on NetWare.

    c. found on UNIX.

    d. used in conjunction with AppleTalk.

8. PCMCIA refers to

    a. a labor union.

    b. a credit card sized NIC.

    c. PCs for the CIA.

    d. a network operating system.

9. D channels under ISDN carry

    a. customer information.

    b. data.

    c. signal and control information.

    d. fourth-priority information.

10. Under ISDN, small capacity devices are served by

    a. the Basic Rate Interface (BRI).

    b. the Primary Rate Interface (PRI).

    c. the Massive Rate Interface (MRI).

    d. the Transaction Rate Interface (TRI).

11. ISDN channels transmit at

    a. 220 kbps

    b. 1.544 mbps

    c. 56 kbps

    d. 64 kbps

12. The major protocol currently used for network management is

    a. CMIP

    b. IPX

    c. SNMP

    d. NetBEUI

Local Area Network Selection

About This Chapter

A company must make many decisions before purchasing a LAN. You examine how a company can do its initial needs analysis, factoring in company information needs, existing resources, and plans for future growth. While most companies will still need to meet with data communications and telecommunications consultants, such early analysis provides a basis for discussion. This prevents the consultants from selecting a system that may satisfy *their* needs, but does not solve the company's major problems.

In this chapter, you look at the steps necessary to develop a request for proposal (RFP) and follow-up procedures. You also consider the problems posed by multiple vendors, and by maintenance and training considerations for both hardware and software.

Solving Problems with LANs

When assessing their LAN needs, companies that already have data communication and telecommunication equipment generally ask this question first: "What problems do we have that might be solved if we implement a network?" When interviewing employees from several departments, you often hear similar problems described. These might include:

- Too much duplication of effort (several salespeople typing form letters, for example)

- Too much paperwork. (Why can't we eliminate most of the memos and use electronic mail?)

> Once problems are identified, the question to ask is, "Will a LAN help to solve these problems?"

● Loss of data integrity because people working on the same project need to swap disks frequently

● Mounting hardware and software expenses, because departments don't share resources but build "kingdoms"

● Inability to obtain data from other departments

● Security concerns over use of computerized information and no regular structured backup

● Growing hardware and line expenses for departments that need to use public information networks

Problems such as these suggest a need for a LAN. The next step is to inventory existing hardware and software resources, to determine whether they are compatible with a LAN solution.

The information gathered could result in a *request for proposals (RFP)*. By analyzing a company's current equipment, it is possible to determine what additional equipment is needed to enable the company to operate more efficiently—as well as what additional functions need to be performed. As you see later in this chapter, vendors reply to an RFP with specific lists of equipment and software to address the company's needs.

● Surveying your company's data communications and telecommunications capabilities can improve the flow of information.

Surveying Telecommunications Equipment

To learn the most effective way to improve the flow of information, companies need to survey their data communications and telecommunications equipment. In some small companies, for example, a survey might take one minute, and consist of looking around the office, to conclude that the company has a simple telephone system (four lines and eight telephones), and two IBM PS/2 workstations (used for word processing and accounting).

In larger companies—with much more equipment—the survey must be formalized, and an instrument developed to ensure standardized answers. Assuming the company has a PBX telephone system, some of the questions that should be asked include:

● Has a traffic study been done to determine peak periods of phone system usage?

● If the PBX were to be used for data as well as telecommunications, how much surplus capacity does the system have at present?

● Would some of the PBX functions—such as its call accounting system (which records each call, keeping track of the resulting expense) be cost-effective if the company's data communications were linked to these functions? In other words, if the company currently uses modems to transmit data over telephone lines, would it save money if these transactions could be tracked, and perhaps re-charged to the departments using these services?

● Is there significant interest in integrating voice and data communications? Is there a proportional need for it?

● If the PBX represents a possible LAN, is there any redundancy (backup hard-ware) built into this proposed switch? What happens if the PBX fails?

● Is a mainframe computer located at the same location? Is it feasible (or even desirable) for the microcomputers comprising a LAN to communicate with the mainframe computer through the PBX?

● What kinds of private networks must be accessed by the LAN? Do these net-works require speeds that are possible with a PBX?

● Does the company need to tie a number of asynchronous PC terminals to its synchronous mainframe? (Because a PBX is an excellent way of linking synchro-nous and asynchronous devices—and providing protocol conversion—a com-pany that already has a PBX should consider this question very carefully.)

● Perhaps the most critical question of all "What kind of information needs to be shared and transmitted through a network?" If the information consists of lengthy files, it might well be that the PBX isn't fast enough to accommodate the network.

Note: People are accustomed to a brief delay when accessing a computer, but they expect instant telephone response. It is necessary to estimate the degree of degradation that would result if telecommunications and data communications were combined. Because some older PBX systems require two dedicated data lines for a single voice terminal, it is essential to estimate the number of terminals (and lines) the company will need for the future.

In most cases, a PBX will prove inadequate to handle all data communications, because its speed cannot approach that of a dedicated computer system with data-grade cabling. Most major PBX companies (such as AT&T and Northern Telecom) offer LAN interfaces to their digital PBX systems. A company with a PBX might consider using it primarily for features such as modem pooling and automatic route selection while handling heavy data communication over a computer-based LAN.

Surveying Hardware and Software

Before investing in any new system, it is important to take inventory of any existing hard-ware and software that could be put to use on the LAN. The marketing department's in-ventory of current hardware and software might look like this:

1	IBM 750 with 16M of RAM
2	old IBM ATs with 640K of RAM and 40M hard drives
1	Compaq 486 with a 240M hard disk
1	Dell 486DX 33-MHz with 500M hard drive
1	HP Vectra 386 with a 120M hard drive
1	Hewlett-Packard LaserJet 4 printer
3	Epson LQ model 24-pin dot-matrix printers

The department currently uses a word processor, a spreadsheet, and a database manager program. Its list of present computer activity—as well as what it would like to be able to do in the future with a LAN—might look like this.

Lotus 1-2-3 worksheets for forecasting future sales

FoxPro customer list that everyone could access

FoxPro customer sales histories

WordPerfect sales form letter

Ability to merge form letters with customer lists

Ability to print sales contracts

Lotus 1-2-3 commission worksheets

Ability to access MRP manufacturing information (from mainframe)

Electronic mail

Remote ability to inquire on product availability

Ability to input an order on-line

Ability to track salespeople's phone expenses

Ability to switch salespeople to the least expensive long-distance carrier

Ability to share resources such as laser printer and dot-matrix printers

Ability to print envelopes as well as letters

Ability to track salespeople's performance and produce graphs available only to the salesperson involved

After having each department make a "wish list" that includes present activity as well as these future capabilities, you need to decide whether the present software can be networked. This assessment involves evaluating present capabilities and estimating what problems a LAN might pose.

For example, if the accounting department has a single-user program that cannot be upgraded to a network version with record locking, then a new program might be needed—and buying it might be prohibitively expensive. Even if the present accounting program uses ASCII data files, extensive programming would be needed to format this data so that it corresponds to a new program's field-and-record parameters.

The marketing department's desire to have remote access to the LAN is understandable. Salespeople would like to be able to view current inventory levels, and perhaps even place their orders over phone lines. If the company decides this capability is essential in its LAN implementation, it must include this requirement in its RFP.

Not all major LAN software can support remote entry. Even those networks that do may have their own requirements (such as a dedicated gateway workstation), and these can add to the expense.

The marketing department also expressed an interest in being able to access (or at least view) manufacturing data currently residing on a mainframe computer. Before deciding that a micro-mainframe network connection is desirable, the network administrator must determine whether or not this mainframe information is important enough to marketing's performance to justify its access.

A complementary question can be applied to the departments using the LAN. What programming would be necessary to download the information directly from the mainframe into one of the network's programs? Of the departments that will be linked by the LAN, which ones have sufficient reason to view mainframe information to warrant the security problems that could result from establishing the link?

A major concern in many companies is the variety of computer models within departments. Not all IBM-compatibles are actually compatible enough to use the same network adapter circuit cards, some may be Microchannel, others ISA, for example. As you will see shortly, the RFP needs to address this issue, and place the burden of proof on the network vendor to guarantee its network will work with all present equipment.

The Nature of Data Transmission

Before selecting the media and network hardware and software, you need to analyze the work that will be done on the network. We just saw what the marketing department has in mind, but we need to know how large the FoxPro customer lists and Lotus 1-2-3 worksheets are. Very large FoxPro file transfers consume valuable network time. The company may have to eliminate from consideration some of the slower LANs (1–2 mbps) in favor of a faster network (6–20 mbps).

Once this determination has been made, the company can look at related issues—such as geographic considerations and security requirements.

Geographic Considerations

Once a company has an idea of the software it plans for its network, and a clear picture of its present resources, the next step is to determine the geographic parameters of the network. Will the network encompass several departments, a single building, or multiple buildings? There are many different physical network topologies in use, and some of those topologies—such as a bus topology—are limited to short distances. A network adminis-

When contemplating installing a LAN, a company must consider what type of data will be transmitted and must address geographic and security concerns.

trator needs to look at the physical limitations of the various network media (cabling) when choosing cabling and physical network design.

If the LAN is to extend into other geographic locations—across the city, state, or country—the company must consider how it will link the networks in each office into a Wide Area Network (WAN). There are many unbounded media types to consider: microwave, laser, and satellite, for example. Likewise, there are also several types of bounded media open to consideration. One popular way to link local networks together into a WAN is a leased line (56kbps or T-1).

Media Selection

The network medium might be directly related to the company's geographic requirements. If the network will be installed in an environment where there is a good deal of interference, fiber optics might be required. If the building already has unshielded twisted-pair telephone wire installed, it might be cost-effective to determine whether a network could handle the data transmission requirements using this medium. If the company wants simultaneous voice and data transmission, then a medium capable of such transmission must be selected.

Security Considerations

LANs and network operating systems vary in the degree of security they offer. There are a variety of network management software programs—some based on Simple Network Management Protocol (SNMP)—to monitor network activity. There are also software programs that allow the network administrator to audit file and directory access (such as Auditware or Novell's Auditcon). Network operating system software such as Novell's Netware, for example, establishes several levels of network security beyond simple password protection. The network administrator has the ability to assign user access to files and directories by making trustee assignments for individual users and/or groups of users. These files and directories can be further secured with file system attributes such as Read Only and Shareable, for example.

It is also important to consider whether it is possible to change user access quickly. Novell's concept of user groups is beneficial in situations where people's assignments change frequently, requiring changes in network access.

There needs to be some concern for the security and integrity of data. What happens if a user turns off the workstation without properly closing his or her files? Sophisticated network software prevents files from being damaged in such situations.

Another security concern is the ease with which certain network topologies and media allow unauthorized entry (eavesdropping). Most of the copper-based network media are susceptible to eavesdropping because the electrical signals transmitted can be intercepted by special devices and then decoded by an intruder. The intruder then uses the intercepted information to breach the security of the network. Fiber-optic media offers the best protection against eavesdropping because this media type uses light spectrum, not electrically grounded signals to transmit information, making it immune to eavesdropping.

If security is a great concern, the network administrator should consider incorporating additional security measures in the RFP. One such measure is the purchase of terminal locks to protect unattended workstations from unauthorized entry.

Another safeguard is the use of callback modems. In this system, a remote user must provide a password which the network checks against its list of authorized passwords. If there is a match, the network hangs up and calls the remote user back using a telephone number that is stored next to the authorized password. This practice ensures that only authorized users can access sensitive network files, and—with the use of inexpensive WATS lines—offers substantial savings. Unhappily, not all networks permit this security measure.

Backing Up the File Server

The RFP should require a backup system so that the file server is backed up on a regular basis. Will backup software permit unattended backups? Can the network administrator flag certain files that will be backed up at specified intervals or whenever they change? Can files be restored easily if the version running on the file server is damaged?

The RFP should also require an *uninterruptible power source (UPS)* for the file server. If power is lost abruptly, the UPS (and appropriate software running on the file server) should shut down the file server properly, quickly, and efficiently, so that no open files are damaged.

Developing a Request for Proposals (RFP)

You have seen that a company must conduct a thorough needs analysis before it can begin the process of inviting vendor proposals. In the example, the company first determined which software was currently being used, and then which software it planned to use under network conditions. To ensure complete compatibility, the company also surveyed its present computer workstations and printers.

Because of the limitations inherent in many networks, the company also determined the maximum size of the network, the potential for expansion, and the type of information and size of files that it wanted to transmit over a network. It also examined the security measures it might want to require to ensure only authorized access. Now the company can develop a formal RFP.

●
A request for proposals to implement a LAN must solicit vendor information on network hardware, software, and applications programs.

In order to receive viable vendor proposals, we must provide information in a logical order. A basic outline follows for the heart of the RFP—to which we will add several important sections (with explanations) shortly.

When the company has gathered information for its RFP up to this point, it is in a better position to determine the extent to which the prospective LAN requires a networkable upgrade (or replacement) of existing software.

I. Hardware
    A. Microcomputers
        1. What is currently on hand (brand, configuration)?
        2. Additional workstations required.
            a. IBM compatibility?
            b. RAM requirements?
            c. Number of disk drives required:
                i. For security reasons, do you prefer no disk drives and a remote boot PROM chip?
                ii. If disk drives are required, what size and capacity (720K, 1.2M, 1.44M, 2.88M)?
            d. If a hard disk is required:
                i. Size (megabytes)
                ii. Mounted in what kind of microcomputer?
                iii. Formatted with which operating system and version?
            e. Monitors and monitor adapter cards required?
                i. Color or monochrome
                ii. Resolution capability
                iii. Size
                iv. Dual mode
                v. Graphics capabilities
                vi. Other features required
            f. Other I/O cards required?
                i. Parallel or serial cards and cables
                ii. Multifunction cards
                iii. Accelerator cards
                iv. Others
    B. File Servers
        1. Size required
        2. Processing speed
        3. Additional Specialized System fault tolerance (if required)
        4. Number of tape backup units
        5. Other features required
    C. Bridges to other networks
        1. Other networks to be connected
        2. Adapter cards and cabling required
        3. Software required

D. Backbone networks required to connect multiple bridges
   1. Description of bridges to be connected
   2. Processing speed required
E. Gateways to mini/mainframe environments
   1. Local or remote connections
   2. Protocols required
   3. Number of concurrent sessions required (licensed connections)
   4. Terminal emulation hardware or software required
   5. Local printer emulation required
   6. Amount of activity to be handled
F. Minicomputers
   1. Currently on hand (brand, configuration)
   2. Need to integrate information with LAN
G. Mainframe computer
   1. Currently installed (brand, configuration)
   2. Need to integrate information with LAN
H. Printers
   1. Currently on hand (brands, buffers, accessories)
   2. Additional printers needed
      a. Speed required
      b. Type (laser, dot-matrix, etc.)
      c. Availability of printer drivers?
      d. Connection type (parallel, serial)
      e. Distance from workstations
      f. Other special features
         i. Special language or downloadable fonts
         ii. Letter-quality and fast dot-matrix modes
         iii. Which workstations/areas will need to access which printers?
         iv. Any unusual printing requirements (color, multiple copy, specific accounting forms, etc.)?
         v. Do any software packages require a specific printer?
I. Modems
   1. Currently on hand (brand, speed, special features, etc.)
   2. Needs for additional units with the LAN
   3. Transmission mode required (simplex, half duplex, full duplex)
   4. Interconnections required (point-to-point, multiple drops)
   5. Special features needed
      a. Auto-dial
      b. Auto-logon
      c. Auto-dial-back-on-answer
      d. Other

    J. Plotters
        1. Presently on hand (brands, configuration)
        2. Additional units required
            a. Speed
            b. Number of colors
            c. Programs to drive plotters?
    K. Optical scanners
        1. Currently on hand
        2. Additional units required
            a. Speed
            b. Types of documents to be scanned.
            c. Which programs will need access to this data?
    L. Other hardware required
        1. Cash registers (for retail environment)
            a. Connection type (serial, parallel)
            b. Compatibility with which point-of-sale accounting program?
        2. Badge readers (for manufacturing environment)
            a. Will employees clock in and out of several jobs in the same day?
            b. Must this information be interfaced with an accounting program's payroll module?
        3. Multiplexers
            a. Devices to be attached
            b. Device location
            c. Type of transmission required
            d. Speed required
        4. Protocol converters
            a. Devices to be attached
            b. Protocols involved (SNA, IPX, BSC, ASCII, etc.)?
        5. Power protection required (UPS)
            a. Voltage regulation
            b. Limits sags, surges
            c. Prevents common-mode noise
            d. Provides battery backup
II. Software
    A. Operating system and utility programs
        1. Operating system
            a. Which system and version?
            b. Multiple versions on the network?
        2. Electronic mail
            a. Menu-driven
            b. Help screens available
            c. Display messages
            d. Distribution lists

  e. Message receipt notification

  f. Message forwarding

  g. Ability to define multiple user groups

  h. Ability to print and file messages

  i. Ability to attach files including graphics, sound and video?

  j. Other features desirable

 3. Network calendar

  a. All workstations may access calendar features

  b. Ability to schedule rooms and hardware resources

B. Network management

 1. Ability to perform diagnostics

 2. Ability to add and delete user groups

 3. Password protection

 4. Maintain user statistics

 5. Ability to handle remote dial-in users

 6. Ability to handle multiple operating systems

 7. Ability to handle bridges to other networks

 8. Ability to add and delete printers

 9. Security provided

  a. Log-in level (time, station, account restrictions)

  b. File System (directories and files; attributes)

  c. Printing system

 10. Menu-driven, but sophisticated users may bypass the menu and use commands

 11. Log-in scripts or other facilities (such as batch files) permitted to make it easier for novice users to log in

 12. Printer server software

  a. Number of printers supported by print server

  b. Print queues

   i. Storage location on the server

   ii. Multi-user/operator capable

   iii. User ability to control own print jobs

  c. Printer redirection commands available to network users

   i. For setting parameters of specific print jobs

   ii. For disabling network sharing of printers temporarily

  d. Printer types supported

   i. Parallel

   ii. Serial

   iii. Laser

   iv. Line printers

   v. Direct Network Attach

 13. File server software

  a. Size and number of volumes supported

  b. Network drives permitted (mapped drives)

           c. Virtual drives (transparent to users)

           d. Restore tape to disk capability

           e. Directory and file allocation tables duplicated for fault tolerance

           f. Directory and file allocation table caching for performance

  14. Network communications server software

        a. Protocols supported

           i. IPX

           ii. TCP/IP

           iii. SNA

           iv. AppleTalk

        b. Ability to handle call-back modems

        c. Automatic dial-out

        d. User statistics provided

  C. Current software that the network must support

    1. Word processing

    2. Spreadsheets

    3. Database management

    4. Accounting

    5. Other application software

Trying to Avoid Starting Over

It is possible a new LAN will not support a company's current software. Your request for proposals should detail which programs and the operating system platforms (WordPerfect for Windows, WordPerfect for Macintosh, for example) are currently being used. If the word processing program is cross-platform compatible, the network will allow easy exchange between the various OS platform data files. Many of the most popular programs (WordPerfect, for example) are network aware and can easily be installed to run in a multi-user, shared, network environment. Rather than selecting new software programs, you should try to select a network upgrade so that no additional training is necessary for this portion of network activity.

Accounting is a far more complex area. Some programs have networkable upgrades. A company fortunate enough to be using a single-user version of such a program can upgrade to a network version without having to worry about file transfers or training. In most cases, however, as you saw earlier, moving from a single-user accounting program to a network accounting program means starting over.

In such a case, the company probably will choose to run the single-user program until the fiscal year's accounting cycle is complete, while gradually adding more and more customer information to the network software. After running both programs concurrently for at least a couple of months (to ensure the accuracy of the new program), the company can switch to the new system.

Software Licenses

Virtually all software packages restrict their usage—sometimes to one user, and sometimes to one machine. The RFP should provide for site licensing (software licensing for the network site), or specify a network version licensed for a specific number of users. This consideration leads us to add another section to our RFP outline:

    D. New application software required
        1. Word processing
            a. Compatibility with current software
            b. Features required
            c. Training to be provided
        2. Spreadsheet/financial analysis
            a. Compatibility with current software
            b. Features required
            c. Training to be provided
        3. Database management
            a. Compatibility with current software
            b. Features required
            c. Training to be provided
        4. Accounting
            a. Compatibility with current software
            b. Features required
            c. Training to be provided
        5. Custom software required
            a. Compatibility with current software
            b. Features required
            c. Training to be provided

Vendor Requirements

In order to complete this outline of information in our RFP, we need to examine the relationship between the company and the prospective LAN vendors. A number of questions need to be asked of vendors before a network is purchased and installed. It is an excellent idea, for example, to require that a vendor demonstrate its network's ability to run the software your company plans to install. Often companies will require a "benchmark showdown" of sorts, in which competing vendors are asked to perform under similar conditions.

Even if a vendor's equipment is capable of providing a LAN that meets your company's speed and compatibility requirements at a reasonable cost, the equipment may not prove to be sufficiently reliable. As shown in our outline for an RFP, it is imperative to request references to vendors' customers with installations similar to the one you are considering.

It is also essential to secure information about the equipment's reliability—including a mean time between failures (MTBF), maintenance contracts, and service response time.

Frequently network vendors will offer a variety of maintenance options—including a guaranteed response time, a repair-or-replace designation, or even a guarantee to provide a "loaner" file server if the vendor is unable to repair the network within a given length of time. Before issuing an RFP, your company must determine how long it can afford to be without network services—and then require vendors to meet a response-time requirement that suits your needs.

Because a LAN includes computer hardware, network hardware and software, and third-party software, it is possible for vendors will pass the buck, and not accept responsibility when a network problem arises. Part of the RFP should require the principal vendor to take overall responsibility for the network's maintenance. If a software problem suddenly develops, for example, the principal vendor should act as a liaison with the software company to solve your problem.

The possibility exists, unfortunately, that none of the vendors have practical installation experience with the precise network configuration your company requires. At that point, you may offer to serve as a beta site for the vendor (and perhaps the manufacturer). A beta-site user tests the new product in a real-world work environment. By beta testing software and hardware, you will be helping the vendor/manufacturer discover problems before the products are released into the market. You may also be able to form special relationships with both your vendor and the product manufacturers that may allow you to assist in development of future products. Usually, in exchange for the experience you provide the vendor by serving as a beta site (and the referral you may later provide), you may be offered a substantial discount in price.

Your company might want to insist on other safeguards as well. These can include a performance bond to be posted by the vendor, and a payment schedule phased to correspond to the completion level of the network (including software and hardware).

Your safeguards should be linked to the minimum level of performance you specify in your RFP. If you fear serious degradation in response time with heavy activity, you might require a minimum response time for each of a certain number of workstations when all are involved simultaneously in a certain procedure. Several major network software companies (including Novell and 3Com) make benchmark test reports available; these provide excellent "tests" that you can require your vendors to duplicate.

Because LANs' topology and media have a direct effect on their maximum distance, be sure the RFP includes a diagram indicating where workstations will be placed and their approximate distances from each other. Also—and this is essential—indicate where future growth will take place, and whether these future workstations will require additional file servers and other peripherals.

III. Vendor Requirements
    A. Experience
        1. Company history: how long in business?
        2. Customer references from similar installations?
    B. Service
        1. Number of factory-trained service technicians
        2. Ability to provide on-site service:
            a. Repair-or-replace service within 24 hours?
            b. Offers 7-day, 24-hour support options?
            c. Ability to respond within 2–4 hours?
            d. Maintains a sufficient inventory of parts to provide adequate service?
    C. Ability to provide a LAN demonstration
        1. Software to be identical with ordered software
        2. Hardware to be identical with ordered hardware
        3. Benchmark tests to be conducted
    D. Training
        1. Can the vendor provide basic user training?
        2. Can the vendor provide training on all purchased software? Or do they offer recommendations for other training sources?
        3. How much training is provided with installation?
        4. What is the charge for additional training?
        5. Is phone support included in purchase price?
        6. What kind of training should the network administrator receive? How many people should take this training?
    E. If multiple vendors are required for this network, who will assume responsibility for:
        1. Hardware training and network familiarization?
        2. Hardware service?
        3. Software training?
        4. Software service?

Evaluating an RFP

Evaluating an RFP is not difficult—assuming that all key decision makers within a company agree on the criteria to be used for evaluation and (most importantly) agree on the weight each item in the evaluation should have. Table 14.1 shows sample list of criteria, and the weight associated with each one, for a company issuing an RFP.

Table 14.1. Sample criteria list and suggested weight.

Evaluation	Item	Weight (%)
1.	Cost (hardware & software)	20
2.	Quality of hardware & software	10
3.	Database management system	10
4.	Accounting software	10
5.	Productivity software	5
6.	Flexibility of report generation	12
7.	Response time	5
8.	Vendor hardware/software support	10
9.	Rapid implementation by required date	8
10.	Previous implementation record	5
11.	Company's references & stability	5
		100%

What Have You Learned?

1. The first step in developing an RFP is to analyze the company's needs.
2. The geography of a company's proposed LAN determines what kind of network topology and media are feasible.
3. In order to ensure network security, some network workstations use remote boot PROM chips, and do not have any floppy disk drives.
4. Most software generally is licensed for one user. Network applications require special network versions (designated for a certain number of users) or software site licensing.
5. A beta-site user tests a product under real-world conditions.
6. Vendors need to be evaluated on far more criteria than just the price they charge for equipment and services.

Quiz for Chapter 14

1. The first step in an analysis of a company's LAN needs is to

    a. examine the problems that currently exist that could be solved with a LAN.

    b. inventory all current software.

    c. inventory all current computer hardware.

    d. write a request for proposal (RFP).

2. The variety of microcomputers found in most companies creates a potential LAN problem because of

    a. different costs for different components.

    b. service needs.

    c. incompatibility of hardware and software.

    d. different disk drive speed.

3. If a needs analysis reveals that several programs on the network will include large databases, this could mean

    a. you will need a disk server rather than a file server.

    b. problems may occur with file server disk access speed.

    c. the database software had better be able to handle long field names.

    d. the operating system cannot be DOS.

4. The geography of the company's building (including where it will need workstations) has a direct effect on

    a. the network topology

    b. the network's medium

    c. the network's cost

    d. all of the above

5. For security purposes, a network workstation might include

    a. a lock

    b. a remote boot PROM

    c. no disk drives

    d. all of the above

6. In order to have the entire network use a specific software program, the company must obtain permission from the software company. This is known as

    a. site licensing.

    b. software permission.

    c. multiple network copies (MNC).

    d. workstation access to software help (WASH).

7. The major problem with multiple vendors in a network environment is

    a. the expense.

    b. the lack of quality.

    c. the lack of clear responsibility.

    d. network efficiency.

8. Once company officials agree on RFP criteria, these criteria should be

    a. changed.

    b. kept secret.

    c. suggestions that the vendors can change.

    d. weighted.

9. In case of a power failure, the RFP should require a(n)

    a. UPS

    b. SQL

    c. XCOM

    d. Kermit

10. In order to be able to restore damaged files, the RFP should provide for a(n)

    a. file server backup software program.

    b. UPS.

    c. asynchronous communications server.

    d. modem.

Supporting a LAN

About This Chapter

Once a LAN is implemented, there are regular steps that can be taken to ensure that it is always operating effectively and downtime is kept to a minimum. In this chapter you learn about establishing a support routine that keeps your LAN in a healthy state.

All of these items may seem trivial, but they can save valuable time when implemented.

Preventative Maintenance

Just as through life you should take regular care of your body, a LAN needs regular care to make sure that it operates smoothly and efficiently.

Preventative maintenance is a suite of activities done over a period of time that ensure that your LAN gives you, the Network Manager, a minimum of problems. These activities are best arranged on a weekly, monthly, quarterly, and yearly basis. You should feel free to modify the timeliness of these activities to your own, or company's needs, adding or modifying the list as you deem appropriate.

Weekly Maintenance

The weekly maintenance activities include daily and weekly backup, as well as housekeeping.

●
Daily and weekly
backup and
housekeeping are
weekly support
activities.

Daily and Weekly Backup

Each day a backup of the system should be done using the media that you have. The backup does not need to be a full backup, but should at least be an incremental backup of files that have changed since the previous day. Nearly all backup systems allow you to make an incremental backup. Avoid those systems that don't.

At least once during the week make a full system backup including the network operating system and its file areas. Always make sure that you use high quality tape or disk media, because too often companies find that using cheap tape or disk may result in an inability to restore at a later date.

It is good practice to cycle tapes or disks over at least a three week duration. This is normally called *Grandfather-Father-Son* data storage, and allows you to have several complete backup sets in case any one should fail. Also, if possible, try to store at least one set of backups offsite. This means that should a small fire or problem occur you can recover the majority of your data.

Always test the backup you have made by using your backup software's compare feature. This ensures that you can restore at a later date. Too many restores fail because the data was backed up but the backup was not tested.

Housekeeping

Housekeeping entails spending time on the network making sure that standards are adhered to and available files are being regularly accessed. A file server can quickly become a "dumping ground" for users' temporary data. If such an area is required, make one available, but let all the users know that the files in the area will be deleted at the end of each week. It is not good practice to have huge data areas filled with files that people either don't know what they are or won't admit to what they are!

Try to keep a consistent naming standard for user names, network addresses, and configuration. This leads to time-saving when problems occur. System management is considerably easier when you have a good knowledge of the standards in place.

To improve housekeeping, some simple steps can be followed to help. Try to restrict user access to only the areas that they need. This keeps the files that he or she uses in the correct locations. Try to audit files so that when data areas get large you can see which files belong to whom and therefore have a contact name to see if they are still required. Finally, make it policy to back up and archive off the file server data files (not application files) that are older than two years and have not been accessed within that time.

Monthly Maintenance

Monthly maintenance can be broken down into the following areas:

Virus Scanning

It would be a perfect world if there was absolutely zero risk of viruses infecting your network and potentially damaging your data. Regretfully, users may deliberately, or more often, inadvertently, bring a virus in to the company. Some simple steps can significantly reduce the chances of this.

Aim to have all floppy disks scanned before they are used in the company. You should invest in a virus scanning tool such as McAfee's Scan Virus, Norton Anti-Virus Toolkit or Dr. Solomon's Anti-Virus Toolkit. All of these products are regularly updated and can deal with most types of virus. The file server should be scanned at least monthly. Be careful, however, because some virus scanning software can slow network performance if run all the time on a file server. Check with the appropriate vendor prior to purchase.

Purging Novell's Hotfix Area

On a monthly basis you should run the Novell Purge Utility on your file server if you are running Novell. This removes salvageable files from the deleted file listings.

Peer-To-Peer Hard Disks

Main machines that are shared in a peer-to-peer network should have the hard disks checked monthly. This involves running the scandisk and defrag utilities under MS-DOS for example. This has the effect of rebuilding and correcting any errors in the file allocation tables of these machines and also writing the data files sequentially. This keeps the disk organization correct and reduces disk I/O on these machines.

Quarterly Activities

Quarterly activities can be broken down into the following areas:

Cabling

Cabling has an uncanny ability to come free of its connector or socket. It's also probably fair to say that the majority of networking problems are attributable to cabling.

Each quarter, examine your cabling connectors and cabling for loose connections and wear and tear. It is advisable to replace worn or damaged cabling. Where possible, make sure that cabling is firmly screwed into position but not too tightly that you need Arnold Schwarzenegger's arms to remove it again!

Powering Hardware

Most modern file server equipment is designed to run and operate 24 hours a day. It rarely gets switched off. It is a good policy to power off server systems in a controlled manner once a quarter. This allows the diagnostic routines in the machine to run when it is switched back on. These routines can often identify problem areas in a machine before that area fails (often during a very critical time in the working month!).

Hence, any problem can usually be fixed in a controlled manner rather than the panic state that often comes about when a LAN crashes.

Fixes and Patches

Once a quarter, discuss with your LAN vendor what patches and fixes have been brought out for the particular network operating system that you are running. Obtain a copy of these patches, and see if they improve or correct any difficulties that you may be experiencing. You should apply any patches in a controlled manner, and it is advisable to test them on a test machine first *before* updating large numbers of users.

Obtaining updated patches and fixes to operating systems has proved to be valuable, particularly when the LAN is connecting to a midrange or mainframe computer.

CompuServe and the Internet are valuable information networks for this type of information and are also very useful as support tools.

Yearly Maintenance

Yearly maintenance can be broken down into the following areas:

Hardware Maintenance

Physical hardware maintenance contracts are usually reviewed annually. These contracts are for you to have a backup plan if the PC's in your company, including the file server, fail. Usually, you pay a fixed price contract for the year to a 3rd party maintenance company who guarantees repair or replacement of a particular machine within a contracted period. The period of time can vary significantly depending on:

- The equipment to be repaired
- The physical location of the equipment
- The contract

Most companies settle for a next-day fix on LAN workstations and a four-hour fix on LAN servers. This means that the maintenance company will arrive and fix the server within four hours. It is very important in any contract situation that you make sure that the maintenance company has the correct parts for your server in the event of failure. It is one thing to have your 4GB NT Server on a maintenance contract but a real problem if the maintenance company can only fit 1GB hard drives. Verify that any 3rd party support staff is authorized by the server vendor to repair the failed hardware. This gives you some degree of comfort that the support engineer knows what he or she is doing to the machine holding all your corporate data (which you backed up.......didn't you?).

Network Operating System Support Contract

In addition to a hardware maintenance contract, it can prove valuable to take out a Network Operating System Support Contract. This is usually placed with the vendor of the NOS or a recognized support vendor. Typically, this is an annual contract providing you with regular monthly updates, patches, fixes, press releases, unlimited telephone support for a few designated individuals, and sometimes a number of visits from the support vendor to audit (check) your LAN environment. This type of contract can usually be extended to provide support cover and additional resources from the support vendor if needed.

Server Hardware

At least once a year, have the server hardware checked by removing memory and adapter cards, removing dust inside the machine, and reseating all adapters and memory. Do not attempt to do this if you are not authorized to repair the machine. Your hardware maintenance company will usually do it for a nominal fee. This gives your servers a proverbial "spring cleaning."

And Finally...

Once you have your LAN implemented, you should remember these six things:

- LANs are as necessary as death and taxes
- LANs never go away once implemented
- LANs require more investment in computers, not less
- LANs always grow, not shrink
- A LANs capability is determined by its weakest link
- No LAN is an isLANd; someday you will connect it to someone or something else

What Have You Learned?

1. Backups should be made daily and weekly and should be tested regularly.
2. Naming standards can ease security and housekeeping.
3. Virus scanning at regular intervals significantly reduces the potential for damage to data.
4. Cabling should be examined for wear and tear quarterly.
5. Switch off servers periodically in a controlled manner so that the server diagnostic routines can check the machine when it is powered on again.

Quiz for Chapter 15

1. Backup of a network should be done at least

    a. quarterly and yearly

    b. every Christmas

    c. daily, incremental, and weekly full

    d. every three weeks

2. Setting standards for _____ can aid troubleshooting, problem determination, and fault diagnosis.

    a. user names

    b. workstation configuration

    c. network addresses

    d. all of the above

3. Switching file server machines off, and then on allows

    a. the file server hardware diagnostic routines to run and check the machine.

    b. the coffee machine to cool down.

    c. the network to take a well earned break.

    d. the file server to re-engage its hard disk drives.

4. For maintenance support, it is valuable to have 3rd party support contracts for

    a. hardware.

    b. the network operating system software.

    c. hardware and the network operating system software.

    d. fixes and patches.

Appendixes

Directory of Vendors

Apple Computer, Inc.
20525 Mariani Avenue
Cupertino, California 95014

Artisoft, Inc.
575 East River Road
Tucson, Arizona 85704

AT&T Information Systems
1 Speedway Avenue
Morristown, New Jersey 07960

Banyan Systems, Inc.
135 Flanders Road
Westboro, Massachusetts 01581

Datapoint Corporation
9725 Datapoint Drive
San Antonio, Texas 78784

DCA (Digital Communications Associates, Inc.)
1000 Aldermann Drive
Alpharetta, Georgia 30201

IBM (International Business Machines Corporation)
Post Office Box 1328
Boca Raton, Florida 33429-1328

IEEE (Institute of Electrical and Electronics Engineers, Inc.)*
10662 Los Vaqueros Circle
Los Alamitos, California 90720

Microsoft Corporation
One Microsoft Way
Redmond, Washington
98052-6399

Novell, Inc.
122 East 1700 South
Provo, Utah 84601

*Source of information on
IEEE standards

UNDERSTANDING

Glossary

10Base-T: A new IEEE standard for a 10 mbs twisted-pair transmission network.

Access control list groups (ACL): Under LANtastic, groups of users can be assigned the same network access rights.

Active token monitor: The workstation that assumes responsibility for network management in IBM's Token Ring Network.

Apple File Protocol: The suite of protocols associated with Apple's local area network.

AppleShare: Apple's file server software for its local area networks.

Application layer: The layer of the OSI model concerned with application programs such as electronic mail, database managers, and file server software.

ARCnet: A local area network featuring a physical bus and logical star.

ARM: Asynchronous Response Mode. Stations send messages whenever they desire to transmit, without waiting for a poll bit.

ASCII: American Standard Code for Information Interchange. A character code used by microcomputers.

Asynchronous communications server: Provides the capability for network workstations to access ASCII applications via switched communications lines.

Asynchronous Transfer Mode (ATM): A 53-byte switching cell topology that can achieve transmission speeds of 150 mbps to 1 gbps.

Automatic rollback: Under TTS, when a system fails, the database is reconstructed at the point just prior to the transaction during which the failure took place.

Backbone: A high-speed link joining together several network bridges.

Background tasks: The tasks performed by other network users under PC Network.

Baseband: Single-channel, coaxial cable.

Batch file: A file containing commands that can cause several different programs to execute automatically.

Beacon: A special network signal indicating the address of a node immediately upstream from a defective node.

BIOS: Basic Input/Output System. ROM software.

Bit stuffing: The insertion of a 0-bit to ensure that no data contains more than five straight zeros.

BRI: Basic Rate Interface. Under ISDN, used to service small-capacity devices such as terminals.

Bridge: A connection between two networks that takes place at the Data Link layer.

Broadband: Coaxial cable capable of carrying several signals simultaneously on different channels.

Broadcast messages: Messages sent to all computers on a network.

BSC: Binary Synchronous Communication. A synchronous protocol used on many older IBM mainframe computers.

Bus: A data highway. This term is also used to designate a simple linear-shaped local area network.

Call-back modem: Modems designed to call back a remote caller to verify identity for security purposes.

CCITT: Consultative Committee for International Telephony and Telegraphy.

CCITT X.3: Protocol for the packet assembly/disassembly facility in a public data network.

CCITT X.25: A standard for data packets sent to public switched networks. This standard corresponds to the OSI model's first three layers.

CCITT X.28: Protocol governing the interface between a DTE and a DCE, when a DTE in start-stop mode accesses the packet assembly/disassembly facility (PAD) on a public data network situated in the same country.

CCITT X.75: Protocol governing control procedures for terminals, transmitted calls, and the data transfer system on international circuits between packet-switched networks.

CCITT X.400: A set of protocols governing electronic mail.

CCITT X.500: A set of protocols governing worldwide directories for electronic mail.

Centralized file server: A single file server that serves a local area network.

Cladding: A layer of glass that surrounds optic fibers in fiber-optic cables.

Client/Server: A type of network relationship in which a node runs "front-end" (client) software to access the software running on a "server."

Contention network: Workstations competing for the right to send a message over the network.

Copper Distributed Data Interface (CDDI): A network topology that is a twisted-pair wire version of fiber distributed data interface (FDDI) and can achieve transmission speeds of 100 mbps.

CSMA/CD: Carrier Sense Multiple Access with Collision Detection. A method of avoiding data collisions on a local area network.

Data Encryption Standard (DES): A government-sponsored standard for encrypting data to protect it from those with no legitimate rights to view it.

DCE: Data Communication Equipment. Generally refers to modems.

Dedicated file server: A file server that performs only that function, and performs no computing functions.

Directory hashing: File server software that maps all directory files and keeps this information in RAM.

Disk caching: File server keeps often-requested files in RAM for rapid response in workstation requests.

Disk server: A hard disk used to share files with several users. Usually programs are single-user (only one user may use them at a time).

Distributed file serving: Distributed data processing to several computers rather than one central computer.

Domain controller: A file server controlling security for a set of resources under the Extended Services option of the IBM PC LAN Program.

DTE: Data Terminal Equipment. Generally consists of terminals or computers.

Duplexed drives: A system fault tolerance technique in which virtually all hardware is duplicated, including disk controller, interface, and power supply.

EBCDIC: The Extended Binary Coded Decimal Interchange Code. A character code used by IBM's larger computers.

Elevator seeking: A file server determines in which order to execute file requests, based on the current location of the disk drive heads.

EtherTalk: A protocol that permits AppleTalk protocols to run over Ethernet networks.

Fast Ethernet: A version of Ethernet that can achieve transmission speeds of 100 mbps.

FAT: File Allocation Table. A table that helps a disk server or file server keep track of where particular files are located.

FDDI: The Fiber Data Distributed Interface of fiber-optic cabling. A standard for 100 mbs network transmission speed.

File locking: Software that locks a file so that only one user may use it at a time.

File server: A PC that maintains its own FAT and provides files to nodes.

Foreground task: A task a user performs on his or her own machine while using IBM PC LAN Program.

FSK: Frequency Shift Keying. A technique of shifting between two close frequencies to modulate ones and zeroes and speed up transmission.

Gateway PC: A PC containing gateway hardware and software, used as a LAN gateway to another machine (often a mainframe computer).

Headend: That portion of a broadband network that serves as the communications center for transmission and reception of signals.

HDLC: High-Level Data Link Control procedures. This protocol defines standards for linking a DTE and a DCE.

IEEE: The Institute of Electrical and Electronics Engineers.

IEEE 802.3: The industry standard for a bus local area network using CSMA/CD.

IEEE 802.4: The industry standard for a token bus local area network.

IEEE 802.5: The industry standard for a token ring local area network.

IEEE 802.6: The industry standard for metropolitan area networks.

Inbound band: Carries data from a LAN node to the headend.

Intelligent hub: A wiring hub that can be managed by network management protocols such as Simple Network Management Protocol (SNMP).

ISDN: Integrated Services Digital Network. A CCITT model for the eventual integration of voice and data and a universal interface for networks.

ISN: Information Systems Network. AT&T's high-speed network that features integrated voice and data transmission.

ISO: International Standards Organization.

Jam: A signal sent through a network to indicate a data collision has occurred.

LAN Manager: A network operating system under OS/2.

LLC: The Logical Link sublayer of the OSI model's Data Link layer.

Local printer: A printer attached to a microcomputer that prints this computer's documents only, and performs no network printing functions.

LocalTalk: The hardware associated with Apple's local area network.

Login Script: A predetermined set of steps performed to customize a network environment whenever a user logs in.

LU: Logical Units. These can represent end users, application programs, or other devices. Communication under SNA is among LUs.

LU 6.2: A protocol that makes it possible to have peer-to-peer communications under SNA.

MAC: The Media Access Control sublayer of the OSI model's Data Link layer.

Mirrored drives: Two hard drives onto which data is simultaneously written.

MSAU: Multistation Access Unit. A wiring concentrator linking several network workstations to an IBM Token Ring Network.

MTBF: Mean Time Between Failures. A standard used to evaluate a product's reliability.

Multimode fiber: Fiber-optic cabling consisting of several fibers.

NAK: A Negative AcKnowledgement signal.

NAU: Network Addressable Unit. Under SNA, logical units, physical units, and system services control points.

Network adapter card: Circuit card required in the expansion bus of a workstation under most popular LAN operating systems. This is also known as a network interface card (NIC).

Network layer: The layer of the OSI LAN model that establishes protocols for packets, message priorities, and network traffic control.

Node: An individual workstation on a local area network. Generally includes a monitor, keyboard, and its own microprocessor, as well as a network interface card. It may or may not have its own disk drives.

Nondedicated file server: A file server that also functions as an independent microcomputer.

NRM: Normal Response Mode. When a central computer receives a message that a station wishes to send, it sends a poll bit to the requesting station.

Online uninterruptible power supply: An uninterruptible power supply that remains on even when electrical power is available and filters this power while ready to provide battery power should the electrical power fail.

Open Collaboration Environment (OCE): An environment for Apple Macintosh computers that enables programmers to use application programming interfaces (APIs) so that programs can function in a workgroup environment.

OSI Model: Open Systems Interconnection protocols for establishing a local area network.

Outbound band: Carries data from the headend to the LAN nodes.

Partitioning: Dividing a hard disk into several user volumes or areas.

Path control network: Responsible under SNA for identifying addresses of devices that wish to converse, and then establishing a network path for them.

PBX: Private Branch Exchange. A sophisticated telephone system.

Peer-to-peer network: A network in which nodes share their resources (such as printers or hard disk drives) with other network users.

Physical layer: The layer of the OSI LAN model that establishes protocols for voltage, data transmission timing, and rules for "handshaking."

PMD: The Physical Media-Dependent layer of the fiber data distributed interface found in fiber-optic cabling.

Presentation layer: The layer of the OSI model concerned with protocols for network security, file transfers, and format functions.

PRI: Primary Rate Interface. Used under ISDN to service large-capacity devices such as PBXs.

Print spooler: Software that creates a buffer where files to be printed can be stored while they wait their turn.

Protocol: A set of rules or procedures commonly agreed upon by industry-wide committees (such as IEEE and ANSI).

PU: Physical Unit. This represents a tangible part of the system (such as a terminal or intelligent controller) under SNA.

Public volume: An area of a hard disk containing information that may be shared by several users.

Read-Only: Files that can be read but cannot be changed.

Record locking: Software feature that locks a record so that several users can share the same file, but cannot share the same record.

Redundant Array of Inexpensive Disks (RAID): A system in which several disk drives divide up the input/output of a server and also provide parity bits to reconstruct data should there be data destruction.

Repeaters: Devices on local area networks that rebroadcast a signal to prevent its degradation.

Requester: A network workstation that enables users to access shared resources as well as access server resources.

RFP: Request For Proposals.

RJE: Remote Job Entry. The sending of information in batch form, from a remote site (often unattended by a user) to an IBM mainframe.

Roll-forward recovery: Under TTS, keeping a complete log of all transactions in order to ensure that everything can be recovered.

Router: A device that links two networks that are running different protocols.

SCSI: Small Computer Systems Interface. An interface used to connect additional disk drives, tape backup units, or other SCSI-based peripherals to a PC.

SDLC: Synchronous Data Link Control. A subset of the HDLC protocol used by IBM computers running under SNA.

Semaphore: A flag that is set in order to make a file local; this procedure prevents two users from using the file simultaneously, which would destroy it.

Session: Under SNA, a logical and physical path connecting two NAUs for data transmission.

Session layer: The layer of the OSI model concerned with network management functions (including passwords, network monitoring, and reporting).

Site licensing: Procedure in which software is licensed to be used only at a particular location.

SMDR: Station Message Detail Reporting. This type of report uses a computer to analyze telephone calls to determine cost patterns.

SNA: Systems Network Architecture. The architecture used by IBM's minicomputers and mainframe computers.

Spanning tree: A type of bridge where networks with multiple bridges ensure that the traffic transmitted on a bridge flows in one direction only.

Split seeks: A system with duplexed drives checks to see which disk system can respond more quickly.

Splitter: A device that divides a signal into two different paths.

SRPI: Under SNA, the Server/Requester Programming Interface that allows PC applications to request services from IBM mainframes.

SSCP: System Services Control Point. An SNA network manager for a single SNA domain.

Standby uninterruptible power supply: An uninterruptible power supply that only switches on when electrical power fails.

Star: A network topology physically resembling a star. This network, built around a central computer, fails completely if the main computer fails.

StreetTalk: The distributed database serving as a network-naming service for the Vines local area network.

Superserver: A computer that has been optimized for use as a file server. Often it contains multiple microprocessors.

Switching hub: A wire concentrator or hub that provides dedicated transmission channels for each user.

Synchronous transmission: The continuous sending of information in packet form, rather than one byte at a time.

System fault tolerant: Duplication of hardware and data to ensure that failure of part of a network (a system fault) will not result in network downtime.

Token: A data packet used to transmit information on a token ring network.

TokenTalk: A protocol that permits AppleTalk data to be transmitted over a token ring network.

Topology: The physical arrangement or shape of a network.

Transient error: A "soft" network transmission error, often intermittent and easily corrected by retransmission.

Transport layer: The layer of the OSI model concerned with protocols for error recognition and recovery, as well as with regulation of information flow.

TSI: Time Slice Intervals. The way a file server divides its time.

TTS: Transaction Tracking System. A way to ensure data integrity on multiuser databases.

Twisted-pair wire: Two insulated wires twisted together so that each wire faces the same amount of interference from the environment.

Wire center: Connections that enable network administrators to add and remove network workstations without disrupting network operations.

Wire hub: Another term for a wire center or wire concentrator.

Workgroup software: Software that enables users to work on documents and data cooperatively and view each other's contributions.

Workstation: A network node. Often such nodes do not contain disk drives.

Bibliography

3Com Corporation. *3+ Administrator Guide for Macintosh.* 3Com Publication 3283-8145.

American Telephone and Telegraph Company. *Introduction to Information Systems Network (ISN).* AT&T Information Systems Publication 999-740-101IS.

_____. *STARLAN Network Application Programmer's Reference Manual.* AT&T Information Systems Publication 999-802-215IS.

_____. *AT&T STARLAN Network Custom Guide.* AT&T Information Systems Publication 999-350-00115.

_____. *STARLAN Network Design Guide.* AT&T Information Systems Publication 999-809-101IS.

_____. *STARLAN Network Introduction.* AT&T Information Systems Publication 999-809-100IS.

_____. *STARLAN Network Technical Reference Manual.* AT&T Information Systems Publication 999-300-208IS.

Apple Computer Corporation. *AppleTalk Network System Overview.* Addison-Wesley Publishing Company, 1989.

Artisoft. *Complete Guide to LANtastic.* 1993. Artisoft Publication 6280.

Banyan Systems, Inc. *Vines Administrator's Reference.* Banyan Systems Publication 092047-000.

_____. *Vines User's Guide.* Banyan Systems Publication 092002-002.

Bartee, Thomas C., ed. *Data Communications, Networks, and Systems.* Howard W. Sams, 1985.

Digital Communications Association, Inc. *10Net Software Reference Manual.* 10Net Communications (DCA) Publication 001908.

Dixon, R.C., Strole, N.C. and Markov, J.D. "A Token Ring Network for Local Data Communications." *IBM Systems Journal* 22 (1983): 47–62.

International Business Machines Corporation. *An Introduction to Local Area Networks.* IBM Publication GC 20-8203-1.

_____. *IBM LAN Server 2.0 New Functions and Features.* June 1992. IBM Publication GG 24-3875-00.

_____. *IBM Local Area Network Server version 3.0: Information and Planning Guide.* IBM Publication G 326-0162-01.

_____. *IBM PC Network Program User's Guide.* IBM Publication 6361559.

_____. *IBM Token Ring Network: A Functional Perspective.* IBM Publication G520-6062-1.

_____. *IBM Token Ring Network Decision.* IBM Publication G320-9438-1.

_____. *IBM Token Ring Network PC Products Description and Installation.* IBM Publication GG 24-173900.

Microsoft. *Schedule+ User's Guide, Windows for Workgroups version 3.1. 1992.* Microsoft Publication WC 33892-0992.

_____. *Windows for Workgroups Mail User's Guide version 3.1.* 1992. Microsoft Publication WG 33891-0992

_____. *Windows for Workgroups version 3.1 Getting Started.* 1992. Microsoft Publication W 132394-1092.

_____. *Windows for Workgroups version 3.1 User's Guide.* 1992. Microsoft Publication W 132404-1092.

Novell, Inc. Menu Utilities. Novell Publication 100-000323-001.

_____. *Supervisor's Guide.* Novell Publication 100-000425-001.

O'Brien, Bill. "Network Management: Tips, & Traps." *PC World* (September 1986): 228–237.

Sant'Angelo, Rick. *NetWare Unleashed.* Sams Publishing, 1994

Schatt, Stan. *Linking LANs.* Tab/McGraw-Hill, 1991.

_____. *Microcomputers in Business & Society.* Charles Merrill Publishing Company, 1989.

_____. *Data Communications For Business.* Prentice-Hall, 1983.

_____. *Understanding NetWare.* Howard W. Sams, 1989.

Schatt, Stan and Keith Fuller. *Using AppleShare.* Prentice-Hall, 1992.

Schatt, Stan and Steven Fox. *Voice/Data Telecommunications.* Prentice-Hall, 1988.

Stamper, David. *Business Data Communications.* Benjamin/Cummings, 1986.

Strole, Normal C. "A Local Communications Network Based on Interconnected Token-Access Rings: A Tutorial." *IBM Journal of Research Development* 27 (September 1983): 481–496.

Sun Microsystems, Inc. *TOPS DOS Version 2.1.* Sun Microsystems, TOPS Division (now Sitka Division), 1988.

Answers to Quizzes

Chapter 1:
1. a
2. b
3. a
4. b
5. a

Chapter 2:
1. c
2. c
3. b
4. b
5. b
6. b
7. d
8. a
9. b
10. c
11. a
12. c
13. a
14. b
15. c
16. b
17. b
18. b
19. d
20. a

Chapter 3:
1. b
2. d
3. b
4. a
5. c
6. b
7. c
8. a
9. c
10. d
11. b

Chapter 4:
1. c
2. d
3. a
4. c
5. b
6. b
7. d
8. b
9. c
10. a
11. b
12. b
13. c
14. c

Chapter 5:
1. b
2. a
3. b
4. d
5. c
6. b
7. d
8. c
9. a
10. d

Chapter 6:
1. b
2. b
3. d
4. c
5. b
6. c
7. a
8. d

Chapter 7:
Windows for Workgroups
1. d
2. b
3. d
4. b
5. b

6. d
7. c
8. b
9. b

Windows 95
1. c
2. d
3. a

LANtastic
1. d
2. a
3. b
4. c
5. d
6. b
7. d
8. c
9. c

Apple
1. c
2. b
3. c
4. d
5. a
6. b
7. c
8. d
9. c
10. d
11. b
12. d
13. c
14. b

Chapter 8:
1. d
2. c
3. b
4. a

Chapter 9:
1. c
2. b
3. d
4. a
5. b
6. a
7. a
8. b
9. b
10. c
11. a
12. c
13. b
14. d
15. b
16. b
17. d

Chapter 10:
1. d
2. a
3. a
4. d
5. c
6. b
7. a
8. d
9. b
10. b

Chapter 11:
1. c
2. b
3. a
4. d
5. c
6. b
7. a
8. b
9. c
10. c

Chapter 12:
1. b
2. d
3. c
4. a
5. d
6. b
7. d
8. c
9. a
10. b
11. d

Chapter 13:
1. d
2. c
3. d
4. c
5. d
6. c
7. a
8. b
9. c
10. a
11. d
12. c

Chapter 14:
1. a
2. c
3. b
4. d
5. d
6. a
7. c
8. d
9. a
10. a

Chapter 15:
1. c
2. d
3. a
4. c

Index

N

Add to Your Sams Library Today with the Best Books for Programming, Operating Systems, and New Technologies

The easiest way to order is to pick up the phone and call

1-800-428-5331

between 9:00 a.m. and 5:00 p.m. EST.

For faster service please have your credit card available.

ISBN	Quantity	Description of Item	Unit Cost	Total Cost
0-672-30481-3		Teach Yourself Netware in 14 Days	$29.95	
0-672-30712-X		Netware Unleashed, 2nd Edition (Book/Disk)	$45.00	
0-672-30501-1		Understanding Data Communications	$29.99	
0-672-30549-6		Teach Yourself TCP/IP in 14 Days	$29.99	
0-672-30486-4		Rightsizing Information Systems, 2nd Edition (Hardcover)	$40.00	
0-672-30473-2		Client/Server Computing, 2nd Edition (Hardcover)	$40.00	
0-672-30173-3		Enterprise-Wide Networking	$39.95	
0-672-30448-1		Teach Yourself C in 21 Days, Bestseller Edition	$24.95	
0-672-30620-4		Teach Yourself Visual Basic 4 in 21 Days, 3rd Edition (September release)	$35.00	
0-672-30655-7		Developing Your Own 32-Bit Operating System (Book/CD)	$49.99	
0-672-30667-0		Teach Youself Web Publishing with HTML	$25.00	
0-672-30737-5		World Wide Web Unleashed, 2nd Edition	$35.00	

❏ 3 ½" Disk

❏ 5 ¼" Disk

Shipping and Handling: See information below.	
TOTAL	

Shipping and Handling: $4.00 for the first book, and $1.75 for each additional book. Floppy disk: add $1.75 for shipping and handling. If you need to have it NOW, we can ship product to you in 24 hours for an additional charge of approximately $18.00, and you will receive your item overnight or in two days. Overseas shipping and handling adds $2.00 per book and $8.00 for up to three disks. Prices subject to change. Call for availability and pricing information on latest editions.

201 W. 103rd Street, Indianapolis, Indiana 46290

1-800-428-5331 — Orders   1-800-835-3202 — FAX   1-800-858-7674 — Customer Service

Book ISBN 1-672-30840-1

PLUG YOURSELF INTO...

MACMILLAN INFORMATION SUPERLIBRARY™

que

SAMS PUBLISHING

Hayden Books

que COLLEGE

NRP

alpha books

Brady

ADOBE PRESS

THE MACMILLAN INFORMATION SUPERLIBRARY™

Free information and vast computer resources from the world's leading computer book publisher—online!

FIND THE BOOKS THAT ARE RIGHT FOR YOU!

A complete online catalog, plus sample chapters and tables of contents give you an in-depth look at *all* of our books, including hard-to-find titles. It's the best way to find the books you need!

- ● STAY INFORMED with the latest computer industry news through our online newsletter, press releases, and customized Information SuperLibrary Reports.

- ● GET FAST ANSWERS to your questions about MCP books and software.

- ● VISIT our online bookstore for the latest information and editions!

- ● COMMUNICATE with our expert authors through e-mail and conferences.

- ● DOWNLOAD SOFTWARE from the immense MCP library:
    - - Source code and files from MCP books
    - - The best shareware, freeware, and demos

- ● DISCOVER HOT SPOTS on other parts of the Internet.

- ● WIN BOOKS in ongoing contests and giveaways!

TO PLUG INTO MCP: → **WORLD WIDE WEB: http://www.mcp.com**

GOPHER: gopher.mcp.com

FTP: ftp.mcp.com